INTEGRITY

*How I Lost It, and My
Journey Back*

INTEGRITY

How I Lost It, and My Journey Back

by

Richard W. Dortch

First Edition — January 1992
Second Edition — March 1992

Library of Congress Catalog Number:
ISBN: 0-89221-217-9

Jacket Design: Terry Dugan Design, Bloomington, MN

NOTE: Some names have been changed to protect their privacy.

Contents

Dedication 6

Acknowledgements 7

Author's Preface 9

1. A Mysterious Call 13

2. I Was Made to Know 19

3. James Orsen Bakker 29

4. An Uncertain Sound 41

5. Behind the Scenes at PTL 55

6. Blackmail 79

7. The Unraveling 115

8. Ankerberg, Swaggart, and Falwell 137

9. Jim Gives PTL to Falwell 157

10. Forty Days and Forty Nights 177

11. Confessions of Failure 193

12. Under Siege 205

13. After Midnight 223

14. Pleading Guilty 231

15. Eight Years! 259

16. Eglin Prison 275

17. How Long, Oh Lord? 289

18. Integrity 309

19. Free at Last 339

Epilogue 346

Endnotes 347

Index 348

Dedication

To my
Princess of peace, my jewel, my friend,
Mildred,
I lovingly dedicate this book.

To Deanna and Rich and their families,
our gifts from God.
Thank you for walking with us
through the storm.

Acknowledgments

Without my family, there would be no book.

After having read over two thousand articles and five books about PTL, I knew the real story, from the perspective of someone at the center of the storm, needed to be told.

Ande Yaktsis, senior correspondent for one of America's fine newspapers, was the first person I talked to about this book. Mr. Yaktsis is known in Illinois as an award winning investigative reporter. I wanted someone whose integrity would speak for itself to guide me. In the initial stages of the book's development, Ande was by my side.

Jamie Buckingham is a friend and confidant. He helped me to *not* write the book when I wanted to. He gave me the best advice, to wait until the story was finished. "It will be a different book," he cautioned. Sound advice. It is a different book.

Neil Eskelin had the most to do with this book. He did not help me write it, but he asked me the correct questions to get me thinking. His advice gave meaning to this book. He helped me make it a book with a message, not just a story.

About midway in this project I realized I needed the help of someone to give me, and this text, the depth and perspective it needed. I did not want it to be a throwaway testimony. Dr. Barry Banther, an esteemed former college president became a sounding board and source of wisdom. He is a very special, loving gentleman. I will forever be grateful for his help.

My secretary, Leslie Jones, and my administrative assistant, Gene Shelton, lived through these hours with me. They helped me bear the pain. They will always have a place in my heart.

Dr. and Mrs. Arthur Parsons never gave up on me. Dr. and Mrs. Durward Davis, Mr. and Mrs. Robert D'Andrea, Larry and Sandra Sims, Herman and Sharon Bailey, Frank Urquhart, Bob Moran, Eric and Becky Watt, and Mark and Wanda Burgund gave me the love and inspiration to "go on."

Karl and Joyce Strader would not let us fall into despair before prison. They reached out to us almost every week. During the time in prison they wrote every other week for sixteen months. That is love.

Pastors Larry and Pat Freeman gave me the example of Christian love and grace. My attorneys, the brilliant Mark Calloway, and the efficacious Bill Diehl, in Charlotte, North Carolina, were gifts from God. Attorney George Tragos of Clearwater, Florida, was there at the right time, when he was most needed.

Pastor and Mrs. Ron Meade lived much of those critical days with me. Jim and Rita McDonald, Col. Bill Rimes, his gracious wife, Pam, and Bill and Mary Landreth, were guardian angels to my wife.

Mr. Cliff Dudley and Mr. Tim Dudley, my publishers, were special people encouraging me. The staff of New Leaf Press was a part of the team to make this book what it is. I am their debtor. A host of people advised me, read the text, and offered counsel and suggestions.

To over a thousand people who cared enough to share their love by writing, and to all who loved and prayed, I am most thankful!

Author's Preface

"Pastor Dortch, you need to hire a lawyer."

I didn't know it at the time, but that statement from our in-house attorney at PTL marked the beginning of my way back.

"All you need to do is tell the truth, and things will be all right," she told me. I believed her. I purposed in my heart that was exactly what I would do.

When I met with government officials they repeated the lawyer's recommendation, "Just tell the truth."

The leaders of our church counseled me to "simply tell the truth."

Everyone who cared enough to give me advice, invariably reiterated, "What you need to do is simply tell the truth."

I am not sure that truth is really what everyone wants — especially if it affects them.

That's what this book is about — truth.

The incidents and events written in the following pages are things I lived through myself. I experienced them. I was at PTL when they happened.

During the thirty-four years of my ministry before PTL my personal and professional life was a life of integrity — a life of truth. I know it's the only way to live.

But slowly over time, I lost that quality by not speaking

up when I knew things were going wrong at PTL. I compromised and reaped the painful results. By closing my eyes and refusing to admit to things I saw happening around me, I condoned some people's conduct and arrogantly placed myself above reproach.

I am ashamed and embarrassed about some things that took place at PTL. I am determined to let the truth set me free from the guilt and condemnation of the past. This book is the result of that decision.

"Whoever heeds correction gains understanding... and humility comes before honor" is a proverb for all of us.

In the process of writing and reliving the events in this book, I have tried to face my problem, admit my guilt, and ask a host of people — as I've been doing since 1987 — to please forgive me. I want to be right with God, and I want to be right with man. Whatever it takes to humble myself before God and people, I am willing to do it.

Thousands of people worked at PTL during its fourteen years of existence; thousands more visited Heritage USA; and millions watched the PTL television program. To each of those people, Jim Bakker, and a host of us, represented the ministry and ourselves as Christian leaders. Were we? The public has a right to know the truth about what really happened at PTL.

I wrote this personal account, not out of rancor or bitterness, but with a sincere desire to be as honest and accurate as possible. I have tried to recapture my feelings during the time frame of these events.

I lived what happened at PTL. Within the pages of this book you will learn what it is like to lose your integrity. It is painful; it is ugly. I am a composite of all that I have experienced, read, and instinctively know. In writing this book I have been helped by many people. They gave me ideas, material, and the best of what they know. For the past two years I have read, searched, and obtained as much as I could acquire about the subject of integrity. It has become a part of me. I am sure that much of what I have studied has so assimilated into my spirit that I can't really know what is mine or others. No attempt has been made to take credit for anything. I am sure that whatever I have put into this book, from any source, all of us want to lay at our Master's feet.

My prayer is that you will receive this book in the same spirit in which it was written. When light shines in dark corners everything is illuminated. I want all of us to be better people because of this book. The truth will set all of us free.

The royalties of this book are being given to Life Challenge, a non-profit agency that assists professionals who are going through major crises in their lives. I work for Life Challenge. I want it to be effective. I have walked this road. I know the hurts and realize how much it helps to have someone stand with you through the pain. Our vision is to make Life Challenge a caring place of refuge for people in crisis.

1

A Mysterious Call

The phone rang in my office.

"Pastor Dortch, there's a woman on the line," the switchboard operator said, her voice shaking. "Pastor Dortch . . . She's making accusations against Rev. Bakker. I think you'd better talk to her."

Bizarre phone calls were not unusual at PTL. I had often dealt with disgruntled viewers making complaints. Without much concern, I picked up the phone. "This is Richard Dortch. How may I help you?" I asked politely.

I listened to the caller's shrill, panicky voice as she almost screamed, "My name is Jessica Hahn. I live in New York!" She then repeated her shocking allegation. "I want you to know that Jim Bakker raped me. He's ruined my life."

Because of the lateness of the hour and the severity of her allegations, the hysterical caller had gotten through the network of telephone counselors who usually handled distressed people. Having filtered into the private phone system of the World Outreach Center, the mysterious intruder had reached the sacred domain of PTL's executive office suite, the private inner sanctuary of Jim and Tammy Bakker. As the senior executive vice president, I alone shared the floor of luxurious offices that shielded the famous couple from the public.

Within the pyramid-shaped executive complex, security guards protected Jim from outsiders. An armed bodyguard went everywhere with him. There were threats on his life. Once the FBI overheard a radio message from someone plotting to harm the PTL leader. On another occasion, a briefcase, reportedly with a ticking device, was found in the front yard of Jim and Tammy's home. Police evacuated the neighborhood, but the bomb proved to be a hoax.

Jim felt secure in his third floor headquarters. He could see the beauty of the South Carolina countryside and Heritage USA — the family recreation park and spiritual oasis for thousands of visitors. Jim had asked me to share in his dream to build the ministry into a worldwide outreach center. After several months on the job, I had discovered that my duties involved much more than administrating the huge complex.

Now an unknown woman, who identified herself as Jessica Hahn, was confessing to me that Jim had a secret past. This strange, puzzling caller slandered the character of PTL's president and spiritual leader and attacked the integrity of the ministry. I knew for a fact that Rev. James O. Bakker, pastor of Heritage Village Church, had condemned the sin of sexual immorality before millions of viewers. Now a stranger was claiming that our pastor's character was tarnished by sexual infidelity.

Jessica Hahn? I was puzzled, having never heard the name. I did not even consider the possibility that her story could be credible. Jim Bakker? Never!

"Jim Bakker and John Wesley Fletcher (an evangelist who had appeared on their show many times) tricked me into going to a hotel in Florida," Miss Hahn continued to rant.

She accused Jim of sexually assaulting her, in reality, a criminal offense. Miss Hahn's story was astonishing. "They drugged my wine; they humiliated me," she cried.

Miss Hahn, a follower of "The Jim and Tammy Show," insisted she knew Jim, the co-host, in an intimate way. Her portrayal of his behavior did not fit the picture of the Jim Bakker I knew. Her accusation was ludicrous. I was his trusted friend, his second in command, and often his spiritual counselor. I knew him as shy, withdrawn, usually fearful of others.

Before the TV cameras, Jim's charisma charmed millions of faithful viewers; but in private, I'd seen him stare at the floor like a shy school boy in order to avoid conflict. He was not a sinister character who lured women into hotel rooms.

I had watched Jim become one of the most successful entrepreneurs of the electronic ministry in the world. Certainly, he was vulnerable to blackmail. Was Jessica Hahn a pawn in a conspiracy to blackmail Jim? A sexual scandal could ruin him, his marriage, and possibly cause PTL to crumble.

In her bizarre confession, Miss Hahn revealed the sexual episode with Jim. She said that it had caused her mental suffering. She wanted money to pay for medical and psychiatric bills. She wept uncontrollably. I was convinced this was an emotionally disturbed woman, crying out for recognition. It wasn't unusual for women to have sexual fantasies about evangelists on national television. In my years as superintendent of the Assemblies of God in Illinois, I was the spiritual overseer and counselor to nine hundred ministers. I remember women who imagined sexual experiences with pastors or church leaders.

While Jessica Hahn unveiled her fantastic story, I swung my chair around facing the window. Outside, the darkness blotted the cold landscape. Workmen were assembling the lights and flashing them off and on in preparation for the 1984 Christmas season at Heritage USA. Thousands of visitors would make their annual pilgrimage to the grounds to see the spectacle of lights, Jim Bakker's Christmas gift to the world. Soon a million colored bulbs would be glowing outside my window, creating a Christmas fairyland.

My position at PTL was to be one of the highlights of my ministerial life. My only ambition was to obey Jesus' command to spread the gospel to the whole world. Now I was a partner with Jim to beam hope and love on TV to more than fifty countries.

My life was dedicated to helping people in crisis. Miss Hahn was a woman in desperation, and I wanted to help her. I glanced at the placard on my desk. It proclaimed: "You Can Make It," a slogan of PTL. "You can make it," I assured millions of viewers regularly. Now I found myself reassuring Miss Hahn.

I offered to pray with her to ease her distress. She consented and answered, "Amen," when I finished the prayer. Her hysteria ceased, and she became quiet, apologizing for taking my time. "I'm sorry," she said quietly.

I pleaded with her, "Call your pastor, tell him. He's the best friend you have. He will help you." She hung up.

It was past 7:00 p.m. and the staff had gone home. Another day was winding down at PTL. The executive offices were quiet. I glanced at the TV monitor. The morning show of "The Jim and Tammy Show" was being replayed. I saw myself appear on the screen talking to nighttime viewers.

"Good night," I said to the security guard.

"Good night, Rev. Dortch," he acknowledged.

I drove along the autumn countryside toward home. *Who is Jessica Hahn?* I wondered, suspicious of any stranger who intruded into the sanctity of PTL, a ministry blessed by God. It didn't matter. Miss Hahn would never call again. It was another distressed soul who called PTL for prayer. With God's help I was able to console her. Another problem solved, another soul comforted.

I didn't bother Jim with the call; it was so ridiculous. Anyhow, bad news depressed him. Since Jim had a habit of brooding for days over problems at PTL, I shielded him from confrontations with adversaries. Criticism of the ministry hurt him deeply.

I thought about tomorrow. I would be on the show with Jim and Tammy. It was an exciting time at PTL. We were launching into new spiritual programs to help people.

In my rear view mirror I saw the lights of Heritage USA,

a representation of the active faith of thousands of people. As I turned toward my home along the lake, it never crossed my mind that the conversation with Jessica Hahn was the opening scene of a strange drama that would change the course of PTL — and the religious world.

I was beginning a journey into uncharted territory, with danger lurking ahead. Soon the names of Jim and Tammy Bakker and Richard Dortch would become familiar to millions in the secular world. I would be a central character in one of the longest running stories in media history.

Dear Jesus, how did I get myself into this? was my prayer!

2

I Was Made To Know

As the Model A pickup truck bumped along the Illinois back roads, its eighteen passengers sang and fellowshiped, filling the darkness with momentary bursts of loud laughter. On their way to an evening of worship, no one would have guessed how that night in 1928 would end.

Approaching the railroad crossing, Mr. Matthews, the driver, looked up and down the tracks, saw nothing, and slowly started across. Suddenly a black mountain of smoke-belching iron loomed before him. The mammoth steam engine of the train hit the truck, scattering the old vehicle and its precious cargo like feathers in the wind.

Harry Dortch lay unconscious on the ground, his skull fractured by the impact. The engine light on the train had not been working, resulting in the deaths of seven of the eighteen passengers. Harry's wife, Eva, was killed instantly. His five children, some of whom were found lying underneath the train's engine, miraculously survived.

During my dad's long recovery, five families from the church each took one of the children. The John Frederick Brown family cared for his son, Kenneth, and on his visits to see Kenneth, Harry developed a relationship with Mary, one of the Brown's daughters.

They were married on Mary's sixteenth birthday, making the young wife an instant mother of Harry's four sons and one daughter — with the oldest only seven. Two years later, I was born on October 15, 1931, at the height of the Great Depression. Soon after that my oldest brother, Graham, died of rheumatic fever.

My father moved our family to a small farm in Collinsville, Illinois, about ten miles outside of St. Louis, Missouri. Times were hard, but we grew our own food and never went hungry. In fact, my enterprising father was always thinking of new ways to bring in extra money. He'd wake up at four or five o'clock in the morning and make pies from the fruit grown on his own trees. Then, loading all five kids and baskets of pies into the back of the pickup, he'd drive out to the government funded W.P.A. (Works Projects Administration) work site where we'd sell the little pies for a nickel each.

Whenever I think of my father, I am reminded of his devotion to God and the loving commitment he had to his family. In fact, I cannot remember my father being away from home for even one night while I was growing up.

Today, as I look back over my own life as a parent, that memory confounds me. During my years as an evangelist, pastor, missionary, and denominational leader, I was away from my wife and children often, sometimes fifty percent of the time.

At the outbreak of World War II, my father took a job in a defense factory, and our family moved to Granite City, Illinois. We began attending the First Assembly of God Church where the pastor instilled a missionary vision in the congregation, telling them not to focus on "the pulpit" but to create new pulpits all over the world. As a result, over 140 young people from that church went into the ministry, some becoming outstanding preachers and missionaries.

On December 7, 1947, a young twenty-nine-year-old evangelist, whom our pastor had met in Oklahoma, came to minister. I didn't go to church that Sunday morning, but in the evening, when I went to hear him preach, he prayed a prayer I will never forget: "Lord, don't let a mother's boy or a daddy's girl go to hell who heard me preach tonight. But bring them to Jesus."

That evening, I met two men. Jesus Christ changed my life. Oral Roberts was the evangelist. At the age of fifteen I became a Christian. I put my life on a course that would lead me to serving people all my life.

For as long as I can remember, I knew God had called me to preach. There was a brief time, when, as a young man playing baseball, I considered becoming a professional ball player. But, in my heart, I knew all I really wanted to be was a minister.

To prepare myself for the ministry, I enrolled at North Central Bible College in Minneapolis, Minnesota, where I received my theological training. During that time a group of friends and I formed the Master's Quartet and traveled together for several years. We represented the college and helped to recruit new students. That experience whet my appetite for evangelistic work and gave me a burden for the lost.

After leaving college, I traveled with my friend Daniel Johnson. We called ourselves "Dick and Dan" and spent our time singing and preaching our way across the Midwest. For most of the past forty-one years, hardly a week has passed that Dan and I have not talked and shared with one another. He remains, to this day, my dearest friend.

Not long after Dan and I went our separate ways, I married the love of my life, a precious girl named Mildred Nickles. A few months after the wedding, we moved to Chillicothe, Missouri where I pastored a church for a short time. But my heart longed to be back on the road. That wasn't a good choice for us because our daughter, Deanna, was born and we needed to be at home.

One of our first crusades was in Watertown, South Dakota. Shortly after the crusade the pastor, Grant Wacker, called to tell me he was resigning and the church wanted me

to consider becoming their pastor. Although this new assign-
ment was nine hundred miles away from our families in
Illinois, Mildred and I gladly accepted.

While pastoring in Watertown, I was smitten with
Crohn's disease, a devastating disorder causing painful
inflammation of the digestive tract. I lost sixty-five pounds
and ultimately had to have about seven feet of my intestine
removed. Very few people die with Crohn's disease, and
fewer get well. The doctors told me I would have to learn to
live with my condition.

After several years in South Dakota I received a phone
call one day from Rev. Rudolph McAdams, the pastor of the
Assemblies of God Church in Garden City, Kansas, a remote
town about fifty miles from the Colorado border and fifty
miles west of Dodge City, Kansas.

"Our time here is finished, and the church would like
you to be their next pastor," he informed me.

Several years before, my wife and I, as young evangelists, had conducted a three-week crusade at the Garden
City church. During that time the pastor's wife had said to
me, "Someday you will be the pastor of this church."

I remembered her statement as I considered the pastor's
proposal. These were such good people. This church had
been a great influence on my life and ministry. Still I didn't
want to commit myself.

"I don't think it's the right time for me to come," I told
him.

"Then we will wait to leave until it is the right time!" he
responded.

In the back of my mind I knew that a church in Kansas
City, Missouri also needed a pastor, and that was where I
wanted to go.

To my delight the Kansas City church invited us to
preach and meet with their pulpit committee. Afterwards,
they extended the official invitation for us to come and pastor
the church.

One night as my wife and I were praying, I realized we
were about to make a terrible mistake. I was made to know

that I was getting out of the will of God. (Instead of using the expression "God told me," I always say, "I was made to know.")

Actually, I hadn't really sought the Lord on where He wanted us to go. After all, the larger, more prestigious church in Kansas City seemed the obvious choice. What future would I have at the smaller Garden City congregation out in the middle of nowhere?

That night after much prayer, my wife and I said, "Lord, if the church in Garden City calls us again, we will accept their invitation. You know where we are, and You know where they are. If You want us to go, they will call."

About 1:30 a.m. that same night, the phone rang.

Pastor McAdams said, "Pastor Dortch, there are about sixty people at the church praying right now. We are praying that whomever God has chosen to pastor this church, the Holy Spirit will put a fire under them."

My response was, "Go back and tell them to turn off the heat. We are ready to come."

The following Sunday, three days later, we arrived in Garden City, Kansas. That evening the congregation elected me as their pastor, and Mildred and I began one of the most pleasant experiences of our ministry. What appeared to be the back-side of the desert turned out to be an oasis of love, where problems in the church were quickly quelled by praying people. In fact, the congregation in Garden City probably blessed us more than we ever contributed to them.

We have good memories of all of the churches we have pastored, but Garden City, Kansas holds a very special place in our hearts. I've often said that if I were sick unto death, I would want the people in the church in Garden City to be the ones praying for me. Those people knew God in an intimate way. In that environment I gained a new sense of integrity.

Two significant events took place in Garden City. Mildred delivered our son, Rich, and God birthed in me a new vision — a desire to take the gospel to Europe.

On Easter Sunday 1958, I preached my last sermon in

Garden City. During the following four months, Mildred and I worked hard to raise the funds to go to the mission field, a feat which today takes over two years to accomplish. Soon we would be leaving for Europe to help start a Bible college to train ministers of the gospel.

For the next five years, we worked under the leadership of V.G. Greisen, a man whose vision and faith influenced me tremendously. It was our privilege to help establish what became Continental Bible College in Brussels, Belgium. V.G. Greisen and I, and later Charles Greenaway, were the first missionaries involved in this ongoing educational ministry.

One morning, while we were living in Belgium, I suddenly awakened, feeling a deep pain in my stomach. The Crohn's disease had made me especially sensitive to environmental changes, but this was a different sensation. I don't know how I knew, but I was aware that I was being asphyxiated.

I tried to move, but I couldn't. I tried to concentrate on maneuvering my legs, but my limbs would not cooperate. All I could do was roll back and forth, left to right, right to left. I finally got enough energy to roll off the bed. The jolt of landing on the floor helped revive me, and I could think more clearly. Working my way toward the large floor-to-ceiling European type window near the bed, I was able to swing my body around and knock out one of the panes to let in fresh air.

Crawling on the floor, I tried to wake my wife and daughter, but to no avail. I knew they were in serious trouble because I couldn't revive them. By literally rolling myself down the steps, I was able to knock over the telephone stand and struggled to dial a 2 which brought the people from the Bible college running to our rescue.

We later discovered that the chimney had stopped up and carbon monoxide had filled the house. It was only by the grace of God that we were still alive. One of my wife's lungs, however, had collapsed, but later through rehabilitation her breathing capacity returned to normal. Our daughter, who was seven years old at the time, revived without incident.

In spite of this life-threatening episode and our weakened physical conditions, Mildred and I didn't want to leave the mission field. But our supervisors insisted, telling us, "You must return to the States where you can take care of yourselves and repair your health."

On our trip back to America, I remember standing on the tarmac at Heathrow Airport in London, England — that was before the days of airport security. Beside me was one of the truly great evangelical leaders of all time — W.T.H. Richards, one of the leaders of the Assemblies of God of Great Britain.

Turning to him, I said, "Billy, I have no idea what I am going to do when I get back to America. But I am as confident as I can be that God is going to guide me."

I didn't consider our return to the States in 1963 as the end of our mission. I felt God was sending us back home the same way He had sent us to Europe — with high hopes and great expectations.

Ten days after arriving home I was "made to know" to call Lloyd Shoemaker, the pastor of the Assembly of God church in Alton, Illinois. During our furlough from Europe the year before, I had preached in Lloyd's church for a month while he was on vacation.

When he answered the phone, he responded, "I know this is Richard Dortch's voice, but you are not here, you are in Europe."

"No, we just got home," I said and explained what had happened.

"Hold the phone a minute," he told me. I could hear his footsteps cross to the office door and shut it. He whispered into the mouthpiece, "I am resigning this church tomorrow. Your call is providential."

Within ten days I was elected the pastor of Edwards Street Church in Alton, Illinois, where I served for several years.

Never, in trying to find out what we should do, did Mildred and I ever have any questions or doubts. We were "made to know" with certainty at every turn. In fact, we had thought we would be in Alton, Illinois for many years, but HE had other plans.

At a specially called business meeting of the Illinois Assemblies of God in 1966 I was unexpectedly elected the state secretary. For the next four years, I assisted Dr. E.M. Clark, the state superintendent. During that time, Dr. Clark put me through his university of day by day schooling, where I learned more about people and the work of the ministry than I had in all my previous years combined.

When Dr. Clark became president of North Central Bible College in 1970, I was chosen to succeed him as the superintendent of our denomination for the state of Illinois.

The morning after I was elected, I lay in bed, remembering my roots and how far the Lord had brought me. Now the fact that the first and founding superintendent of the Assemblies of God in Illinois, Rev. C.M. O'Guin, had dedicated me to the Lord when I was born seemed overwhelmingly significant. As a child from a poor family, I had attended a small church, and in my wildest dreams I could never have imagined that some day I would serve in the same honored post as Rev. O'Guin.

Later I considered an even more noteworthy fact: Of the first sixty years of our denomination in Illinois, over twenty of those years had been under the leadership of someone from First Assembly in Granite City. Looking back, I marvel at the Lord's guiding of the early events of my life.

During the years I was superintendent, the pastors and people in leadership in Illinois made many innovative and progressive achievements. We were the first to create several ministry positions, including a full time director of continuing education for the pastors, a resident counselor for pastors, and a full-time development director. Our state organization developed a large staff of qualified personnel to accomplish the task of training people to do their work.

During that same period of time, 129 new Assemblies of God churches were started in Illinois, and many outstanding young pastors began to emerge. Pastor Robert Schmidgall in Naperville, M. C. Johnson in Springfield, and many others, built outstanding churches with large congregations in Illinois.

Media ministries and outreach, both in radio and television were being developed all across America, and we were the first state Assemblies of God organization to operate radio stations.

It was about that time when Owen Carr, who was then the pastor of the Stone Church in Chicago, told me that he wanted to start a television station.

"I believe you will do that," I quickly responded. We had just begun our radio ministry, and I believed mass media was an important tool for preaching the gospel.

"There is a station with a transmitter already on top of the John Hancock Building in Chicago," Pastor Carr said. "There's only one problem. The transmitter and the permit to build the station are owned by the AFL/CIO Union of Illinois."

I said, "I can't believe that."

"Why are you saying that?" Owen asked.

"The president of the AFL/CIO of Illinois lived across the street from me as a boy, and we grew up together."

He asked, "You know Robert Gibson?"

"Of course." I said. "In fact, his mother and sister attend our church in Granite City."

Owen Carr was surprised. Within a matter of ten minutes I was talking to Robert Gibson at his office in Chicago. I said, "Robert, let me tell you what you need to do with your television station."

He listened, and the AFL/CIO graciously sold that station to the Stone Church. What is now Channel 38 in Chicago was one of the first Christian TV stations in America. I still get blessed knowing I had a part in making it happen!

As my interest in radio and television expanded, I began to know — in the same way that I knew that I was going to be a pastor — that I would someday be involved in media ministry.

One night, during the early '70s, I was flipping through the various TV channels. To my surprise, I saw two men praying with real conviction. It was exciting to see a TV program that emphasized faith. One of the men appeared to be in his forties; the other man, of small stature, appeared to be around thirty. That was my introduction to Christian television and the first time I saw Uncle Henry Harrison and Jim Bakker.

Richard Dortch and Dan Johnson

3

James Orsen Bakker

"You know Fern Olson, don't you?" I asked Jim Bakker the first time we met in 1977.

"Yes," he replied. "She and her husband Russell performed our wedding ceremony while we were students at North Central Bible College."

The invitation to come to Charlotte to appear on the "PTL Club" television program had reminded me that I had first heard Jim Bakker's name from my dear friend, Fern Olson.

When I was a pastor in Alton, Illinois, Fern had asked if I'd like Jim to preach at my church. I remember telling her I'd pray about it, but I honestly don't know if I did or not. I do know that I didn't extend the young Bible school student an invitation. It was my policy not to bring anyone into our pulpit until I had personally heard him preach.

"Fern has had a tremendous impact on my life," I told Jim, explaining that I had known this wonderful woman for many years.

The connection with Fern and Russell Olson gave Jim

and me an immediate point of reference. Our mutual respect for the Olsons and their influence on our spiritual development brought a sense of unity. I suddenly felt more at ease with the dynamic television personality.

As Jim talked about Fern's marvelous ministry, as I remember it, I thought back to when I was a child. Our family attended the Assembly of God Church in Collinsville, Illinois, and Fern Olson had returned to Illinois to preach and minister to the sick. One of our deacons, Mr. Hamm had fallen and broken his leg, but the bone had not healed properly and the doctors had to rebreak it.

When Mr. Hamm hobbled forward for prayer, I remember thinking, *Why go through this? His leg is broken and in a cast.*

But as soon as Fern prayed for him, Mr. Hamm threw his crutches up in the air and ran down the aisle of the church. The next night, he came to the service without the cast — totally healed. I never forgot that miracle.

In fact, at another point in my life the Lord used Fern. The memory of that rebuked me for my lack of obedience.

When I was pastoring in Alton, Illinois, I invited Fern Olson to speak at a church convention. I respected her tremendously and knew that she was a devout person — the result of her deep, confident relationship with God. Fern's bold, no-nonsense demeanor gave true meaning to the word integrity.

Several months before Fern's visit, a lady in our church, Yvonne Moxey, had come with her husband to see me.

"My wife has a serious form of leukemia," the distraught husband told me. We prayed together, and I wanted to believe God was going to heal the young woman. But it seemed the more we prayed, the worse Yvonne got, until she was finally hospitalized.

One day as I was petitioning the Lord again for Yvonne's healing I was made to know: *This woman is going to die. Prepare her for death. Start talking to her about the wonders and glories of heaven. She is not going to get well. She is only going to be healed when she wakes up in God's presence.*

Such a thought did not fit into my theology of healing, deliverance, and miracles I had been taught and had preached for years. How could I tell someone they were going to die? I tried to ignore the struggle within and instead looked for ways to bolster my faith.

When Fern arrived, I reminded myself, *Remember, this is the lady who prayed for the man with the broken leg and he was healed.*

On the way to the hospital, I told Fern about Yvonne's condition and also indicated my concern that perhaps Yvonne wasn't going to get well. By failing to mention what I sensed in my spirit, I knew I was not being totally candid with Fern. My zeal for the ministry got in the way of my obedience and integrity.

Once in the room with this great "miracle worker," Fern prayed for Yvonne, reaching out to her in love. Yvonne was obviously blessed by the visit but showed no signs of having been healed.

When we walked out into the hallway, Fern suddenly squared around in front of me and said, "Richard, what has the Lord told you about this woman?"

I was so stunned and shocked, I could only mumble some kind of trite answer. Obviously irritated, Fern admonished, "It is clear in my mind this woman should be prepared for death."

I had not used that expression with Fern before. Now here she was, a total stranger to the situation, saying, "Prepare this lady for death."

That experience humbled and chastened me. It forced me to realize we mortals do not determine the future.

I also learned something about faith. Faith is not determined by winning or losing but by simply resting in the plan God has for us. When that plan is in effect, we have all we need. God is sovereign, and the outcome is in His hands and only for His glory. The miracle is in doing God's will.

In the years ahead, I wish I had continually reminded myself of that important lesson in integrity, but it was later lost in an environment where miracles were demanded and failure wasn't tolerated.

PTL itself was a miracle. Who could deny that? That's the question I asked myself as I was driven to the studio that day in 1977.

I'll never forget my first appearance on the "PTL Club" program. On the air Jim and I discussed personal relationships and the importance of forgiveness — topics that came easily to me.

At the time I was known across the country as a pastor to pastors and was often called in to deal with difficult church situations. In my position as the Illinois state superintendent of the Assemblies of God, I acted as a bishop serving over nine hundred ministers, caring for them and their families. My energies were focused on helping pastors develop their ministries and work through any problems. I loved my job and couldn't imagine doing anything else.

I saw my appearance on national television as an opportunity to share some of the principles I knew would help people involved in crisis situations. The program began at ten o-clock in the morning and ended at noon. I felt drained but exhilarated.

As Jim and I were leaving the studio, which at that time was housed in a former retail facility, he asked, "Can you stay a while, Pastor Dortch? I'd like to show you around Charlotte."

The unexpected invitation surprised and flattered me. *Why would this young, charismatic televangelist want to spend the day with me, an old-line denominational executive from Illinois?* I wondered.

"Sure," I answered. *Maybe I can find out who Jim Bakker really is,* I thought, hoping to put to rest many of the rumors about PTL circulating at the time.

After touring the city, we stopped for lunch. Throughout the afternoon, I tried to piece together everything I knew about Jim Bakker.

I had often watched the early "700 Club" programs that Jim had hosted for over seven years. When he resigned that responsibility, I knew he had moved to California to begin a new ministry called "PTL" — "People That Love" or "Praise The Lord" — which later became Trinity Broadcasting Network. After only a short time with that ministry, he had come to North Carolina and started the Charlotte based "PTL Club."

The remainder of the day passed quickly. At five o'clock Tammy Faye joined us for dinner at a restaurant, and I met her for the first time.

"Why don't you spend the night with us at our home?" Jim suggested. "That will give us more time to talk. You can re-schedule your flight and leave in the morning."

Captivated by their charm and friendliness, I agreed and changed my travel plans.

After their two children were in bed, Jim and Tammy began to share with me some of the problems they were facing. I listened politely, humbled that this famous couple would confide so readily in me.

Soon after I returned home to Illinois, Jim began to call me and share his vision for PTL. Whether I was in Vermont, California, Montana, Florida, or at home, it was not unusual to get a phone call from Jim and Tammy in the middle of the night. Both of them would be on the line, pouring out their hearts and seeking my counsel.

My pastor's heart sensed a deep need in Jim and Tammy that at the time I could not put my finger on. Maybe it was loneliness. Maybe it was insecurity hidden behind Jim's in-control personality and Tammy's flamboyant behavior. I don't know. But whatever it was, their need gripped my heart, filling me with compassion and making it impossible for me to turn my back on them.

At the same time, I was struck by their magnetism and outstanding talents. They appeared to be two young people who sincerely wanted to do something to help people. Their purposes seemed noble. Yet, in spite of their professional demeanor and creative abilities, I sensed a childlikeness in Jim and Tammy Bakker that made them seem so vulnerable.

The more I got to know the Bakkers the more their

generosity astounded me. They were the largest contributors to the Goodwill program in Charlotte and gave to the Boy's Ranch in North Carolina. It was not unusual for Jim, who may have just gotten a luxurious new car, to give it to a pastor who had come to PTL with an old, beat-up vehicle. From the very beginning of my appearances on the program, I sensed that Jim and Tammy were giving people.

Before long Jim began asking me to come to Charlotte on a regular basis, and soon I was appearing on "The PTL Club" almost every month. When the Bakkers were out of town, I occasionally acted as substitute host on the program.

About a year after our friendship began, Jim called one day. "Some of our board members are resigning. Pastor Dortch, would you consider coming on our board?" he probed.

"Let me check with the board I am accountable to in Illinois," I replied. "If they say yes, I will gladly be a member."

I asked my superiors if I should serve on the PTL board. Their response was, "Yes, we think that would be a good thing. The Lord knows they need help."

I was serving as one of the executive presbyters of the Assemblies of God, the highest elective body of the denomination. I didn't ask for their permission to serve on PTL's board. I simply informed them, and they made no response other than, "We hope you can be a blessing to them."

The PTL board met more regularly than most boards I was serving on at the time. In fact, we had five or six board meetings each year, more than the average college required. This put a real strain on my time since I was also chairman of the board of Evangel College, serving on the Board of Education of the Assemblies of God, and on the boards of Central Bible College and North Central Bible College.

In addition I was a member of the Home Mission board, the Foreign Mission board, and the board of the retirement fund for the Assemblies of God Minister's Benefit Association. During that time, I was learning a great deal from Dr. Thomas Zimmerman, the general superintendent of the Assemblies of God, whose leadership skills were recognized by many other outstanding churchmen, including Billy Graham.

I served on the PTL board from 1978 to 1987 during its greatest period of growth and expansion. I realized Jim Bakker is, without question, a genius. He was constantly presenting us with fresh ideas and innovative programs. Anyone who worked with him and was involved at the beginning of Heritage USA observed firsthand Jim's creative brilliance.

I well remember the day Jim took the board members — Efrem Zimbalist, Jr., Aimee Cortese, Dr. Charles Cookman, A.T. Lawing, and myself — out to view an Industrial Park that was for sale. As Jim drove around the site, he gave us a glimpse of his vision, explaining how he wanted to purchase the property to build "Heritage USA." Jim's foresight and attention to detail astounded us.

The following page of checklist items is an example of Jim's thoroughness. Sometimes he would dictate as many as ten pages of these items in a given day.

PTL Television Network Charlotte, NC 28279
Office Of The President
Jim Bakker

ADDITION - CHECKLIST - JUNE 23, 1986

- One of the lights is burned out on the Jim & Tammy sign on Highway 21.

- Have Sam McLendon check out the Safari Campgrounds for our overflow for the Fourth of July weekend or any other time; and also to just give me a report on what he thinks of the place and the possibility of putting people who want to live permanently in travel trailers in that park.

- Check with Grounds concerning the dirt piled up at the entrance of Heritage USA . If they're going to spread that out, it should be done right away.

- Some of the lights that go around the Welcome Center are burned out, and need replacing right away.

- Something needs to be done about the grass where
  you walk up from the parking lot at the Welcome Center.
  Either put a fence or some bushes or shrubs in there.

- Have someone pick up the cigarette butts at the
  Welcome center DAILY.

- Install a sound system in the Water Park. The wires
  are run but not the speakers. They need to put water-
  proof speakers in the Water Park -- they should be built
  into the rocks, but they need to be put into the bushes
  and all areas so we can give messages and also run
  Hawaiian instrumental music throughout Heritage Island.
  So make sure Heritage Island is wired and have the
  speakers and amplifier wired in for it.

- We need to get the lawn in, lanscaping in around Kevin's
  House.

- The head end of the lake needs to be landscaped, and
  no parking is to be allowed there.

- There are to be NO reserved spaces around the Grand
  or anywhere else. It is totally against ministry policy.

A flow of enterprising energy exuded from Jim that appeared miraculous — of a child-man doing superhuman feats. How else can you explain two people, with the limitations of Jim and Tammy Bakker, taking 2,300 acres of land and building a multi-million dollar facility that captured the imagination of America?

The idea of developing a family theme park in an environment where parents could leave their children alone and be assured nothing would happen to them was a stroke of creative genius. In all those years of Heritage USA, nobody was ever beaten up, robbed, or harmed in any way. Millions came to enjoy the Christian atmosphere, the pleasant accommodations, the theme park and especially the water slide, the magnificent parades, and to meet the hosts of "The PTL Club" television program.

Whenever we came to Charlotte for board meetings, Jim always encouraged the members to have access to anything they wanted to see or do. He not only took us around and showed us different aspects of the ministry but told us to strike out on our own. We were urged to talk to the PTL personnel and to ask any staff member questions.

In my presence, he gave orders to the division heads to answer any inquiries the board members might have. I never had the feeling that Jim had anything to hide. In fact, he seemed to want everything out in the open so we could advise him on any problems we encountered.

At one of the board meetings, Jim informed us that the *Charlotte Observer* had been running articles on the new budding ministry. PTL was getting an extreme amount of publicity, and any new project solicited some kind of a reaction from *The Charlotte Observer.*

Since I did not live in Charlotte until 1984, it was impossible for me to know all the details this local paper found to be newsworthy. Still a reporter from *The Charlotte Observer* began phoning me at home in Illinois. He would cite certain rumors he had heard and make questionable innuendoes, but I refused to respond.

Whenever he called, I replied with one standard answer from which I didn't vary: "I am a board member of PTL and my accountability is to the board not to the press. When the board decides to speak to the press, the board will have someone speak for them. I have not been chosen by the board to speak so I have nothing to say."

I have always believed that the people who support a ministry should have access to any information they want about its operation. They have a right to know. I am *not* convinced, even as I write this book, that the *Charlotte Observer* has a "right to know" what any ministry is doing!

In fact, even when things were going well at PTL, the *Charlotte Observer* set out on a mission to discredit Jim and Tammy. One of their reporters would, on some occasions, park his car in front of the Bakkers' house and take notes about what he saw happening. In my opinion, *The Observer's* continued attacks on other evangelical Christians, especially its biased and negative reporting about charismatics, proved to me their agenda went beyond the scope of journalism.

When I first began visiting PTL in '78, I noticed that a

web was building in Jim's mind concerning the whole concept of security and his protection. I wasn't convinced that all the security measures were necessary. Later I learned that anyone appearing regularly on national television attracts a certain element of people who are potential security problems.

In fact, one day while I was hosting "The PTL Club," a man watched and made up his mind to come to Heritage USA to "get me." When he arrived on the grounds, the security guards had to restrain the man and ask him to leave. That incident gave me some insight into the fears Jim and Tammy lived with day after day. We had a security force of over seventy full time officers. They were well trained professionals who did their job well. We had a retired secret service agent as a consultant to us. He was with President Reagan when he was shot.

Jim's obsession and fascination with security, however, did appear quite eccentric. Wherever he went, security people accompanied him, watching whatever Jim and everyone around him did. I should have said something to Jim and asked him why he had to have so much security. But I didn't question his reasons because I wasn't living the same fishbowl existence. PTL was a world unto itself, and I was just a frequent visitor.

In the world of television, people feel like they know you and your family personally. This was especially true with the Bakkers. Jim and Tammy talked freely about their lives, and you seldom had to guess what was on their minds. I could see, even in those early days, that what you see is what you get with Jim and Tammy Bakker.

I have been asked many times what kind of people the Bakkers really were in those years when I served on the board and spent time in their home. Jim and Tammy were doting parents, obviously fascinated with their two youngsters. Their lives revolved around Jamie Charles and their daughter, Tammy Sue. In fact, I remember playing kid's games on the floor with all four of the Bakkers, laughing and crawling around.

Jim and Tammy loved children, having created and performed in children's programs during their earliest days on television. Maybe that's why their hearts were so tender and openly loving toward everyone. It was this special childlike quality that captured the hearts of millions who viewed "The PTL Club."

As the Bakkers' commitment to the ministry increased, I noticed, the less real their world became. That was true, not only of their relationship with Jamie and Tammy Sue, but also in other aspects of their lives. Of course, the same can be said of many television personalities, and frequently with very busy pastors and business executives.

As Christians, however, our commitment must first be to God, secondly to our spouse, and thirdly to our children. The last priority should be to our work. God's work must never come before God. Our ministry must never come before our family or our health. If these areas of our lives are not in the proper order, the imbalance will cause us to malfunction, limiting our ability to be used by God and help mankind.

I wish I could say my priorities were always in order, but that's not true. If they had been, maybe my experience at PTL would have turned out differently. Perhaps I would have had more discernment or been more cautious if I had put God first instead of my work. If there had been more balance to my life, maybe I wouldn't have been so completely drawn into the alluring temptations that come from being in the spotlight.

The fascinating aura surrounding television can suck you in like quicksand if you let it. Almost every time I went to PTL for a board meeting, I made a television appearance. It didn't take long for me to be captivated and enchanted by the experience. Surrounded by cameramen and sound people who focused on my every word and movement, I enjoyed the exposure and attention of television — not realizing its dangers.

A transformation takes place when that red light on the TV camera goes on. It affects people in different ways. For most it brings out the best; for others, the worst. A person whose lifestyle and character are questionable can suddenly receive unmerited prominence from one well-placed television appearance. Frail, weak, ordinary people appear strong and powerful. Most are perceived as something they are not.

At times the camera is not a friend, magnifying every characteristic for good or evil. For some, the camera has resulted in their stardom; for others, their downfall. For Jim and Tammy Bakker television highlighted their finest qualities, but it also magnified their imperfections for all the world to see.

I saw the humanity of Jim and Tammy Bakker. So did most people who knew them personally. But I never observed anything in those years that indicated evidence of any kind of aberration. I did, however, notice a change.

With the advent of the satellite network, the number of outlets through the cable systems exploded. Jim and Tammy began to be seen regularly across the nation — not just on isolated stations. Their visibility increased dramatically, giving them access to millions of people daily. The PTL Network was in about sixteen million homes, twenty-four hours a day.

Toward the advent of Heritage USA, something did begin to change in Jim Bakker. I noticed it but said nothing.

Now I have to answer to God myself, as do others who had spiritual authority over him. Did we fail Jim by not using that authority? Perhaps we were more concerned about the effects of his ministry than we were about Jim as a person.

I wish I had fully understood then what I know well now: When *what we do* is more important that *who we are*, we are in trouble. Big trouble!

4

An Uncertain Sound

In my position as the superintent of the Illinois Assemblies of God, I did a lot of traveling and attended several meetings a week. Many people knew about my involvement with PTL, so they often used me as a sounding board for their opinions.

Most leaders that I met not only had a theory about PTL, but they felt they had a word from heaven, a word from God. Yet many of them had never been to PTL; some had never even seen the "The PTL Club," but they were experts on what was wrong with Jim Bakker and his media ministry.

It was in the midst of these early rumblings that Jim and Tammy began pleading with me to accept a full time position on the PTL staff, citing how much they needed my help. The media ministry was expanding rapidly, and it seemed that the Heritage Church congregation increased every Sunday. It was difficult, if not impossible, for Jim and Tammy to keep up with the accelerated pace of growth.

In spite of my hedging, the Bakkers persisted. It's a bit heady, quite frankly, to be wanted and desired for any position, especially when someone says, "You can help us make this operation work. We must have you." I was flattered by their constant praise and enthusiasm over how much I could benefit their organization.

In April, 1983, Jim and Tammy formally asked me to become the executive director of PTL, overseeing all aspects of the ministry and co-pastoring the church. For the next six months, I struggled, weighing all the facts, sorting out my motives, and addressing every concern in an effort to make the right decision.

I constantly talked with people, the executives of my denomination, my contemporaries, and my colleagues, about what it would take to get the PTL ministry under control. Interestingly, none of these friends ever put up a red flag concerning PTL. Perhaps they didn't want to hurt me, or maybe they just did not know what to say. I understand that.

I know that you can't determine the authenticity of a ministry, the character of a minister, or seeking God's will by taking a poll!

During this time, I submitted myself to others, asking, "What do you think I should do?" Over the years, I tried to have a broad-based group of people whom I trusted — friends who loved me and whose judgment I respected to counsel me.

I've never been afraid to say to people, "Tell me if I'm doing something wrong." Nobody thinks of everything, and all of us have blind spots. I was always open to advice.

That doesn't mean my friends are responsible for my mistakes. But, I believe I would have listened if someone had told me that PTL was not the place for me. "The wounds of a friend are better than the praise of an enemy" (Prov. 27:6; my paraphrase), certainly applies to the subject of integrity.

I wanted answers, and I was searching for truth. If they knew, I wish someone had had the courage to be honest with me.

"If the trumpet gives an uncertain sound, who shall prepare himself to the battle?" (1 Cor. 14:8). There was an uncertain sound I was receiving and I didn't quite know what to make of it.

I was trying to find the right thing to do, using the same principles I had applied for the past thirty-four years of my life. With every move I had ever made — whether it was leaving Bible college, speaking at conferences or conventions, ministering in local churches, pastoring a church, or becoming a denominational official — I always knew in my heart, from the moment that the situation presented itself: "This is the way, walk ye in it" (Isa. 30:21).

I've learned that the way we determine what is "right" in one given situation may not be the standard by which the next decision should be made. We must consider every new set of circumstances with its new involvements and new players. Each experience, each decision, and each encounter at life's crossroads demands a new commitment to God and a fresh approach in determining the right direction to take.

But I couldn't get any definite direction about going to PTL. The complexity of the issues involved, the contradictions within my own mind, and the enigma of the whole situation made my decision very difficult. Besides, there was a part of me that really wanted to go to PTL.

I can't write a book about integrity and not be totally candid. Television holds a fascinating attraction for anyone. A minister who tells me that he has no interest in appearing on TV would be a rare find. I'm not saying he's not telling the truth; I'm just saying he's one in a million, and I haven't met him yet.

Who wouldn't want a highly visible ministry that involved not only managing a media organization but also included the opportunity to appear on a daily nationwide television program? I admit that my ego got in the way. I enjoyed preaching and talking to millions of people via the media of television. Where else could I minister to so many people at one time?

I let my pride get in the way. I do know the status and public exposure that came with the PTL position were very tempting. In fact, it is difficult for my wife and I, to this day, to go into a shopping mall and not be stopped several times by people who recognize us.

At the time, I couldn't properly evaluate my motives although I believe I did sincerely try to be honest with myself. Thoughts came at me from every direction, presenting opposing views in my own mind. One day practical issues would control my thinking; the next, I would be swept away by high-level emotion, caught up in a whirlwind of excitement that made rational decision-making impossible.

PTL owned one of America's outstanding TV production buildings. Few, if any, television studios in America had the space for an audience of 1,800 people. Whenever one of the major networks wanted to evaluate the newest state-of-the-art equipment or the latest technique, they came to Heritage USA. The caliber of television production was top-notch, with the finest quality control rooms and computer editing suites in the business. All of the equipment at PTL in those years was RCA, the best in television electronics at the time.

These facts impressed me and figured into my decision-making process. My prior experience in radio and television programming made me appreciate PTL's high standard of expertise.

While the technical side of television intrigued me, the aura surrounding the studio often made me uncomfortable. I wondered how I would fit into the ethereal land of emotions that characterized "The PTL Club" at the time. Everything seemed based on outward appearance — how you looked and what people would think. The producer's motto was: Do it the way that gets the best results. Remember millions are watching.

The chain of command at PTL was another matter of grave concern to me. At the time, I was working in an institutional, denominational environment where the lines of authority were clearly defined through constitutional bylaws. Pages of responsibilities told me: Here's what your job is, and here's what your job is not.

It disturbed me to think of giving up my role as a professional churchman, knowing I would be forfeiting on a daily basis the stability and security of well-established friendships. I was considering launching into another world and leaving behind a committed group of quality people whom I trusted implicitly. I often shared my heart with them.

In Illinois I had developed a close relationship with a team of outstanding leaders. My administrative assistant, Al Cress, who managed me and my office, had a keen sense of organization that kept me on track. Another valuable member of my staff, Mark Burgund, an M.B.A. graduate and an outstanding, godly man was a superb administrator.

Others, like Bill Snider, a University of Illinois graduate who also had a degree in theology provided excellent insight into difficult situations. Dr. James Cobble, an outstanding educator, brought his gift of counseling to our staff. Richard Peterson, Mary Ellen Grell, and outstanding youth leaders had great ability. They were great leaders and trusted friends. These people loved me and would tell me if I was wrong in a decision or if I was doing something out of line. We were committed to one another.

I knew I might not have that same strong bond among the employees at PTL. It was common knowledge that the turnover rate among staff personnel and those in high-level positions was high. These facts troubled me.

On the other hand, I knew Jim had a reputation for hiring highly qualified people. In fact, PTL was seen as a forerunner among television ministries in America. They were the first to hire a full-time lawyer and had a number of CPAs on staff.

Jim Bakker constantly pressed me for a decision, offering me more and more opportunities to expand my gifts of leadership. Sometimes I felt overwhelmed by his generosity and insistence that I was the only man for the job. He told me I could make any changes necessary to get PTL under control. All these uncertain sounds reverberated within my spirit, making each new possibility more difficult to refuse.

On the other hand, I wondered if Jim could share the leadership of PTL with anyone else. I knew he could put his ideas down on a piece of paper for an architect to build or explain to the television director how he wanted a program shot. He could develop an organizational flow chart, lay out a fund raising program, and design the concept of a great park. But, when it came to turning over the operation of PTL to someone else, I'm not sure if Jim Bakker himself knew whether or not he could do it.

Jim was like a vehicle, speeding down the road of life. You couldn't get your hands on his back bumper. He was always ahead of you. Try as you might and insist as you would to get him to listen to why he shouldn't do something — that was almost an impossible task. I knew that from having worked with him on PTL's board of directors. In fact, I found Jim Bakker to be one of the most complex individuals I have ever known.

What were simple, understandable realities to most people became emotion-filled, complex dilemmas to Jim Bakker. From his perspective, every problem took on the proportions of an overblown crisis.

At times Jim's secretive nature created some of the problems we had to deal with. On other occasions, he publicly disclosed information that should have been kept private. We were continually putting out fires started by Jim's lack of discretion in disseminating information.

I realize now that the warning lights were flashing all around me, signaling, "Be careful! Watch out! Danger ahead!" But I did not see them.

The question I must ask myself is: Did I even want to see them? Was my mind already set on going to PTL, making me unwilling to acknowledge the alarms sounding in my heart?

While still in the throes of trying to make a decision, Jim asked me to speak at a PTL seminar during the Fourth of July celebration in 1983. That week Heritage USA was the center of much activity with parades and fireworks and other special events such as Christendom had never known. Being there during this time gave me an opportunity to observe Jim and his staff in action. Mildred and I could really see what was occuring at PTL.

In my years as a denominational leader, one of my

responsibilities, when called into a difficult church situation, was to assess what was actually going on and isolate the problem. I put those same principles to work, attempting to get a feel for what was happening behind the scenes at PTL.

I didn't have to look too deep. My presence set off some fireworks of its own when the inner rivalry between PTL department heads came to the surface. There were some rumblings created by rumors that Jim and Tammy were considering bringing me on staff. In a setting like PTL, keeping new appointments confidential was practically impossible for the Bakkers.

Since I had not yet made a decision and did not want to jeopardize my work in Illinois, I had been very selective concerning who I told about Jim's offer. The fact that some of the PTL staff knew disturbed me.

Apparently, some staff members at PTL believed I wanted to take control of the ministry, and a few of Jim Bakker's strong supporters considered me a threat to his position of leadership. To me that seemed ludicrous. I had a great deal of respect for Jim Bakker; he was the mind and impetus behind the whole operation. Who could ever replace him? Still, when I finally accepted the position of executive director at PTL, there were already what I would describe as, "armed camps" prepared for attack.

Jim and Tammy Bakker were never a part of that. I believe they genuinely wanted me to come to PTL. They were at the end of themselves and simply needed help. By not making a firm, clearly understood declaration of why he had chosen me to assist him, Jim did leave a vacuum that led to clamoring among the staff. His erratic leadership style, although not intentional, often created misunderstanding and dissension.

I knew some of the division supervisors and department heads considered me a possible competitor. As for myself, I didn't feel in competition with anyone. Beyond the threat that I posed to the organizational leadership, there were inner-ministry rivals that were developing. Everybody was trying to protect their own turf.

Jim and Tammy lived above that, and I didn't see myself as a rival to anyone. Why should I? Having served for many years as one of our denomination's top officials, I didn't view my move to PTL as an advancement or a demotion. To me it was a lateral move. One of my understandings with Jim Bakker was, while on staff, I could still go out preaching in different churches and events around the country.

A competitive environment existed at PTL unlike any I'd ever seen before. For some reason this type of ministry attracted people who were trying to find out what God wanted them to do. They assumed that because they had a great burden for a particular ministry, it qualified them for certain positions. PTL was so big and so broad that a place was found for almost anyone who wanted to be involved in a ministry — any kind of ministry. The sad part was — most of them were in over their heads. When Jim and Tammy made a trip somewhere, he often hired people on the spot, wherever he was.

What these people, and those who hired them, failed to realize is that you cannot develop ministry from your vision, your burden, or your dream. Ministry is the result of who you are. It flows out of your character and your relationship with God. Ministry doesn't just happen because you're put into a certain position of leadership.

I encountered another group of people working at PTL. This group tried to live vicariously through Jim Bakker. They wanted to be something and somebody, but they weren't, so they lived out their fantasies through Jim. It reminded me of the father who didn't make it as a football player so he pushes his son to the extreme, hoping to indirectly bolster his own ego through his son's success.

Also working at PTL were people who were literally running from God. They had discovered that sometimes it is easier to go someplace else than to face the problems you have where you are. People came to PTL, wanting, expecting, and sometimes almost demanding a job because they weren't happy where they were. They had supported PTL in some way and felt entitled to a position.

I took all this information into account, along with everything else I was hearing, observing, and learning about while trying to make a decision about becoming part of the staff at PTL. It seemed the more I knew, the more confused I became.

One of my primary concerns was to know absolutely what was right for me. With any move we had ever made, my wife and I both knew spontaneously exactly what it was that we were to do. For the first time in our lives, we were having difficulty making a decision. Finally, I brought myself to the place where I was willing to do what was best in this situation.

Several weeks before I made my final decision, I flew to Charlotte just to spend the day. I wanted to spend more time with Jim to see if I could get a feeling of assurance in my heart. During our time together, I tried to perceive Jim's true motives and understand his needs.

On several occasions, Jim said to me, "Pastor Dortch, you probably know me better than anyone else."

Whether he told ten other people the same thing, I don't know. I do believe I knew Jim well, and during my tenure at PTL, I did not have any facts that made me question the personal life and teaching of this man. In private discussions he was always proper, he read his Bible daily, and he had a kind heart. In spite of his many fine qualities, Jim Bakker remained an enigma to me and to other people who were close to him at different periods in his life.

Unquestionably, I think anyone who had a friendship with Jim would agree: Nobody really knew Jim Bakker. I don't think even Tammy totally understood Jim.

During the day that I spent with Jim, I also tried to tap into my own emotions to see if I felt comfortable in the working situation at PTL. On the return flight to Illinois that night, I analyzed my feelings and decided I could be happy there.

On September 28, 1983 I was scheduled to be on "The PTL Club," and Jim wanted my answer by then. Just prior to that date, I called Jim at his office but he wasn't there.

Then someone, I can't remember who, told me that the IRS was coming to PTL to begin an extensive audit. That certainly wasn't something I was looking forward to as soon as I started working there. But the idea of becoming part of the general audit didn't concern me because I knew that I didn't have anything to hide.

I did, however, feel a check of concern within my spirit. But I chose to ignore another silent warning, telling myself that Jim needed me and I had an important job to do at PTL.

It wasn't until later, when the ministry came crashing down around me that I realized: **Knowing** God and being submissive to His will is more important than **doing**. Success is illusive, and the real test of who a person is resides in his character. What God intends us to **be** is more important than **what we do** in life. That element is essential to living a life of integrity. **Being is far more important than doing.**

Because I still had some questions, I returned to Charlotte a day early — on September 27 — and spent the evening at the office visiting with Jim and Tammy.

Later, when we went to their house, I distinctly remember asking, not really knowing why I was posing the question, "Jim, is there anything I should know?"

"Nothing else I can think of," Jim assured me, indicating there were no hidden problems and we could go forward.

After the fall of PTL, many people asked me, "Did Jim Bakker have a design? Did he have a plan? Was there some kind of conspiracy?"

Did the Bakkers have an evil strategy to get me to PTL, as some have suggested? I don't think so. I believe Jim simply had a gut-level feeling that the ministry was no longer manageable, and he needed my help.

Having reached that conclusion and confident Jim had been open and honest with me, I accepted the position. On September 28, 1983, Jim announced to the television viewers that I would be coming to PTL.

On the air that day I said to Jim, "God has given you a vision for a work to be done, and I hope and pray that I will be able to assimilate your vision in my spirit. Together we can work for God and accomplish what needs to be done."

Jim Bakker and I made a commitment of five years to each other that could not be broken unless the other gave permission. I signed a contract, stating that Jim could not dismiss me for any reason whatsoever unless I was kept on the payroll for five years. On the other hand, I could not resign my position with PTL without Jim's permission for five years. That was the only "deal" I ever made with Jim Bakker.

I have never "made a deal" with anybody for anything that was questionable. While I was involved in denominational work, I never negotiated with a pastor, or anyone else, to cover up anything. Even if that person were a special friend, I simply refused to overlook any problem that needed correction. I did my best to deal lovingly and compassionately with all people — and to do what was right.

I can stand before God and men and say: In every area of my life — personal, professional, and morally — I did what I said I was going to do. The goal of my life has always been to be of value, to be used in service to others, and to do what is honorable.

On December 14, 1983, my wife and I flew to Charlotte after a very gracious farewell to Illinois and seventeen years as a state official.

My duties as the co-pastor of Heritage Village Church and Missionary Fellowship and the senior executive vice president of the PTL Ministry did not begin until January 1, 1984. Mildred and I were looking forward to spending the holiday season resting and settling into our new home.

I desperately needed a break from the hectic pace I had been keeping. The Crohn's disease had sapped the energy from my already weary body, and my physical condition cried out for relief.

For the past fourteen years, I had probably preached as much as any executive of the Assemblies of God who was serving as a state official. I traveled constantly all over the country and, at the time, served on many boards of directors.

When you're serving in a responsible position, you become a decision-maker, like it or not. I used to say to my wife, "Honey, I'm so tired of making decisions." The responsibilities of leadership often make for a lonely life. Your motives are questioned and your good intentions are often misunderstood.

In addition to my administrative duties at the Illinois headquarters, the care of the churches and my love for the pastors drove me to spend as much time as possible with them.

I would arrive at a church whose pastor had failed, either morally or personally, and have to sort through the rumors and comfort the families. I couldn't just view things as I saw them — that would be a very pleasant way to live. Instead, I had to constantly examine situations, people, events, and circumstances, trying to uncover the story behind them without causing further damage to those involved.

Many nights I spent weeping with a pastor and his family, counseling them on how to pick up the pieces and go on with their lives. They would bid me farewell and say, "How wonderful to be in your position," not realizing I would carry the burden of their problem with me to the next crisis at another church across the state.

In making the decision to come to PTL, one thought had continuously lingered in my mind: If I went to PTL, no longer would I have to go to the people. Because of the television program and the nature of Heritage USA, the people were coming to us. No longer would I have to drive hundreds of miles every week or fly thousands of miles every month. I could stay at home and still do what I loved most — ministering to the needs of people.

My weariness and fatigue certainly influenced my decision. I should have known that no one should make a decision when they are physically and mentally exhausted. I wish now I had taken time to get away and quiet my spirit, soul, and body before deciding the most important move of my career — and of my life.

Jesus said: "Come ye yourselves apart . . . and rest a while!" (Mark 6:31). If we don't come apart, we may fall apart. That is reality.

The Bible also warns us about being weary in well doing. It says, ". . . we shall reap, if we faint not" (Gal. 6:9). It's up to us to make sure we don't faint.

That holiday season, Mildred and I did rest — for three or four days — but it wasn't enough to release the pressure that had been building up for years.

In making the decision to go to PTL one event did surface in my memory. It was a one-of-a-kind experience. Entering the parking lot at my office after lunch one day I felt restrained from getting out of the car. After turning off the ignition it was as if I just couldn't find a release to leave my seat. What it was I don't know, but in my mind something opened up before me about the future. I was afraid! Within myself I was made to know that I was going to go through a deep tragedy, a severe loss, and would suffer much. I knew that my spiritual life was secure, but I knew my world was going to crash, and that I should be in peace. I did not know what had happened, but it was very real in my mind. Was it an indication of things to come at PTL? Was I prepared for it?

*Henry Harrison, Tammy and Jim Bakker, Richard Dortch
and four other board members.*

5

Behind the Scenes
at PTL

What was PTL? National media, secular writers, and former staff members have tried to describe the phenomena of PTL, but the image remains elusive, even to me.

Legally, PTL was not a corporation. Merely a logo, PTL was a registered trademark, meaning Praise the Lord or People That Love. Those three letters, however, represent much more than a catchy slogan.

PTL began as Jim Bakker's vision, a mixture of reality and fantasy. A born dreamer and the master designer of PTL and Heritage USA, Jim Bakker created the vast Christian complex that remains today unsurpassed in modern facilities.

Heritage USA combined a spiritual oasis and a fantasyland into a unique Christian community designed in the extravagance and architecture of the Victorian period. Comparable to a city, the 2,300 acre site had its own utilities, television studio, shops, restaurants, campground, recreational complex, and television network. Heritage USA also had subdivisions of contemporary and fashionable homes.

What attracted people to PTL? Without question, Jim and Tammy Bakker supplied the magnetism that drew devotees, vacation seekers, and the curious to Heritage USA. They were the super celebrities, the "stars" of "The Jim and Tammy Show," which, at its peak, was carried by more television stations than the "Johnny Carson Show."

Life at PTL revolved around this live TV program, a sparkling hour of spiritual hope and religious entertainment. Music, famous Christian guests, and appeals for money to pay for Jim's multitude of building and missionary projects filled the daily format.

Jim Bakker was a master TV host who could mix all the ingredients of televangelism — the interviews, the script, music, and a Christian message — into a masterpiece of entertainment and ministry that appealed to a wide range of viewers.

Providing a worldwide audience of millions, "The Jim and Tammy Show" lured entertainers, evangelists, actors, and politicians. Oral Roberts, Robert Schuller, Jimmy Swaggart, and Billy Graham all appeared on the TV show.

Unintimidated by famous guests, Jim related to actors as effortlessly as to preachers and evangelists. A glittering list of show business personalities — Mickey Rooney, Carol Lawrence, Pearl Bailey, Gavin MacLeod to name a few — appeared before the cameras with the Bakkers. Jim and Tammy easily identified with the famous people they interviewed, relating to their celebrity status, their high visibility, and their public recognition.

Actors found a new surge of popularity after an appearance on PTL. Songwriters enriched themselves in royalties when their songs were introduced on the show. Christian entertainers and evangelists got a flood of invitations to sing and preach at churches after they were seen on PTL.

Bakker, unsurpassed in his unbiased insight, had the ability to relate to viewers and visitors on the issues of life — loneliness, divorce, addictions to drugs and alcohol. He identified with the forgotten people who were hurting from the tragedies and conflicts of living.

Most people came to PTL to have their spiritual needs met through prayer, camp meetings, seminars, and personal ministry. Few left disappointed.

Behind the scenes of the PTL cameras thrived a different and distinctive culture, with its own vocabulary, idioms, attitudes, and fantasies.

I stepped into this inner sanctum, hoping to find unity and Christian commitment to the common goal of serving God. Instead, there awaited me a bubbling caldron of jealousies, struggles for prestige and authority, and runaway spending.

My job description as the senior executive vice president at PTL came to a brief half page statement of vague responsibilities. Rather unorthodox, I thought, for such a large organization. That, however, turned out to be the least of my worries.

When I arrived, I was told all staff members except Jim and Tammy, David Taggart (Jim's administrative assistant), and Shirley Fulbright (Jim's secretary) were my responsibility. For administrative purposes everyone else would work under me.

I considered the chain of command very important since I knew from experience that clear-cut vertical lines of authority in the workplace make horizontal relationships better. Trouble comes when you don't know who does what or who answers to whom.

A few weeks later, one of the major division heads explained she was not under my authority.

"I have my own arrangement," she told me.

It did not matter to me who she worked for, but I could foresee complications. Apparently, she answered to no one except Jim Bakker and was permitted to operate outside of budget constraints. That was the real problem — a lack of discipline and restraint in spending.

It was not unusual for her to impulsively spend tens of thousands of dollars each month. Because no money had been alloted for such expenses, we struggled from month to month to know where the cash was going to come from.

It didn't take me long to realize that Jim Bakker did not have an established protocol for dealing with staff or difficulties. Jim impulsively discussed whatever current problem was on his mind with whomever happened to be available.

Instead of going directly to the person in charge, Jim would engage the vice president of TV production in a three hour conversation about handling the real estate at Heritage USA, leaving the TV executive totally confused. Then he would discuss data processing with the vice president of Heritage USA, a subject completely foreign to the administrator.

Few, if any, pre-determined procedures, in hiring practices or day to day operations, were followed consistently. Having left behind a staff of highly skilled professionals to come to PTL, I was dismayed by the number of unqualified people in management positions at Heritage USA.

No one frustrated me more than the "Walt Disney man." That's what everyone called Bobby Miller because he carried out Jim Bakker's dreams at Heritage USA.

His first job at PTL involved cleaning the warehouse facilities, but somehow he had been made the director of one of the enterprise's largest divisions. Everyone who worked on the grounds at Heritage USA — about 600 people — came under his authority.

Yet, the responsibility of this position was beyond his training and maturity to carry out. To make matters worse, his character and conduct were constantly in question. In fact, Bobby Miller was so out of touch with life's demands that he could hardly function at living.

For some reason, PTL often sacrificed character for ability and spirituality for personality. It troubled me to realize that the lives of some staff people were not commensurate with the jobs they were doing.

On one occasion Bobby Miller called a day of fasting and prayer for all of his staff, and many of those good, wonderful people conscientiously went to the Upper Room or to the church to pray. Bobby Miller, we later discovered, had used the day to take a pre-planned canoe trip with his friends.

When completion of the water park looked questionable because of over spending, Bobby Miller rushed into my office and blurted out, "Pastor Dortch, we can finish the water park for $600,000."

I was stunned and grateful at the same time. "That's wonderful news, Bobby!"

The estimates we had received indicated it would take at least two million dollars to finish the project. Now I was told we could do the whole job for $600,000.

Regaining my sanity, I asked, "How did you find this out, Bobby? Who told you we could do it for $600,000?"

"God told me," he said simply.

"How do you know God spoke?" I questioned, remembering the canoeing incident.

"I just felt a spirit come upon me that said $600,000."

Ultimately, it cost about three million dollars to finish the water park.

On another occasion, Jim Bakker gave a very nice lady, Mary Nelson, whose job consisted of maintaining Heritage USA's appearance, the title of executive vice president.

I asked Jim, "Why in the world did you give her that title?"

"Because I like her," he responded, "and I knew it made her feel good."

It's true that Mary was quite likable and did exceptional work, but the exaggerated title gave her a heightened sense of importance that sabotaged the true chain of command. She had no idea how to operate a facility like Heritage USA within the required budget constraints, and overspending for new purchases became chronic.

There were people throughout the organization with important titles, who administratively, spiritually, emotionally, temperamentally, and educationally, were incompetent to serve in the positions they'd been assigned. Their lack of professional training and experience left them inept at managing other people or their departments.

One of the most misplaced department heads was Sue Becker, who Jim Bakker assigned to be in charge of the pastoral staff of thirty-one ministers. Although she was a lovely and capable person, her background in secular work did not qualify her for this extremely important and sensitive position.

Ninety percent of the pastors working at Heritage Village Church and Missionary Fellowship had been in the ministry for at least fifteen years — some for thirty. If Sue had been experienced in the ministry with proven qualities of leadership, I would have been extremely pleased about her appointment. She had never pastored a church, never been an evangelist, and never been a church administrator, yet all our pastors were accountable to her. I was glad women were in key places of leadership. PTL was far ahead of other ministries in making women leaders in its ministry.

It broke my heart, for PTL and the people involved, to see so many staff members floundering at their jobs when their talents would have been so much more effective in the proper role.

There were exceptions. Paul Ferrin, PTL's music director and a truly qualified professional, performed his duties with spiritual integrity and outstanding talent. He was not treated with the respect he deserved. I made it known on many occasions I was displeased with his talents being wasted. He deserved better use.

Aside from the staffing and management dilemma that occupied a great deal of my time, my biggest headache was most often Jim Bakker himself.

Jim never faced a problem head-on. He decided vital issues by his feelings. When Jim got depressed — a frequent state of mind — he brought employees and others down with him. The spiritual, emotional, and corporate disposition of the PTL empire plummeted with Bakker's depression. I found his erratic mood swings overwhelming, making it impossible to keep PTL on a stable course. Jim was unable to handle medication. When he took it we all knew.

When Jim found a new hero, a champion, or a fresh

philosophy to follow, he would emerge from his sullen moods. At one point Bakker asked all the staff to read the book, *In Search of Excellence*. But the "instant cure" management tools they prescribed didn't last. He soon jumped to another inspiration for cooperate success. This time PTL leaders were expected to meet in small "quality circles" to promote ideas for ministry growth.

On another occasion, Jim slipped out of an "emotional down" by discovering the book, *Tough Times Never Last, But Tough People Do!* by Robert Schuller. He made it required reading for the entire staff. On another occasion the time clocks were thrown out — traded for a new work concept.

By the nature of his leadership — or lack thereof — Jim Bakker created more problems for the ministry than he solved; all of us knew it but did very little about it. Jim's personal secretary, Shirley Fulbright said, "Jim creates a crisis so that he can solve it. That's one of his self-needs."

When I first came on staff, Jim and I had an understanding that neither one of us would make any financial commitments unless we had cleared it with each other.

"We need to put restraints on spending," he told me.

"Okay, Jim, I will not make any kind of commitment over $10,000 without running it by you," I suggested, and he agreed to do the same.

In the normal course of operating a huge complex like Heritage USA, $10,000 is not a large sum. Such expenditures were necessary, but in order to trim expenses, we had to keep a tight reign on day-to-day spending or it got out of control.

Jim knew he needed limits set for him. Often on the air, spontaneously, without talking to anyone, Jim had made million dollar commitments. This put a financial strain on the ministry time and time again.

Not long after we made the agreement, I arrived for work one Monday morning at my regular time of 7:30 and noticed Jim's car at his parking place behind the general office. This surprised me since Jim normally drove from his house directly to the television studio.

That's highly unusual, I thought to myself. *Something must be up.*

I had been away all day Sunday for an out-of-town speaking engagement and hadn't been informed of any new developments.

I always came in early to go over the work orders for the day and review the program list for the daily broadcast.

Entering my office, which directly faced Jim's, I could see him working. After a few moments, he came in and sat down across from my desk.

"I have an apology to make to you," he began slowly. "I did something yesterday that broke our commitment."

"What happened?" I asked, holding my breath.

In his unique Jim Bakker style, he put his head down like a child expecting to be disciplined.

"It was for over a million dollars — for Kevin," he said meekly.

Kevin, a bright, engaging but handicapped seventeen year old was Jim's second cousin by adoption. Kevin loved Jim Bakker and PTL.

Like Jim and everyone else on the staff, I adored this special young man and believed he was certainly worthy of anything that could be done for him. But I couldn't imagine what Kevin needed that would cost a million dollars. Besides, Jim had given me his word.

"What do you mean?" I probed. "We had an agreement."

"Yesterday, we were standing in front of the Heritage Grand Hotel," Jim explained sheepishly. "Kevin was getting ready to go back to Michigan with his parents when he turned to me and said, 'I wish I didn't have to leave PTL, Jim. I wish we could stay here and live.'"

Jim paused for a moment to catch my reaction. Then he continued, "Before I thought about it, I said, 'Kevin, I'll build you a house in thirty days!'"

I closed my eyes and stared up at the ceiling, trying to think rationally. *Someone has to,* I thought to myself.

"It will cost a million dollars to do that," Jim said with a sigh.

The problem wasn't building a house with special features to meet Kevin's needs. It was the thirty-day time restriction that escalated the cost. If we'd had six months — the normal time it would take to build that house — the cost would have been half the amount. In fact, as it turned out, we could have built a house half the size for probably $200,000. It would have been more than sufficient for Kevin and his family. In the end, the house cost about $1,600,000.

After all the extra expense, we were horrified to discover the builder had not obtained the proper permit, and the house was not properly permitted, as far as the state was concerned. It needed a certain kind of permit, and it did not have it. Had rational thinking prevailed, we could have had a home for Kevin and his family for the rest of his life. However, it worked out for awhile. Kevin and his family were able to live there until the fall of PTL.

Such impulsive, irrational decision-making by Jim Bakker was not unusual. In fact, it was a common occurrence at PTL.

This brings me back to the question of integrity.

What was my sin in the building of Kevin's house? I know now it was one of consensual integrity. I agreed to something when I should have objected.

What should I have done? I should have screamed.

I should have cried out and said, "Yes, let's build Kevin's house. But let's tell him we can't do it in thirty days. He'll understand. Let's take time to raise the money, find out Kevin's needs, and also look into the state requirements for handicapped facilities."

The words of Jesus haunt me everytime I think about the house we built for Kevin: "For which of you, intending to build a tower, sitteth not down first, and counteth the cost . . . " (Luke 14:28).

Another cost-saving measure I tried to introduce also ran into difficulty. I decided to require three bids for every outside contract. After the administrative staff went over the list of regular spending, we began to take three bids from all suppliers and contractors.

One day when speaking to the head of our insurance department, I reminded him of our new policy. "Remember, we must take three bids before awarding our insurance contract for the new year."

His eyes widened. "I'd like to get bids, Pastor Dortch, but I can't. Jim Bakker wants the contract to go to one of Eddie Knox's friends."

Knox was the mayor of Charlotte, a candidate for governor of North Carolina, and PTL's attorney.

"That seems odd," I said, remembering that Jim Bakker had twice told me he was offended and incensed at the fees Eddie Knox was charging the PTL ministry.

In Jim's words, "We're paying champagne prices for 7-Up." We were being charged Eddie Knox rates for the work his nephew was doing. In Jim's opinion, the nephew's limited experience did not compare to Eddie's, who was the senior partner of the law firm.

"Please go ahead and get three bids for the insurance," I told the department head. "I'll speak to Mr. Bakker."

I went to Jim and asked, "Jim, why are we buying our insurance from a firm who hasn't submitted a bid?"

"I have this arrangement with Eddie Knox," Jim said nonchalantly, explaining that the owner of the insurance firm in turn helps Eddie Knox with his political campaign contributions.

"I still plan to take three bids for the insurance," I replied unwaveringly.

"If you're going to do that," Jim shot back, "you're going to take the blame for it."

"Fine," I responded. "That's no problem."

Jim quickly repeated, "You're the one who's going to have to answer the questions when they come up and take the blame."

"I'm prepared to do that," I said, standing my ground.

Eddie Knox was incensed.

That came as no surprise to me. When I first came on the PTL board of directors, Mr. Knox had questioned whether or not I should be a member. Maybe he thought I would uncover some of his dealings and thus threaten his position as PTL's attorney. I did, and we no longer used him.

By taking a stand, I was trying to give Jim Bakker the strength to resist further efforts by Eddie Knox to solicit contracts for his other friends — all of whom it seemed wanted to do business with PTL. One day it was a mobile park, the next a housing development or some other major project. Eddie Knox constantly brought us proposals. The record shows that.

This confounded me. Any lawyer I had ever worked with in the past made it clear it would be difficult for them to give a neutral opinion if they were in business with the corporation they represented. Eddie Knox apparently didn't view his working relationship with PTL as unethical. To me, however, it appeared to be a breach of trust.

At the same time that Eddie Knox was trying to enter into business arrangements with Jim, he was publicly criticizing the ministry and constantly making negative statements about PTL to the press. As the mayor of Charlotte and a gubernatorial candidate, Mr. Knox played both sides as only a politician can. His comments later hurt PTL tremendously. Jim was angry, but pleased that Knox was gone.

It was strange how many times I tried to keep things on the up and up and make Jim accountable — those were the incidents that backfired on me.

During 1985 and 1986, PTL enjoyed its greatest years of blessing. The arms of the vast ministry began to stretch out around the world. Millions of dollars were given to missions both at home and abroad. New outreaches developed almost daily.

Heritage USA became a haven for the downtrodden in life. The New Wine Fellowship, a rehabilitation center for drug abusers and alcoholics, provided treatment and spiritual ministry. The Heritage House, a million dollar facility, was built to house and care for young unwed mothers who wanted to give birth to their babies.

To help street people, PTL designed Fort Hope, a village where the homeless could come to live and be trained in a vocation. Scores of young men took advantage of that program, bettering their lives as a result.

Eight hundred "People Who Love Centers," where the needy could get jobs, food, and clothing, were built all over America. In addition, many prisons in the United States received satellite dishes so that they could have Christian television twenty-four hours a day.

The Upper Room, a twenty-four hour sanctuary for prayer and telephone counseling, ministered to thousands of people every day.

The marriage workshops at PTL enrolled ten thousand plus people a year. Couples came to Heritage USA for counseling and help for their marital problems. Other seminars conducted by the well-known Christian authors and big-name preachers drew thousands of people. A continuous stream of ministry and Bible teaching flowed from PTL's many conference rooms. It was something to behold!

The incredible number of charitable, humanitarian causes supported by PTL in the '80s would make an exhaustive list.

When a historic church in South Carolina, attended predominantly by black people, was maliciously burned to the ground, PTL provided the funds to rebuild that church. Scores of other churches facing financial difficulty were given sums up to $100,000. North Central Bible College, where Jim Bakker and I attended, received over $200,000 in contributions during those years. The unwritten policy at PTL was, if you see a need fill it, and be as generous as possible. An undesignated offering of $250,000 was given to the Assemblies of God. I believed it was the right thing to do, and Jim agreed.

The immense outreach at PTL, the tremendous ministry taking place at Heritage USA, and the popularity of "The Jim and Tammy Show" established 1985 and 1986 as the "glory years."

Viewers nationwide heard the inspiring testimonies of celebrities like Roy Rogers, Dale Evans, and Pat Boone. I could mention dozens of other household names—Christian leaders and preachers — who shared the spotlight on "The Jim and Tammy Show," blessing millions with teachings from Scripture and stories of God's deliverance. In return, their ministries benefited and prospered from exposure to PTL's vast audience. The greatest testimonies came from wonderful, ordinary people who were helped. They loved PTL.

Jim and Tammy loved to discover new talent and promote musicians who had great potential. Mike Adkins, the celebrated gospel singer and songwriter, was a PTL favorite, and his public ministry skyrocketed as a result. Dr. Evelyn Carter Spencer of California, BB and CC Winan, the PTL Singers and Orchestra, and many others — all got their start on "The Jim and Tammy Show."

Every Fourth of July, Heritage USA planned huge parades. In July of 1985 over 50,000 people came to PTL to celebrate our nation's birthday. It was not unusual on any given day to have fifteen to twenty thousand people on the grounds. In 1986, 6,200,000 people visited Heritage USA, making it the third largest tourist attraction in the United States — second only to Disneyland and Disney World.

While the public beheld the outward signs of the glory years, the administration and leadership of PTL agonized over a dilemma eating away at the internal workings of the organization. The problem resulted from one man's vision racing out of control and beyond financial accountability. That is the fact, but the motive behind Jim's vision tells a different story.

Jim Bakker possessed a remarkable gift. Just by talking with people he could grasp their need and envision the dream God had put in their heart. Then, for some reason, he took it upon himself to do anything he could to help make that dream a reality.

I don't believe Jim was motivated by a desire to win man's approval; I contend it was Jim Bakker's genuine love for mankind that moved his heart and compelled him to reach out in incredible ways. Thousands reaped the benefits of Jim's sincere and magnificent generosity. No wonder so many people loved him.

The employees worked long and hard hours, partly because they enjoyed their work, but mostly because they, too, loved Jim Bakker. I know because I was one of them.

Behind the scenes and behind the cameras, however, an atmosphere of high tension in responsibility and operations generated unimaginable stress among the staff. Many couldn't handle the pressure. Burnout casualties took a high toll, and the employee turnover increased dramatically.

This constant flushing of people, department heads, and personnel created chaos in the organization. It seemed we went from one emergency to another. To make matters worse, the financial crisis in management and operations remained constant.

Every Wednesday morning, I met regularly with the department heads for prayer. On Fridays I met with the division heads and their financial officers. Each week it became more evident that we needed to cut back on operations and outreach and live within PTL's income.

In spite of the caliber of people involved in PTL's top administration, we couldn't overcome our greatest hurdle — Jim Bakker.

Jim's vision always outstripped our ability to manage PTL's affairs. Many times funds were not used wisely because of Jim's urgency to complete a project as quickly as possible. The words "wait" or "let's check it out first" never fell from our leader's lips. No time was set aside to assess the project's purpose or determine its real benefit to the organization, or people.

Once Jim caught the vision of something new, a sense of urgency took over. That meant: It must be done and done now. Construction costs often doubled as a result.

Although PTL's income had more than quadrupled, we struggled to bring the finances up to the level of Jim's ever-increasing vision. Those of us in administration were privately expressing to Jim our deep concern about the inability of PTL to meet its obligations.

The record shows that I met with the chief financial

officer, Peter Bailey, regularly.

"Pete, why are we bouncing hundreds of checks every month?" I would ask, frustrated to the point of confusion. "I don't understand why we can't live within our income."

It was not unusual in a given month to have three, four, or five hundred checks bounce, simply because more money was being spent than received.

With five CPAs on staff and three MBAs, I knew the financial problems at PTL were not the fault of the accounting and finance department. These highly qualified people managed their departments with great expertise and consistently warned Jim Bakker about the need to cut back on spending.

The accountants informed Jim and me over and over, "Jim, we're taking in enough money, but we're not cutting back our outreach. The television program isn't the problem, it's the other non-essential areas that are killing us. Our expenses aren't commensurate with the amount of money we're receiving."

Enough money was coming into PTL, but there were no controls in place to limit spending.

Jim Bakker was given the facts and repeatedly warned. Contrary to what was reported in *The Charlotte Observer,* many of us spoke up privately. We weren't trying to embarrass our leader, we were trying to stop the spending. Apparently we weren't getting through.

It was not my style to chew Jim out in business meetings or publicly ridicule him before staff members about the overspending. Besides, that method didn't work with Jim. Instead I encouraged him to work toward the intended goal of less spending and challenged Jim to do what was best for everyone.

Privately, in the dressing room, in the car, walking around Heritage USA, and on more occasions than I can remember, I advised Jim Bakker to cut back. I can take you to exact spots where I sat and had serious talks with him.

I'd say, "Jim, unless we cut back on what we're doing, the results will be financially devastating." My record as an administrator was that we did pay our bills. To the best of my knowledge we were never a day late on any payments in all those years, unless someone had an oversight and had forgotten something, but it was not because we did not have the funds to pay.

On one occasion I specifically used a personal illustration. "You know, Jim, since Mildred and I were first married, we've had a perfect credit rating. By perfect, I mean that every expense we have ever incurred has been paid — and paid on time. We've got to be more consistent with paying the bills at PTL."

Jim agreed with me. It was common knowledge that he and Tammy personally paid their bills faithfully and promptly. Somehow, Jim couldn't carry that policy over into the ministry. Both in Charlotte and around the country, PTL was known as a "slow pay" operation.

"Jim," I pleaded. "I just cannot bring myself to accept the fact that the ministry has a bad reputation. We've got to do something about our pay schedule."

In the television industry, PTL's pay rating was considered one of the worst among Christian media.

Television ministries are rated, by commercial enterprises and the media outlet, according to their ability to pay. Surprisingly, the best payer of their accounts, both to the stations and businesses, was Ernest Angley, who traditionally bought air time and paid for it in advance. As a result his ministry received an A-1 rating and the largest discounts.

It was also traditionally known that the Oral Roberts ministry paid well as did Robert Schuller's. The Jimmy Swaggart ministry was a little slow, but they paid.

The undeniable facts are that the hardest to get money out of were the PTL broadcast stations and the Jerry Falwell ministry. This statistic was presented to me, again and again, by Walter Richardson who had the responsibility of seeing to it that the stations were paid, and that we were paid by those using our network.

Walter, a man of impeccable Christian character, had to live with the daily harassment of telephone calls and the constant threat of lawsuits from our suppliers. Peter Bailey and the finance staff also took a lot of heat from angry customers who were tired of waiting for their money.

"What is our problem?" I cried, again and again.

The answer from our financial advisers was always the same, "We must cut back on operations and outreach, and stretch what we're doing."

"How do we do that?" I asked, pleading for some solution.

"There is one way," the CPA staff replied. "With Jim's thrust to get projects finished quickly and because of PTL's slow pay reputation, all our loans are on a short-term basis. The struggle to pay a consistent $50,000,000 debt in a three-year time frame — a feat no business would ever consider — is killing us."

"So what's the answer?" I probed.

"With a four to one debt ratio, assets at $200,000,000, and debts of $50,000,000, it's crucial to find long term financing to restructure the debt to fifteen years," they explained. "If that's possible, we would be in a livable position. That is, providing Jim restrains himself."

"How can we convince Jim to hold down spending?"

"There's only one way to force Jim to do that," they said. "Let's hope that whoever agrees to lend us the money demands that we not create any additional debt. That would be the leash we need to corral Jim Bakker and bring PTL's finances under control."

Hope rose in my heart, and we began preparing proposals to present to lending institutions. We chased money across the country and in foreign lands, trying to obtain long term financing so we could cut our debt service dramatically and live within our income. At times, just when we thought a loan would come through, the prospect vanished before our eyes.

Relief remained elusive, and our hands were tied.

Getting Jim Bakker to cut back on a program or building project was literally impossible. He wouldn't adhere to it. No one could slow down his dream.

When it came to financial difficulties, Jim erected an emotional barrier, making any discussion about the matter merely one-sided.

"Jim, we've got to deal with these mounting bills," I told him. "The finance department doesn't have the money to pay them."

I'll never forget his reply.

"Richard, what we need is a greater program. We don't need more money; we need bigger ideas. If we attract more people, the money will come in." Then he got up and walked out of his office, leaving me frustrated and worried about how to pay the TV stations and keep PTL on the air.

When things were at their worst, and it seemed PTL was set on a collision course with disaster, I'd look around me and see the thousands of people coming to Heritage USA every day. Then I'd think, *Maybe Jim is right after all.*

The national media promoted the myth that PTL was a corporation that owned a giant "theme park" with $170 million in assets and thrived on a tax-exempt status. I tried to untangle the public confusion and explode the fallacy that PTL wasn't paying any state and federal taxes.

The only corporate name for PTL was Heritage Village Church and Missionary Fellowship, Incorporated. This ministry had a tax exemption on four small pieces of property, less than thirty acres out of the total 2,300 acres. Fort Heritage Campground, Inc. was a separate profit corporation that operated the commercial enterprises like the theme park, the shops, the restaurants, and the other enterprises. Millions of dollars were paid in property, sales, and federal taxes.

Several months before I took the job as senior executive vice president, Jim and I were discussing fund raising projects for PTL, when he asked me, "What do you think of this idea?"

He obviously wanted my opinion on a new project and began to explain. "If the people were to give $1,000, we could let them have four days and three nights every year for the rest of their lives to stay in the Heritage Grand Hotel that we are going to try to build."

I responded, "I think it's a good idea."

He asked, "Why?"

"Well, you just took a few seconds to explain the program to me," I replied cautiously, "and I can understand it. But I think you need to run it by the finance people and see if the numbers come out right."

"I've already done that," he said. "If we dedicate fifty percent of the rooms in the facility to lifetime partnerships and the other fifty percent for cash customers, it would be the same as financing the project."

"How does that work?" I questioned.

"Because about fifty percent of the income for that kind of facility usually goes to debt retirement."

During my first week on the job, Jim announced the lifetime partnership program to the employees. Most of the pre-planning and a lot of the printing for the program had been completed prior to my arrival at PTL. That's when I learned the final details of the arrangement, and saw the brochures for the first time. I strongly objected when I saw the language in the beautiful colored brochures.

In the beginning, the use of the lifetime partnerships was not transferable. One day on the air, however, Jim Bakker announced that a friend or a family member could also use the lifetime partnership. This immediately lessened the value of the memberships.

That made it difficult, if not impossible, for the ministry to be adequately compensated for all that the partners were receiving. The rules of the program were repeatedly changed to benefit the partners, making it necessary to offer more lifetime partnerships.

The limit, that Jim had set in the beginning of 25,000 memberships for the Heritage Grand Hotel, moved to 30,000, and ultimately soared to over 65,000. By that time, the commitment to hold the memberships to the original levels had been forgotten or ignored. Because Jim believed he could manage the people's trips to Heritage USA he wasn't overly concerned.

Providing enough rooms available, however, was not the major problem. The squeeze came because too many people desired accommodations on certain holidays. Everyone wanted to come to PTL on the Fourth of July and

---

HERITAGE USA

DAILY ACTIVITY REPORT

DATE 4-24 87   GRAND TOTAL 16,840

PAGE 1 OF 2

* Brock ** Timeshare PTL

OCCUPANCY #6440

	Rooms	People
*Heritage Grand	476	1090
*Heritage Inn	93	209
*Campgrounds	166	380
*Log Inns	1	3
**Lakeside Lodges	19	42
**Chalets	4	22
**Tennis Villas	0	0
*Bunkhouse	13	30
Total Occupancy	871	1776

UPPER ROOM 2423

2:00 am	3
6:00 am	55
8:00 am	31
Sat only 11:00 am	0
2:00 pm	131
4:00 pm	65
5:30 pm	95
10:00 pm	110

HGH Water Baptism
(Tues. Only)

Total 466

SEMINARS 2395

| Wednesday 9:00 | 62 |
| Wednesday 3:30 | 97 |

Workshops
Total 159

STUDIO 2453

Heritage USA Program	453
Overflow	
Telethon	
Total	452

BARN AUDITORIUM 2050

Church Service	
Overflow	
Campmeeting	546
Concerts	
Theater Program	
Total	546

AMPHITHEATER 2506

Passion Play Paid	419
Complimentary	17
Silver	193
Total	629

OTHER INFORMATION

RESTAURANTS

9-544-5240 *Tone* 131	
Grand Palace	1566
Popcorn Trolley	481
Trolly Main St.	1064
Susie's Ice Crm.	1174
McMoose's	376
Tony's Cafe	290
Bentley's	580
Heritage Court	140
Room Service	70
Granny's Kitchen	192
Little Horse	50
Rec. Village Ice Cream	0
Sea Cave	0
Dockside	0
Dinner Theater	0
Theater II	0
Total	5883

Christmas.

The hotel, managed by the Brock Corporation of Dallas, Texas, found itself hard pressed to limit fifty percent of the rooms for lifetime partners and fifty percent for cash paying

HERITAGE USA		-2-		DAILY ACTIVITY REPORT	
MAIN STREET HGB/OTHER RETAIL		**TICKET SALES 2360**		**BUFFALO PARK 2227**	
Victoria's	71	Cars	18		
Heritage Gift Shop	355	Carousel	22		
Ye Old Book Store	176	Trains	119		
Jerusalem Shop	177	1 Day Pass	265		
General Store	563	4 Day Pass	74		
Gas Island	63	Heritage Tours	188		
Victor's Music	209				
				Total	
		Total	686		
				WATER PARK	
		FAMILY CENTER 2564		Silver	
		Bible Studies	0	Paid	
		Table Games	71		
		Board Games	16		
		Video Games	213		
Total	1614	Academy	31		
		Special Events	0		
TOURS 2100		Skaters	94		
Billy Graham Home	115	Individuals	363	Total	
Studio Tour	0				
Tram Tour	219			**RECREATION VILLAGE**	
		Total	363		
Total	334	**HERITAGE FARM 2770**		Total	
		Trail Rides	83		
TRANSPORTATION 2507		Pony Rides	40	**OTHER**	
Trams	746	Camel Rides			
Buses	2989	Petting Zoo			
		Kennel			
		Carriage Rides	60	Total	
Total	3735				
		Total	183		

customers. The matter was under constant review, and a report was given to us daily on what was happening at each facility.

To make matters worse, guests often did not show up at the hotel to claim their lifetime partnership stay, or they made reservations and did not claim them. These discrepancies created monumental booking problems for the hotel.

To add to the confusion, information about the status of the partnership program was controlled by "The Jim and Tammy Show." On the air Jim encouraged partners to come when space was available and tried to discourage guests from booking on certain special occasions and holidays when the facility would be packed.

Why didn't the lifetime partnership program work? First of all, the partners were not informed of the total number of lifetime partnerships that had been offered.

Secondly, the rules, as originally set forth in the brochure, were not strictly adhered to. Jim changed them constantly. The limitations on availability of space should have been communicated more explicitly. Guidelines for use of the facilities should have been clearly defined. Then the partners would have known what they were actually getting for their $1000 gift.

Thirdly, the twenty-one story Heritage Grand Towers, slated to be our largest hotel facility with 524 rooms, did not get completed. Why? The answer is simple.

Jim Bakker wanted to build Farmland USA, where children from the inner city could come and see firsthand a real working farm. I thought it was an excellent idea, but I knew such a project would require an initial investment of approximately eight or nine million dollars.

I suggested to Jim that we complete the hotel first, which would require another six or seven million dollars, and put the Farmland project on hold. I had no aversion then, later, or now, to Farmland USA. I did oppose building an eight million dollar facility when the Towers was not finished.

Had the Heritage Grand Towers been completed with

the money that was spent for Farmland USA, it could have accommodated approximately 35,000 lifetime partnerships for four days and three nights each year. At least, we could have kept our heads above water. But without the Towers — we were making problems for ourselves.

Those of us who knew what Jim was doing stood by and watched the situation deteriorate, all the while warning Jim over and over again. But somehow we failed to take control of the situation.

In the beginning I do not believe that Jim Bakker intended to defraud his lifetime partners. That thought would never have entered his mind. I testified to that under oath in Federal Court. His greatest faults were his inability to accept advice and submit to the people he had hired to help him, and his insatiable desire to build.

Jim Bakker often said, "I want to be committed and submitted to those who are over me." But he failed to listen to those around him.

Our character is tested, not by our submission to those **over** us, but our willingness to submit to those **under** us.

Richard Dortch with Jeanne and Bob Johnson.

6

Blackmail

The autumn of 1984 set the Carolina countryside ablaze with color. I appreciated the view from my office window at Heritage USA. I often took time to admire the beauty of the frost-bitten foliage. This would be my first fall season as a local resident.

As the days grew shorter and darkness came earlier, it was Christmas, not autumn, that occupied the minds of the Heritage USA grounds staff. In preparation for their spectacular Christmas City display, which began at Thanksgiving time, they had been putting up lights since September.

The dusk of the early evening provided enough darkness to pre-test the results of their labors. I watched from my office window intrigued by the snowmen and manger scenes flashing on and off all over the complex. *What a place to be during the holiday season!* I thought.

At least that's how I'd felt on the evening I received the first phone call from Jim's mysterious accuser.

After a few days, she called again.

"Pastor Dortch, this is Jessica Hahn," she said.

"Yes?" I asked, waiting for more information. The name seemed vaguely familiar but held no significance for me.

"I talked to you a few days ago. I'm the woman from New York," she reminded me.

"Oh, yes," I commented. The call surprised me since she had indicated she wouldn't call again. I had assumed that was the end of the matter.

This time her conversation moved from accusations to complaints about the emotional turmoil she was going through.

"I'm having to go to the doctor for medication," she sobbed. "I've even been admitted to the hospital for treatment."

I listened, agitated because I felt she was lying, and yet moved by her pathetic weeping. Once again I offered comfort and counsel, trying somehow to help her.

But the calls kept coming. It became obvious that Jessica Hahn was not going to go away.

I did what my training and experience taught me to do — get another minister and confront the person. That seemed to be the scriptural and common sense approach to take.

I had not spoken to Jim Bakker about the matter. First of all, I did not believe the story. Secondly, I knew such an accusation would make him very depressed. If that happened, the entire ministry would be affected, not to mention what it would do to his work on the television program. I saw no need to tell Jim. Besides, I was handling all kinds of other problems. This would just be another one to add to my agenda.

I made arrangements to go to New York and talk with one of our board members, a pastor living in New York City. Jessica Hahn agreed to meet with us at the Holiday Inn across the street from La Guardia Airport.

As we sat and talked in the hotel dining room, Miss Hahn repeated her accusations of abduction and rape to the pastor. A lady, whom Jessica said was a paralegal, had accompanied her.

Then on the verge of tears, she lamented, "I have all these medical bills that I can't afford to pay. I'm so worried. I don't know what to do."

After some discussion, she appeared more relaxed and expressed an interest in even helping the pastor in some way.

At that point I made a recommendation.

"I think it would be good for you to meet with Pastor Smith and get the help you need," I suggested. I felt confident she would probably follow any advice the pastor gave her.

As we were preparing to leave, Jessica Hahn said, "I'm so sorry for taking up your time, Pastor Dortch, and making it necessary for you to come all the way from Charlotte."

I simply stared at her in reply.

We had already been subjected to a wide range of emotions in her statements that evening. I couldn't figure out what was going on.

When we got outside the hotel, I asked my pastor friend, "What do you make of this?" I felt the local pastor could size up the situation better than I could.

"Without question, this is a New York heist. A con, plain and simple," was the answer.

As a New York native, these folks should know, I thought.

"Would you serve as an intermediary if that becomes necessary?" I asked.

When it was agreed, I said, "If you need to give her financial help for hospital expenses and things like that, we will reimburse you."

Then I did a very foolish thing. I gave the pastor two thousand dollars so the church would have the cash to help her if she continued to complain.

My great mistake was throwing money after the problem.

That was not unusual at PTL. I knew spending money was not the way to solve problems, but there were times when we did it, hoping for a quick cure. Although there was nothing illegal with such tactics, it did show lack of good judgment.

I thought if two thousand dollars would resolve the problem with Jessica Hahn, let's do it and get it behind us. That money did not come from PTL funds, it was out of my own personal account and I was not reimbursed.

I returned to Charlotte, somewhat assured that the pastor in New York would handle the situation.

Then I received a letter from Jessica Hahn stating how much she appreciated my meeting with her and indicated how sorry she was for burdening me with her problems.

Miss Hahn went on to say, "I would like to do something to help the pastor who has been helping me."

She wanted me to give the pastor four hundred new chairs for his church. The pastor was a wonderful person, she wrote, and she was thankful the church was reaching out to her.

We have this licked, I thought. *Everything is under control!*

About two months later I went into Jim's office to talk to him about some current PTL matters that needed his attention.

At the end of our discussion, as I walked out the door, I said spontaneously, "Oh, by the way, I have been dealing with a woman who says that you raped her."

I had not planned to report to Jim about Miss Hahn. It just came out of my mouth. In my heart, I must have believed the matter was solved, or I wouldn't have told him. I still didn't believe her. I thought it was a hoax.

"Pastor Dortch," Jim said (he always called me pastor), "you know I didn't do that. I've never raped anybody."

"I know that, Jim," I chuckled. "If I believed her allegations were true, I would have talked to you a couple of months ago."

"Where is she from?" he asked.

"New York," I responded.

"What's her name?"

"Jessica Hahn."

He turned to stare silently out the large window behind

his desk. This kind of pensive, reflective posture was not unusual for Jim.

After a long gaze at the beautiful autumn foliage, he turned slowly and said to me, "Pastor Dortch, I never raped anybody."

I repeated, "I know that."

"But there is a problem."

"What is it?" I asked, anticipating a logical reply.

To my surprise, Jim Bakker began to cry. "It's hard for me to talk. Would you speak to Dr. Gross?"

At the time, Dr. Gross was the head of the PTL counseling department.

"Would you call and tell him it's all right for him to tell you about Jessica Hahn?"

Stunned, I left Jim's office and phoned Dr. Gross.

"Jim has been under my counseling and discipline since the incident took place," the doctor said in response to my questions. "He came to me immediately after it had happened."

Vi Azvedo, the head of the pastoral staff, and I went back to Jim's office. I wanted Jim to describe the episode to me himself.

He told me his version of the story.

"When Tammy left me, it hurt me deeply," he explained. "I hated being separated from her, and I wanted to get even. That's why I did it."

It was common knowledge that Tammy and Jim had been at odds a few years ago, resulting in a brief separation.

I couldn't believe what I was hearing.

"John Wesley Fletcher arranged for Jessica to come down to meet us in Florida. I met her there; that's where it happened."

I stared at Jim in disbelief.

My mind flashed back to the year before, when I had asked Jim, "Is there anything you haven't told me about PTL? Anything that might surface down the road I should know about?"

At the time, I didn't know why I was asking since I didn't

have anything specific in mind.

For a year or two prior to that question, I had heard all kinds of rumors about PTL. Stories had circulated in the newspapers, but nothing specific had been mentioned — and never anything about sexual aberration or allegations of financial impropriety.

Before making the final decision to come on staff at PTL, I wanted to find out, one on one, any hidden secrets that might create problems later. Jim assured me, at the time, there was nothing.

Now I reflected on his answer.

The Hahn incident had happened in 1980, four years prior to my employment at PTL. I could understand why, after four years, in Jim's mind he believed it was over. Since Jessica hadn't tried to contact Jim, he assumed nothing would ever develop from the incident.

It's been difficult to come to grips with why Jim Bakker didn't tell me about Jessica Hahn. If I had known, I would have handled the situation differently. As it was, I had been dealing with a ticking time bomb and didn't know it.

In my seventeen years as an Assemblies of God official, I never once made an "arrangement" with a wayward preacher to withhold correction from him. Whenever a pastor broke his wedding vows or committed some act of immorality, our denomination had strict procedures of discipline.

I am convinced, if I had been informed about the situation, I would have followed those same guidelines with Jim Bakker. I would have encouraged Jim to ask Tammy to forgive him. In addition, I would have suggested he come forward with a public confession, asking his congregation and supporters for forgiveness.

If those procedures had been adhered to, the Jessica Hahn case would have been defused. Then there would have been no ugly story lurking in the shadows for Jim's enemies to use against him.

No one knows how to handle every situation. If Jim had sought the counsel of trusted friends and spiritual leaders, I believe the matter would have been addressed quickly and effectively without all the legal ramifications that developed. There is strength in the wisdom and counsel of others.

I realize that a man in Jim's position has to be careful about whom he confides in. It's not always easy to determine when to be transparent and when to keep things to ourselves. That kind of discernment has to be built into our values and our sense of judgment. We have to develop the kind of sensitivity that considers, "Who is this person and can they be trusted?" before we start to unload our innermost secrets.

In the mid-seventies, during one of my out-of-town trips, a businessman whom I had known for years approached me with an offer.

"Pastor Dortch," he began, "I am purchasing a business together with some of your friends. Would you like to have part ownership in that business?"

I chuckled to myself and thought, *If he knew my net worth, he wouldn't be asking such a ridiculous question.*

"You've got the wrong guy," I replied. "I don't have the funds needed to become a partner in a business."

"But you don't need any cash up front," he explained. "The business will loan you the $160,000 necessary to become one of the owners. Through directors' fees, stock, and dividends, you can earn enough money to make the payments on the loan."

"I don't know," I said, hesitating to make a commitment. "That's something I want to think about long and hard."

At the time, I had been in the ministry for almost thirty years, and Mildred and I had no money to speak of. We had never even owned a home. The offer sure sounded attractive.

After questioning the businessman at length, I still felt troubled in my spirit.

During my return trip, I began to think about the offer. Then it dawned on me. Richard W. Dortch was not being asked to become a director or part owner in the business. It was the state superintendent of our denomination and an executive of the national denomination's board that this man wanted.

"My titles and reputation are not for sale," I mumbled to myself.

When I arrived home, I told my wife about the offer.

"I just don't feel right about it," I expressed to Mildred. "I don't think I should get involved." The other people involved were in the businessman's community. That was different for them; but for me, I was hundreds of miles away.

There was nothing wrong or illegal about the offer, but for me something was not quite right either.

At the time I shared the situation with our son, Rich. As I explained the ethical reasons that made it impossible for me to take part in the offer, I said, "It's a question of integrity, and I feel it's best to refuse."

It was not unusual for us to discuss such matters with Rich and our daughter, Deanna. I believe children learn from being part of the decision-making process. Mildred and I have always shared family matters with our son and daughter, knowing they could be trusted to keep the information within our household.

Within a month or so, something happened that confirmed I had made the correct decision.

During a state board meeting for the denomination, which I was attending, the other members asked me to leave the room. I knew they were discussing some kind of compensation for me. Finally, after two hours, I was called back into the meeting.

"Pastor Dortch," they explained, "you have served faithfully for many years as an officer of this denomination, and we would like to make it possible for you to buy the home you have been living in at a reasonable price. You can make the payments using your housing allowance."

Tears filled my eyes. This was far beyond anything that I could imagine.

When I got home, Mildred and I rejoiced.

Then I called the children in and said, "For the first time in our lives, we are going to be able to have a home of our own, and not just live in a parsonage"

Remembering the decision I had made the month

before, Rich suddenly realized its significance. Hugging me, he said, "Dad, it certainly pays to do what is right."

I'll never forget those words and how much it meant to have the respect of my wife and children, the people who know and love me best — and trust me implicitly. It was gratifying to be respected for simply doing what was right.

That decision and the wonderful outcome had seemed so simple.

Now, as I pondered the events of the past year at PTL, I asked myself: *How had my judgment suddenly become so clouded? Why did the options always appear so complex? Why couldn't I just do what I knew to be right? Why wasn't I listening to my heart?*

Somehow I realized my integrity was slowly eroding, but I felt powerless to flee from the slippery slope.

For a while we were at a stalemate in the Jessica Hahn matter. Her very gracious and kind letter seemed to indicate everything was going as expected.

Then, suddenly, she became angry at the pastor from New York City, and we were back to square one. The demands for help resurfaced with new intensity. She called repeatedly, insisting on some kind of action. It appeared to be a form of harassment designed to wear us down. I was very concerned yet unsure about what to do next.

Then we received the following letter from her paralegal:

> I represent Jessica Hahn. Miss Hahn has advised me that she has attempted to contact you on numerous, separate occasions, and you, sir, and Mr. Bakker have failed to return her calls. So now I am contacting you because this is a final attempt.
>
> We do not, absolutely do not want any trouble. All we want is for you to listen. We have to discuss a matter of mutual importance, and I'm afraid we cannot put it off any longer.
>
> Unfortunately, this involves unpleasantness which I believe you are aware of. To be more to the point, this conversation is in reference to the events of the afternoon of December 6, 1980, and an incident that took place in Clearwater

Beach, Florida at the Sheraton Sands Hotel in room 538.

Now, the situation is this: Miss Hahn has confided in me just as Mr. Bakker has confided in you. I have details of the incident that took place on December 6, 1980, and I have been assured by Miss Hahn that these details are true.

There have been some problems, some additional problems, and to tell you the truth, they are from your end. There's still talk. Comments about Miss Hahn are still being passed along in someone's casual conversations. Please find who it is and have it stopped, please! It seems to go on and on, and she has tried to put up with it. We know it is coming from down there because it has gotten back to us. Everything here was kept quiet. Here in New York, it's been held in confidence, in the strictest confidence, and those confidences were never broken. Can you explain any of this?

Also, sir, I want you to be aware of the numerous effects and ramifications this has caused this young lady, and if I may remind you, I am talking about a twenty-one year old girl, who has never been married, who lives with her parents, and I don't know if you're aware of this, but her father is a police officer for the County of Nassau here in the State of New York. I think it becomes necessary at this time to emphasize her age. She's not thirty or thirty-five years old with a couple of ex-husbands or a couple of children.

In view of the fact of her young age, I believe Mr. Bakker led her into making a wrong decision. I contend that he enticed her and coerced her into making a wrong decision to act against her better judgment, on that afternoon of December 6, 1980; a decision which, at that time, she did not yet possess the essential emotional and physical maturity to make. I charge this because he helped arrange and finance her flight to Clearwater Beach and hotel accommodations intended to serve his personal pleasure and convenience. The occurrence that followed was horrible. I truly hesitate to say these things to you because it hurts me as a Christian and as a lady to say them, but I must make certain you are aware that I have had to insist Miss Hahn disclose the facts to me, as painful as they may be.

Mr. Bakker did visit Miss Hahn's room at the Sheraton on the afternoon in question, and he appeared wearing only a very small swimsuit. He then did disrobe, seduce and sodomize her by legal definition, in the strictest legal sense . . . [I have omitted explicit comments here describing what happened.]

Has Mr. Bakker explained these details to you? They are

true. Now, perhaps he has never done this with a stranger before or since, but I'm led to wonder if he has, or if this is a common, everyday occurrence with him. And as if this incident wasn't tragic enough, then this girl continues to be talked about. Something is very, very wrong.

Now I must make another point. I must discuss with you the damages and suffering incurred by Miss Hahn. I want you to be made aware that she has suffered an injustice here. She's been through a tremendous shock. She hasn't been the same since. I know her personally, and I can vouch for the fact that this has cost her over and above what it should have.

She has to be compensated for her injuries of being socially disgraced. The town in which she resides in is a closely knit community; the church community here is even more closely knit. I cannot emphasize to you enough that it was talked about up here and repeated because one of your people revealed this secret to someone. You must know also she has suffered spiritual damages as well. She was just at her strongest point in her walk with the Lord when all this happened to her. Furthermore, she has sustained permanent psychological and emotional damages. Her job may be at stake. She is unable to perform her duties at the same level of productivity as before. It has cost her in her womanhood. She is unable to respond to and sustain any romantic attachments. This all has the potential of ruining her chances to enjoy a full and normal life. She doesn't even have the usual anticipation of marriage and a happy future.

In view of all these facts, it is my belief Miss Hahn has the right to be duly compensated for this series of emotional setbacks.

These are Miss Hahn's requests:

First: Please locate the source of the information that continues still to be talked about, and have it stopped once and forever.

Second: An apology from Mr. Bakker.

Third: Miss Hahn's family is to be protected from any future embarrassment just as Mr. Bakker's family has been protected.

Fourth: A monetary settlement; Miss Hahn requires and deserves an opportunity to pick up the pieces of her life and to rebuild it; to make a fresh start, and she needs the financial means to accomplish this. We're giving you the opportunity to settle this matter justly and privately, according to what you perceive to be a rightful settlement. $100,000.00

(one hundred thousand dollars) is not excessive in view of what happened here. That amount would not seem excessive to you if it had been your daughter or my daughter who had been violated.

And I think sir, it is very important for you to know Miss Hahn's motives for seeking compensation.

Miss Hahn contends it was the method used to handle this, or lack of handling it, that was so personally heartbreaking to her; that no one there would even return her calls; that she was just used like an animal and then totally forsaken and ignored. It leads her to wonder if this has happened before to another girl, and perhaps if Miss Hahn had known it, she would have been sufficiently forewarned to stay away from Mr. Bakker, if his reputation has preceded him. But she trusted him not to hurt her. That is the only reason she accepted his invitation in the first place.

Also, that afternoon of December 6, 1980, Mr. Bakker was unclear as to the purpose of the invitation extended to Miss Hahn. She was led to believe she would join him socially in the company of others for a luncheon and to observe a television show being taped on location from the hotel or nearby studio.

Now, if Mr. Bakker hasn't done this before to others, Miss Hahn is willing to try to believe it, but she is also willing to take a stand to demonstrate to him that he was wrong to hurt *her*, and then simply walk away, free from assuming any of the responsibility for his actions; . . . so Mr. Bakker henceforth will employ foresight regarding such activities, and think at least twice or three times before he even considers to be tempted to take advantage of any young girl.

Now if he has done this before and since, then he has got to be stopped. If he **has** secretly engaged in illicit sexual activity with others, and it was kept quiet, **how was it kept quiet?** If others were quieted with a cash gift then Miss Hahn too is deserving of a similar settlement. If another girl walked away with nothing, Miss Hahn wants it known **she will not.** She desires to help to see that it is stopped. Miss Hahn will not just walk away, and Mr. Bakker must be made aware of this. She was left broken-hearted. It is unrealistic, unjust, and unwise of him to presume she will walk away empty-handed as well.

You must be wondering why Miss Hahn waited three years before coming forward. Well, quite frankly, the pain doesn't go away. She has tried and tried to forget, but then someone else opens a mouth to gossip, and yet another lends an ear, and so it goes. It goes on and on and on with reminders at every turn. The worst, most degrading and permanent effects are just now truly manifesting themselves.

What if Miss Hahn was Mr. Bakker's daughter? Would he want **his** own child, **his** own flesh and blood to just walk away from the person who is the source of her torment? I think not.

You all seemingly have survived most of this. You all appear to be managing well enough down there. No one there seems to be suffering. You are fortunate this never did blow up sky-high. Fortunate indeed the details of what happened that afternoon of December 6, 1980 were never made known by Miss Hahn. Mr. Bakker's colleagues and family have been protected. You're blessed that you are building up instead of tearing down; you're prospering, and that is as it should be, if Mr. Bakker acknowledges his wrongdoing to Miss Hahn and takes the responsibilities for his actions; that he too pays the required consequences, just as others have paid with their tears and their suffering and their anguish and their frustrations.

The last, the very last thing Miss Hahn wants is a scandal, but if Mr. Bakker chooses to ignore her requests, she will have no recourse but to:

- Reach Leon Miles, Assistant Superintendent of the Assembly of God, and inform him of the incident in its entirety.

- We absolutely do not want the press and network news media involved in any way. PTL has more at stake here than Miss Hahn if this information becomes public knowledge. At this point in time, it would be wiser for you to ease the mind of one person than to appease all the mainline churches and the entire public.

- Miss Hahn will be instructed to seek formal legal counsel, and commence a legal action. Thus far, she says she would do this only as a final solution, since retaining an attorney would entail confiding in yet **another** person who would have to be apprised of the explicit details of the case; a person who employs a staff, replete with the hazard of breaking client/attorney confidences, and thereby creating the potential of the possibility of the unwanted, massive public scandal she so thoroughly dreads. But Mr. Bakker will leave her no option but to:

- File formal charges against him.

I urge you to work with us to arrange a settlement, at your earliest possible convenience, so that we may resolve this matter once and for all and forever. I plead with you, take time now rather than later in court. All of Miss Hahn's charges can and will be tried and proven in a court of law. She is willing, if need be, to submit to a polygraph test, to submit a sworn statement or deposition, to provide evidence, and to give testimony, if it should come to that.

We sincerely want to settle with you privately. Please know it is our belief that everyone's best interests will be served if this is carried out immediately and briefly. It would be best for everyone if this anticipated settlement took as little time and as few words as possible. You should use the trusted representative of your choice. Miss Hahn trusts you since she knows your name, your voice, and your whereabouts. She would prefer you to handle it, if possible.

It would be to your benefit and overall advantage to meet our terms, but if you fail to respond, I have no alternative but to advise Miss Hahn to pursue this matter in another way. I represent her, and it is my responsibility to protect her and to safeguard her interests. You may as well know she is despondent; she's at the end now; nothing else matters to her any more. But even so, you people have a lot more to lose, even more than she has already lost.

In return for your immediate consideration, Miss Hahn:

- Promises to forego all intentions of filing formal charges.
- Promises this will conclude the entire matter.
- Is willing to swear to absolute and total silence. I suggest she has previously established she is capable of keeping quiet.
- Promises Mr. Bakker he will be forever absolved of any contact from her, and she will disclaim any association with him whatsoever.

We look forward to hearing from you. You may reach me through Miss Hahn at her private number . . . anytime after 5 p.m. or before midnight. Her address for mailing purposes is . . . for the next thirty days. [We have eliminated the phone number and address for obvious reasons.]

Thank you for your time and attention.

This letter makes it abundantly clear that blackmail was in progress. I believe much of it was orchestrated by her former pastor, Eugene Profeta, (not the PTL pastor) in New York. Jessica had been a secretary in his church. We had received allegations of a romance between Profeta and Jessica.

Contrary to what has been reported on the ABC television program "Nightline," it was evident Jessica Hahn was trying to blackmail Jim Bakker.

The few people at PTL who talked on the phone to Miss Hahn were concerned about her agitated state of mind, but no one believed she was serious about her threats. Their assessment was the same as I had made initially: This is an emotionally disturbed woman who needs spiritual help.

Still she persisted!

I came to the point where I dismissed her requests and returned to matters I felt were of greater importantance to the ministry.

For a while, things quieted down, and we thought, perhaps, the problem with Jessica Hahn had been resolved.

Then, one day in January, 1985, my administrative assistant brought me several legal documents in black folders and stacked them on my desk.

"Looks like a lawsuit," he said. "Here's your copy. I'll see that the others receive theirs."

"I guess Jessica Hahn found an attorney," I replied, shaking my head in dismay and opening the document.

The lawsuit requested damages of $12,300,000.

The plaintiff was Jessica Hahn.

The defendants were James Bakker; PTL, Inc.; Richard Dortch; Assemblies of God, Inc.; the PTL pastor in New York; and the Sheraton Sand Key Hotel in Florida.

The allegations were the same ones she had initially made to me: battery, kidnapping, rape, and all manner of abuse.

Since we had not been keeping contact with Miss Hahn, I did not give the matter too much attention. I felt, as did others, that the proposed lawsuit was an attempt to scare or extort money from us.

Surely this young lady will not do anything to identify herself, I thought. *If she makes this kind of allegation against Jim Bakker in court, she will also expose herself to public scrutiny.*

Although I put the proposed lawsuit in the bottom of my desk drawer and went about my business, the matter remained in my subconscious like a dull pain. The lawsuit had not been executed, it was just there — like a time bomb waiting to explode.

One day, in the middle of taping a live program in the studio, Phoebe Connoway, a lady who was the guest hostess, approached me on the set.

What's Phoebe doing here? I wondered. Apparently, she had gotten clearance from the scores of security guards and production staff to bring me a message. Under normal circumstances, it is impossible on a national television broadcast to have access to a person sitting on a set in front of the cameras.

Phoebe slipped in beside me and whispered, "There's a man on the phone who has one of the most vile tongues I have ever heard. He is angry, and he wants to talk to you."

Because of the violent nature of the telephone call, she felt it required my immediate attention.

I didn't respond and tried to brush off her sense of urgency.

As soon as the television program ended, she grabbed my arm and said, "Pastor Dortch, please, you've got to talk to this man because he's very upset. His language is horrible."

I went to the telephone, and someone identified himself as Eugene Profeta, the pastor of a gospel church in Massapequa, New York. His opening words were filled with filth and vile language, threats, and innuendoes.

"You're going down! Jim Bakker's going down! I'm going to castrate you!" he screamed, all the while cursing and using vicious language.

I finally got his attention and simply said, "You've got

the wrong man. I've never had any kind of a relationship with Jessica Hahn. So don't talk to me this way."

As we had expected, Jessica Hahn had disclosed to him the stories of her tryst with Jim Bakker. It had been alleged that the pastor had an ongoing relationship with Jessica Hahn. We'd also been told that Eugene Profeta was a dangerous man.

"I know you haven't had anything going with Jessica Hahn," he continued. "But Jim Bakker has. I can't get to Jim Bakker, but I can get to you! So I'm telling you, I'll come down there and get you, or I'll send somebody. But you guys are going down." Then he once again threatened me with castration.

I did not doubt the ability of Profeta to perform any kind of violent act. We had been warned by people in the New York area that this man carried a gun in a holster on his leg. I knew he was capable of carrying out his threats. If he didn't personally follow through, he had the contacts to do it for him.

He made it clear to me that, either we respond to this proposed lawsuit, or there would be violent action taken against Jim Bakker and myself.

I was afraid; I was concerned; I was bewildered and very, very nervous.

That night I went to my desk and took the proposed lawsuit out of the drawer.

"If you want to resolve this issue," the letter accompanying the proposed lawsuit read, "call this number." Paul Roper, the California connection, represented himself as Jessica Hahn's "attorney in fact." That term was unfamiliar to me, so I thought he was a lawyer.

I called Paul Roper and told him who I was.

"You had better get out here and get yourself a lawyer," he commanded, "because we're coming after you."

Paul Roper, we came to know through our contacts in California, had become a self-appointed watchdog over certain pastors and churches in southern California, giving thumbs up or thumbs down as to their conduct. Pastors and

Paul R. Roper

January 14, 1985

Defendant:

The enclosed package of material has been prepared with the intention of placing it in the hands of legal counsel in the appropriate jurisdictions for filing and prosecution. If you feel you would like to discuss this situation prior to it becoming a filed lawsuit and a public record you may make such arrangements by leaving a message for me with the secretary at 516-798-1920.

This courtesy is extended to you until January 21, 1985 at 8:00 a.m. at which time we will utilize every possible legal remedy.

You are notified herewith that you are not to make further contact with Ms. Hahn. Any contact of any kind will be noted, recorded, and added to the complaint for damages. If you attempt any contact of any kind we will immediately seek a restraining order without further notification to you.

Sincerely,

Paul R. Roper
(Attorney-in-fact for
Jessica Hahn)

PRR:cr

1 JESSICA HAHN
    4100 Jerusalem Avenue
2 Massapequa, New York   11758
    Telephone:
3

4

5 In propria persona

6

7

8   SUPERIOR COURT OF THE STATE OF NEW YORK

9   FOR THE COUNTY OF NASSAU

10

11 JESSICA HAHN,   ) CASE NO.
)
12   Plaintiff,   ) COMPLAINT FOR DAMAGES FOR
) ASSAULT AND BATTERY,
13 vs.   ) INTENTIONAL INFLICTION
) OF EMOTIONAL DISTRESS,
14 JAMES BAKKER, AKA JIM BAKKER;) FALSE IMPRISONMENT,
    PTL INC., a North Carolina   ) NEGLIGENCE
15 Corporation; RICHARD DORTCH;)
    ASSEMBLIES OF GOD, INC., a Missouri)
16 Corporation; AMY •CORTISE; CROSSROADS)
    CHURCH, INC., a New York Corporation;)
17 SHERATON SAND KEY HOTEL, a Florida)
    Corporation; and DOES 1 through 50,)
18 inclusive,   )
)
19   Defendants.   )
)
20

21   Plaintiff complains and alleges as follows:

22   APPLICABLE TO ALL CAUSES OF ACTION

23   1. Plaintiff is, and at all material times herein

24 mentioned was, a resident of the County of Nassau, State of

25 New York.

26   2. Defendant James Bakker is, and at all material

27 times herein mentioned was, a resident of the State of North

28 Carolina.

3. Defendant PTL Inc. is, and at all material times herein mentioned was, a corporation organized and existing under the laws of the State of North Carolina.

4. Defendant Richard Dortch is, and at all material times herein mentioned was, a resident of the State of North Carolina.

5. Defendant Assemblies of God, Inc. is, and at all material times herein mentioned was, a non-profit corporation organized and existing under the laws of the State of Missouri.

6. Defendant Amy Cortise is, and all material times herein mentioned was, a resident of the State of New York.

7. Defendant Crossroads Church is, and at all material times herein mentioned was, a non-profit corporation organized and existing under the laws of the State of New York.

8. Defendant Sheraton Sand Key Hotel is, and at all material times herein mentioned was, a corporation organized and existing under the laws of the State of Florida.

9. Plaintiff is ignorant of the true names and capacities of Defendants sued herein as DOES 1 through 50, inclusive, and therefore sue said defendants by such fictitious names. Plaintiff will amend this complaint to allege their true names and capacities as soon as the same has been ascertained.

10. Plaintiff is informed and believes and thereon alleges that each of the defendants sued herein was the agent, servant, or employee of each of the remaining defendants and at all material times were acting within the scope of said agency or employment with the permission of the remaining

1 defendants.

2   I

3   FIRST CAUSE OF ACTION FOR
                        BATTERY (Against defendant
4   James Bakker)

5   11. Plaintiff incorporates by reference each and

6   every allegation of paragraphs 1 through 10, inclusive, as

7   though set forth in full at this point.

8   12. On or about December 6, 1980, defendant James

9   Bakker battered plaintiff by causing her to unknowingly ingest

10 a sleep-inducing drug which was mixed with wine prepared at

11 defendant Jim Bakker's request.

12   13. By reason of the wrongful and malicious acts

13 of defendant James Bakker plaintiff suffered extreme and

14 severe nausea, and was rendered incapable of defending herself

15 against the defendant's subsequent advances.

16   14. By reason of the wrongful and malicious acts

17 of defendant James Bakker plaintiff was required to and did

18 expend money and incur obligations for medical services, drugs,

19 and sundries reasonably required in the treatment of the

20 emotional disturbances she sustained. The exact amount of

21 these medical expenses is not now known to the plaintiff; when

22 the same have been ascertained, plaintiff will request

23 permission to amend this complaint so as to set forth the

24 various items and the total of such charges and expenses.

25   15. All of the aforementioned acts of defendant

26 James Bakker were done with malice and ill will and with the

27 design and intent of injuring and oppressing plaintiff, and

28 for that reason plaintiff is entitled to and asks for $1,000,000

exemplary and punitive damages.

II

SECOND CAUSE OF ACTION
ASSAULT AND BATTERY
(Against defendant James Bakker)

16.   Plaintiff incorporates by reference each and every allegation of paragraphs 1 through 15, inclusive, as though set forth in full at this point.

17.   On or about December 6, 1980, defendant James Bakker assaulted and battered plaintiff in her hotel room in Clearwater Beach, Florida, by advancing upon her and forcing her to engage in sexual intercourse and oral copulation.   Said advancing occurred when plaintiff was weak, nauseous, and sedated due to defendant's actions in drugging plaintiff's drink.

18.   By reason of the aforementioned acts of defendant, plaintiff was placed in great fear for her life and physical well being.

19.   By reason of the wrongful, intentional, and malicious acts of defendant and the fright thereby caused plaintiff, plaintiff has suffered extreme and severe mental anguish and physical pain and has been injured in mind and body, as follows: physical trauma from unconsented sexual acts; emotional trauma from said unconsented sexual acts, resulting in severe psychological disturbance and the inability to desire and maintain normal relationships with men.

20.   As a result of the aforementioned assault and battery plaintiff has been damaged in the sum   of $100,000.

21.   The aforementioned acts of defendant were

willful, wanton, malicious, and oppressive and justify the
awarding of exemplary and punitive damages in the amount of
$5,000,000.

III

THIRD CAUSE OF ACTION
INTENTIONAL INFLICTION OF EMOTIONAL DISTRESS
(Against defendants James Bakker, Richard
Dortch, Assemblies of God, Inc., Amy Cortize,
and Crossroads Church)

22. Plaintiff incorporates by reference each and
every allegation of paragraphs 1 through 21 inclusive, as
though set forth in full at this point.

23. On or about November 1, 1984, defendants Dortch
and Cortise, in their respective capacities as agents,
employees and representatives of defendants Assemblies of God,
Inc. and Crossroads Church, Inc., with the knowledge and
consent of defendant James Bakker, induced plaintiff to sign
a "confession" as to the assault and batteries described
herein in paragraphs 11 through 21, inclusive. Said "confession"
was an attempt by defendants to exculpate defendant Bakker
and was signed by plaintiff only after defendants employed
coercion, duress, and undue influence in securing signature.
Defendants Cortise and Dortch made promises to plaintiff
regarding "healing, forgiveness, and obedience to God" which
overcame plaintiff's resistance in cooperating with a deception.

24. Defendants conduct was intentional and malicious,
and was done with a wanton and reckless disregard of the
consequences to plaintiff.

25. As a proximate result of the aforementioned acts
plaintiff suffered humiliation, mental anguish, loss of sleep,

edginess, fatigue, tension requiring physical therapy, and pschological stress requiring on-going psychological therapy, to plaintiff's damage in the amount of $100,000.

26. The aforementioned acts of defendants were wilful, wanton, malicious, and oppressive, and justify the awarding of exemplary and punitive damages in the amount of $5,000,000.

IV

FOURTH CAUSE OF ACTION
FALSE IMPRISONMENT
(Against defendant James Bakker)

27. Plaintiff incorporates by reference each and every allegation of paragraphs 1 through 26, inclusive, as though set forth in full at this point.

28. On or about December 6, 1980, defendant James Bakker siezed plaintiff and forcibly, against plaintiff's will, and without her consent and over her protest, kept plaintiff confined in her hotel room by force and threats of physical violence for a period of approximately two hours. During this time defendant forced plaintiff to engage in various sexual acts as herein alleged in this complaint.

29. Immediately prior to the acts of defendant herein alleged, plaintiff had been peacefully staying in her separate hotel room in Clearwater Beach, Florida.

30. As a proximate result of the act of defendant, plaintiff was injured in her health, strength, and activity, sustaining injury to her body and shock and injury to her nervous system and person, to plaintiff's damage in the amount of $100,000.

31.   The acts of defendant as herein alleged were wilful, wanton, malicious, and oppressive, and justify the awarding of punitive damages in the amount of $1,000,000.

V

FIFTH CAUSE OF ACTION
NEGLIGENCE
(Against defendant
Sheraton Hotel)

32.   Plaintiff incorporates by reference each and every allegation of paragraphs 1 through 31, inclusive, as though set forth in full at this point.

33.   Defendant Sheraton Hotel, being in control of the premises located at Clearwater Beach, Florida, had a duty to protect its guests. Said duty is reinforced by the higher duty of innkeepers recognized at common law.

34.   On or about December 6, 1980, defendant breached its duty by failing to come to plaintiff's aid when summoned.

35.   Defendant's failure was both the actual and proximate cause of injury sustained by plaintiff as described in paragraphs 11 through 21, inclusive, and 27 through 31, inclusive, above, in the amount of $200,000.

WHEREFORE, PLAINTIFF PRAYS JUDGMENT as follows:

1.   For the sum of $300,000 as general damages for assault and battery, battery, intentional infliction of emotional distress, false imprisonment, and negligence.

2.   For the sum of $12,000,000 as punitive damages for battery, assault and battery, intentional infliction of emotional distress, and false

```
 1            imprisonment.

 2       3.   For costs of suit incurred herein; and

 3       4.   For such other and further relief as the court

 4            deems just and proper.

 5    DATED:

 6

 7                                    _____

 8                                    Jessica Hahn,
                                      Plaintiff
 9

10
```

churches rose or fell according to his whim.

My wife and I quickly flew to California and met with the attorney who would be handling the case for PTL.

"Do you think PTL can endure the publicity this kind of lawsuit will bring?" he asked us first off.

"I think it would be extremely difficult for the ministry to survive something like this," I replied.

Our attorney told me that an out of court settlement is an ordinary procedure and that most civil legal actions are resolved in this manner. At that point, I gave the go-ahead for our lawyer to begin negotiations. I spoke with Paul Roper regarding a settlement.

The lawyer and Paul Roper came to an agreement as to how the settlement of $265,000 was to be paid to Jessica Hahn.

In making the arrangements and the negotiations of the proposed lawsuit Dr. Fred Gross accompanied me to the lawyer's office. As soon as I knew the amount of money that was agreed upon, I returned to Heritage USA believing that we had to come up with $265,000.

I went to Jim Bakker and said, "The lawyers have agreed upon an amount to pay Jessica Hahn."

He quickly responded, "I don't want to know."

I said, "Well, you're going to know. If we're going to pay somebody this kind of money and you're the person involved, you're gonna . . . "

"Well, I don't want to know," Jim said curtly.

I repeated, "Well, you *are* going to know." And I explained to him in detail, exactly what the settlement was going to be, how it was going to be dispersed, and all that was involved.

Now all we had to do was come up with the money. Who would be willing to write a check for $265,000?

I began to think. *If the Jim Bakker/Jessica Hahn incident becomes public, who has the most to lose?*

I thought of the Brock Corporation who had the management contract for the hotel. The Morrison Corporation, who provided all the food services at Heritage USA — a multi-million dollar business — also came to mind.

Then I realized who had the most to lose if there were any kind of reversal of PTL's growth. It would be the contractor of the buildings, the developer of Heritage USA, Roe Messner. Besides, I have known Roe Messner for over thirty years, and I felt comfortable going to him. He had been the contractor on the Heritage Grand Hotel, and had completed several other facilities at PTL. At that time in early 1985, he had at least $50,000,000 of work underway.

I went to Roe Messner and told him the nature of the problem.

"Roe, Mr. Bakker had a tryst with a lady," I explained without giving many details, "and she and her cohorts are demanding $265,000 as the out of court settlement. If we don't get the money, we are going to have legal action filed against us."

I don't know why I ever got involved in such a stupid scenario. I actually thought I was helping Roe avoid financial ruin should a scandal cause PTL to fall apart. There was nothing illegal in seeking Roe's help; it was simply a very foolish thing to do.

Roe Messner and I have both testified on this matter in federal court. He and I disagree. My remembrance of this matter is as I have stated. At the time, I explained to Mr. Messner the need and told him if we didn't get the money, disaster could result.

Roe Mesner's testimony is that I told him to over bill a facility known as The Amphitheater at Heritage USA.

Why would I do that when no work had been done on The Amphitheater in over a year? The project was complete. I knew that. Asking Roe to add $265,000 onto a project that was idle would certainly be an extremely unwise and foolish thing for me to do.

Many people have asked, "Did you believe Roe Messner would get his money back?" Yes, I did.

My remembrance and belief is that my agreement with Roe was an unspoken one. He and I did not discuss the specifics, but with $50,000,000 in projects underway, I believed that Roe would get his $265,000 back some way. Without verbalizing it, I assumed we both understood that the money would come from profits on one project or another.

Our testimonies differ, but I believe my motives were right.

As agreed, Roe Messner sent the money to our attorney in California.

The public was led to believe that I, or some other PTL administrator, acted as the "bag" person to take the money to Jessica Hahn in California. That was not the case.

Although I did not attend the settlement proceeding, our attorney informed us that Jessica Hahn came to California and appeared before a judge. At that time the legal documents were signed for the out of court settlement, but we were not sent any of those documents.

In fact, I did not see the documents until Jerry Falwell took over PTL. Our then attorney at PTL, Roy Grutman, called the attorney in California and, with my permission, the California lawyer released those documents.

For the first time I saw the official documents that contained the settlement with Jessica Hahn. She was to receive $20,000 immediately and Paul Roper $90,000. The remaining amount was to be put into a fund and invested.

COMPROMISE AND SETTLEMENT

This Compromise and Settlement agreement entered into on March 27, 1985 between Jessica Hahn (herein after "Hahn") and James Bakker, aka Jim Bakker (herein after "Bakker"); PTL Inc., a North Carolina Corporation; Richard Dortch; Assemblies of God Inc., a Missouri Corporation; Amy Cortise and Crossroads Church Inc., a New York Corporation.

The parties stipulate that:

1. Hahn asserts a claim against Bakker, et al., for damages for assault and battery, intentional infliction of emotional distress, false imprisonment and negligence arising out of an incident that occured on or about December 6, 1980 at the Sheraton Sand Key Hotel, Sand Key, Florida.

2. There is no action presently pending based upon such claim and upon execution of this Compromise and Settlement agreement Hahn agrees that no such claim, or any action arising therefrom, shall be filed in any court of competent jursidiction.

3. Bakker, Richard Dortch, Assemblies of God Inc., Amy Cortise, and Crossroads Church Inc., denies any liability in connection with the alleged claim.

4. The parties wish to reach a full and final settlement of all matters and/or potential causes of action arising out of the facts and claim as herein above set forth.

In so doing:

(a) Hahn, her heirs and assigns, shall not file nor cause to be filed any cause of action in any court of competent jurisdiction arising from the facts and circumstances set forth in paragraph 1 above.

(b) If any such cause of action was to be filed, not only would it constitute a breach of this Compromise and Settlement agreement and bring to an immediate termination the Jessica Hahn Trust to be established as a condition of this compromise and settlement, but a dismissal with prejudice shall be caused to be filed by Hahn.

(c) Hahn shall refrain from contacting, annoying, harrassing or molesting Bakker, Richard Dortch, any member or employee of P.T.L. Inc., any member or employee of Assemblies of God, Inc., Amy Cortise and Crossroads Church, Inc. *Bakker et al shall* ~~*refrain from Contacting, annoying, harassing or molesting Hahn. SSF*~~ *SSF & settled did*

(d) Hahn shall not discuss or otherwise disseminate *to* the public any information or facts with reference to the claim *her* set forth in paragraph 1 above, with the exception of any *direction* licensed therapist, and then Hahn shall direct that the appropriate priviledges of confidentiality between said communications be asserted. This shall not effect Hahn's right or ability to confession. *Bakker, et al shall not discuss or otherwise disseminate to the public any information or facts with reference to this matter. SSF*

1

"her direction" SSF

(e) Hahn shall not attempt to contact or disseminate* information to any media source with regard to this Compromise and Settlement or any of the facts giving to rise to an incident as alledged in paragraph 1 above. Bakker shall not attempt to contact or disseminate to any media any facts with regard to these proceedings SSF J.H

This agreement is executed by the parties hereto for the sole purpose of compromising and settling the matters involved in this dispute, and it is expressely understood and agreed, as a condition hereof, that this agreement shall not consitute or be construed to be an admission on any part or as evidencing or indicating in any degree an admission of the truth or correctness of any claims asserted.

Upon execution of this Compromise and Settlement, Hahn shall deliver to counsel for Bakker, et al, a general release releasing Bakker, et al, from all liability or responsibilities of any character whatsoever, except those of compliance with and in performance of any obligation and duty arising out of the terms of this agreement for Compromise and Settlement.

Each party shall bear their own attorneys fees and costs in connection with this agreement for Compromise and Settlement.

Hahn and Bakker, et al, agree that the failure of either party to carry out any obligation under this agreement will constitute immediate and irreparable damage to the other party not compensable in money damages and will warrant preliminary and other injuctive and equitable relief. It is understood between the parties that upon the failure, breach or default of either party to carry out any obligation under this agreement that the matter shall be referred to binding, private arbitration before the Honorable Charles Woodmansee, Judge of the Superior Court of Los Angeles County, retired, or in the event he is unavailable, before any other arbitrator for Los Angeles County upon mutual agreement of the parties. Hahn shall have no election under the terms of this agreement for Compromise and Settlement to file any action with a court of competent jurisdiction as a result of any breach on the part of Bakker, et al. It is understood and agreed that Hahn's sole remedy is through binding, private arbitration.

In consideration of the mutual convenants and agreements as set forth herein, the parties agree as follows:

1. Upon execution of this agreement for Compromise and Settlement by Hahn, Bakker shall cause to be delivered to Hahn a check payable to the Bank of Yorba Linda in the amount of $115,000.

2. Hahn shall execute a general release releasing Bakker, et al, from any liability whatsoever for any acts alledged to have occurred on or about December 6, 1980 at the Sheraton Sand Key Hotel.

3. Bakker will cause to be established a trust, the duration of which will be 20 years, in the name of Jessica Hahn as follows:

(a) $150,000 will be placed in a trust account with Dean Witter Reynolds, Inc. 9470 Wilshire, Beverly Hills, CA for the purchase of the corpus of the Jessica Hahn Trust.

(b) The corpus of the trust shall consist of securities in the form of government agency issues, treasury bonds, notes and bills, tax exempt funds and insured deposits at the election of Hahn. Bakker will assume no liability for the reliability, viability or return on the aforementioned securities.

(c) Paul R. Roper and Scott S. Furstman shall act as trustees for the Jessica Hahn Trust. The exercise of any powers granted to the trustees pursuant to the trust agreement to be drafted shall be effective only upon the mutual consent by way of written instructions by both trustees. The trustees' powers shall be fully set forth in the trust documents, however, said powers shall include the power to relocate the corpus of the trust property. However, no such powers may be exercised without *J.H* the written mutual agreement by both trustees. *Hahn and Bukstet al waive any conflict of interest between trustee and their respective clients. SSF*
(d) The trustees shall not be required to maintain a bond for their services.

(e) The trustees, by mutual agreement and assent, shall direct that Dean Witter Reynolds, or any other brokerage firm to which the corpus of the trust may be relocated, disburse monthly payments of interest on the trust corpus to any individual so designated by the mutual assent and agreement, in writing, of the trustees.

(f) In the event Hahn breaches said term, condition or covenant of this agreement for Compromise and Settlement and/or the Jessica Hahn Trust the matter shall be referred immediately for private binding arbitration. Either trustee shall have the power to request that this matter be so submitted for arbitration upon alleging a material breach of these agreements. Upon a finding of Hahn's material breach of any term, condition or covenant of the agreement for Compromise and Settlement and/or the Jessica Hahn Trust said trust will immediately terminate and the corpus shall revert forthwith to trustor, Bakker. Upon receipt by either trustee of notice from the other of breach and a request for arbitration it is agreed and understood by all parties that monthly payment to Hahn or her designee of interest on the corpus of the Jessica Hahn Trust shall be paid directly into an escrow account and held until final determination by private, binding arbitration. In the event of a finding of a material breach by Hahn, not only will the corpus revert to trustor, but any and all monthly payments of interest on the corpus held in said escrow account will also revert to trustor.

3

(g) At the expiration of twenty years and a day of the establishment of the Jessica Hahn Trust said trust will terminate and the corpus become the exclusive property of Jessica Hahn, her heirs or assigns.

(h) A trustee to the Jessica Hahn trust may resign or substitute in his place another trustee upon the mutual agreement of the remaining trustee, Hahn and Bakker, at any time by depositing with the United States mail, postage prepaid, a notice of such resignation or nomination for substitution, addressed to all interested parties, including, the remaining trustee, Hahn and Bakker.

(i) This Compromise and Settlement agreement, and the Jessica Hahn trust shall be administered in the State of California, and its validity, construction and all rights thereunder shall be governed by the laws of that state.

The foregoing represents an intent of the parties to the Jessica Hahn Trust. Said trust documents are to be prepared fully setting forth in the formal document the respective rights, obligations and duties of the trustor, beneficiary and trustees of the Jessica Hahn Trust. Upon completion and acknowledgement of said trust documents it will be incorporated herein by reference as though fully set forth.

This agreement shall be binding on Jessica Hahn, and on her heirs, legal representatives and assigns.

Executed this 27 day of February, 1985 at Los Angeles, California.

JESSICA HAHN

SCOTT S. FURSTMAN on
behalf of BAKKER, et al

Witnessed By:

CHARLES WOODMANSEE — Feb. 27, 1985
Judge of the Superior Court, retired

PAUL R. ROPER

The below is stricken SSF - J.H.

This document shall not be copied and shall remain in the custody of Judge Charles Woodmansee. They shall not be released except by Judge Woodmansee upon his order upon application by all outstanding copies of the proposed Hahn Complaint shall be delivered by SSF

Jessica Hahn was to receive the interest on this money for the next twenty years. After the twenty years, she was to get the corpus, the principal amount.

That's when I learned Paul Roper had received $90,000.

Later, when I did the "Larry King Live" show for the first time, I publicly told about the threats of Eugene Profeta. I also made public the fact that the open court records indicated to us that Paul Roper received $90,000.

Paul Roper had made clear to me that he was representing Pastor Profeta. He did not say he was representing Jessica Hahn, who was the alleged victim. His client was Pastor Profeta.

On the Larry King show I asked, "How much of that did Pastor Profeta get? Did Roper and Profeta split the $90,000?"

As for myself, I got nothing out of the settlement except a lot of heartbreak and pain. Throughout the grand jury investigation, the trials, and my sentencing, my testimony under oath has been consistent with what I have stated. Later, over $150,000 of the Jessica Hahn money was returned to PTL. Jessica Hahn had broken her agreement and PTL got the money back.

The settlement for Jim's 1980 episode with Jessica Hahn was completed in February, 1985. Finally, after months of harassment, threats, and legal negotiations, life at PTL began to return to normal.

The Heritage Grand had then been open for about two and a half months, and thousands of people were coming to Heritage USA everyday. The work was nearly completed on the Main Street USA, and different areas of the hotel were in the process of being finished. Plans were being drawn to build the twenty-one story Heritage Grand Tower, and our staff grew from 700 employees to 2,200 employees. PTL's income rose from $40 million to $160 million a year.

Dr. Gross told me that Jim Bakker had submitted to him both spiritually and psychologically and had made good progress. I had not noticed any unseemly conduct on the part of Jim Bakker, nor did I have any reason to doubt that the Lord had forgiven him. That was all behind him. It appeared to me that Jim was on his way to victory and living in submission to a psychologist who was also a spiritual leader.

Toward the end of 1986, I would periodically receive a phone call from some evangelist, pastor, or layman telling me they had heard Jim Bakker had allegedly had a tryst with some woman. Was it true?

In my desire to protect the ministry, I generally avoided the question as best I could, by attempting to protect Jim and Tammy and PTL. I compromised the truth, not by what I said, but by what I didn't say. I let people believe what they wanted to, without involving myself too much in their speculation.

I failed my Lord and myself and others by not setting the record straight or by letting people believe things they assumed to be true.

The truth, however, cannot always be concealed.

In the summer of 1986, I received a telephone call from a man whom I have always believed is one of the few prophetic figures of our time — David Wilkerson. I don't believe Rev. Wilkerson ever knew the tremendous esteem and appreciation I have for him. In fact, I considered him, as I do now, to be more than just a "man of God." I believed he was a principled person who would not compromise his values. He was not for sale at any cost.

His telephone call caught me by surprise. After a few brief pleasantries, in genuinely Wilkerson fashion, he quickly addressed the issues on his heart.

"Brother Dortch," he said solemnly, "you must do something, and it must be done fast. What is going on at PTL is an abomination to God, and it must be stopped. Brother Dortch, you are the hope of getting some of these problems solved."

In a stunned manner I responded and explained, "You may well be right, but we need to hear it from you. I am certainly open to the possibility of your coming and sharing with our entire staff your vision."

Without responding to my invitation, he continued, "If something isn't done quickly God is going to write *ICHABOD* over the doors of Heritage USA. The birds are going to be flying in that hotel within a year — if something isn't done."

I implored him to come, but he said it would be impossible at this time. I pled with him to meet with Jim Bakker and/or me. He encouraged me to address the staff myself.

At the time David Wilkerson called, Jim Bakker was in California. I did my best to get Brother David to come and unburden his soul to us, but he felt that he could not do it.

I called an entire staff meeting for the next Friday afternoon at 2:30 p.m. Everyone was to be released from their jobs and assemble at the PTL television studio.

By that Friday Jim Bakker had returned from California, and I shared with him David Wilkerson's prophetic word. I told him about the scheduled meeting and asked him to introduce me that day before I spoke. I wanted the staff to know that Jim Bakker was standing with me in what I had to say. Jim cheerfully responded and said he would be glad to do so.

I addressed the staff that Friday afternoon in a way I had never done before at Heritage USA. I dealt with every known sin that I felt God leading me to address, including infidelity in marriage, adultery, homosexuality, drinking, pornography, conversation, and language. I discussed the importance of paying our tithes and living a life pleasing to God. I felt it was necessary to cover the fundamentals of Christian living and the conduct expected of believers.

"Our partners and viewers have a right to expect every one of us to have proper moral values in harmony with our Christian witness," I told the PTL staff. "They have a right to expect us to live an overcoming life — a life above reproach."

At the conclusion of my message a holy silence hovered over the auditorium.

Upon returning to the dressing room and sitting down, Jim remarked to me, "If there's anything you missed today, I don't know what it was. And it all needed to be said."

In my soul I felt that I had delivered the message that, in a sense, had been laid upon someone else's heart. But it was a message I knew had to communicated.

I then called David Wilkerson and pled with him once again to meet with us. He kindly consented to meet with Jim Bakker and me on the following Thursday in Chattanooga or Knoxville, Tennessee. The next morning, however, his secretary called to say he would be unable to come. I was extremely disappointed.

Other Christians were also sending warnings to PTL. Some of them, without fanfare, privately attempted to lay a foundation on which to get Jim Bakker's attention. They were unsuccessful.

As the year progressed the rumors, stories, and allegations concerning Jim Bakker and a woman continued. I found myself frequently trying to answer the questions that were coming, never imagining the whole matter would explode in our faces.

As my third Christmas at PTL approached, plans were made for the department and division heads to meet at the Bakker's home. Tammy was quite ill, Jim had been gone a great deal of the autumn. Whether in Palm Springs or Gatlinburg, Tennessee, Jim Bakker still principally directed the projects and the activities of PTL by telephone.

More and more, however, the responsibilities and burdens of the ministry fell on my shoulders. I preached regularly in the church, weekly on national television, and assumed the day by day leadership in the absence of Jim Bakker.

But it was Christmas time at PTL. What better place to celebrate the holidays?

7

The Unraveling

Christmas City at Heritage USA in 1986 displayed 1,250,000 lights — even the national TV networks were impressed. The cars attempting to get into Heritage USA to see the spectacular show stretched for ten miles. Packaged into an eight week presentation, the project required almost twelve months of preparation and was the grandest event of the year.

Coming to Heritage USA for the Christmas season had become a tradition for many families, and the hotels were bursting at the seams. People came to hear the speakers, see the special holiday programs, and participate in the many opportunities for fun and fellowship. It was a magnificent time.

I remember well the evening the staff and management team gathered together to celebrate Christmas at the Bakker home. The house was jam-packed with department and division heads and their companions.

In spite of the festivities, thoughts of Tammy's illness, Jim's recent absence, and the rumors about Jessica Hahn, bounced around in my mind.

I wondered to myself, *What will this "celebration" be*

like?

It wasn't really a celebration I was seeking, it was relief. The Crohn's disease had been acting up, and the resulting weakness had left me feeling miserable. Many nights, after coming home from work, I would lay across the bed and cry — partly from the pain, mostly from frustration.

Most days I was responding to questions I didn't have the answers for and making decisions that were beyond my authority to decide. The ministry had grown so large and cumbersome and involved so many people that I didn't have the power or the will to take much action.

How am I going to answer for all the turmoil here? I asked myself constantly, sensing that some kind of corrective or remedial action might be forthcoming.

I took safety and comfort in my haven — our family. Mildred and our children, Rich and Deanna, were my strength. Whenever I was not working or preaching, I took every opportunity to return to the security of our home and family.

The night of the Christmas event, upon entering the Bakker home, everyone had their picture taken with our hosts, Jim and Tammy. It was a beautiful evening, filled with gaiety and good fellowship.

Yet, a foreboding sense of dread hung over me like an executioner's sword. I knew we were living in a dream world that could soon be jolted into reality.

After the guests had eaten and the activities of the evening quieted down, someone led us in singing several Christmas carols. Then the hushed crowd listened intently as Jim Bakker began to speak.

"We need the Lord during this Christmas season more than we've ever needed Him before. I sense that we, as a leadership team, need to call upon God tonight more than ever. I am going to ask you to do an unusual thing tonight, even with your nice gowns on, ladies. Men, I'm going to ask all of you and your companions to get down on your knees and pray. We must call upon God for forgiveness, mercy, and strength."

My heart exploded with joy at this celebration of prayer and praise. The management team's Christmas celebration at the Bakker's had turned into a prayer meeting!

Perhaps there is light at the end of the tunnel after all, I thought. *There is always hope when people are on their knees.*

The response of the team left me overjoyed. We were all in a dry, weary place. How gracious God was that night to do more for us than we expected or deserved. It was the best Christmas gift I received that year.

After the Christmas celebration came to a close, Mildred and I remained behind. I quietly tried to assure Jim and Tammy that this was one of the best evenings we had ever spent together. I was encouraged to think that perhaps 1987 held new hope for PTL.

During the following week on the telecast and when I spoke in the church, I described the blessings of that evening in great length. I wanted people to know — and I needed to remind myself — that God had not forsaken us.

Tammy left for Gatlinburg, Tennessee, following the groundbreaking service of the Heritage Crystal Palace in the first week of January. Promising to be the largest church in the United States, seating 30,000 people, the Palace would be Jim's most extensive undertaking.

Tammy had become very ill, and Jim wanted to spend much of January in Tennessee with her. We began to plan accordingly.

"No matter what the cost, I'm going to be there for her," he said.

An important meeting had been scheduled in January with the York County commissioners. They wanted to see a long-term plan of PTL's operation instead of the usual bits and pieces we had been giving them. Jim and I were planning to outline to the commissioners — in the presence of the PTL staff, management, and residents — our vision for Heritage USA.

Jim had decided that, even though Tammy's needs were urgent, he would take the days necessary to prepare for the presentation and see that things went as planned.

The day of the meeting, Jim received a call from Gatlinburg telling him that Tammy was so sick she needed to be hospitalized. As I recall, Jim phoned a dear friend in California, Dr. Nichols, and urged him to fly to Gatlinburg and take care of Tammy. When he arrived, Dr. Nichols determined that Tammy needed treatment immediately.

An airplane was chartered, and on the day of our meeting, Tammy was flown to Palm Springs, California to enter the Eisenhower Hospital. As soon as Jim finished his presentation with the county commissioners, he flew to Palm Springs to be with Tammy.

Jim Bakker departed that day — never realizing he was leaving Heritage USA for the last time as the leader of the PTL ministry.

While in California, Jim remained in constant contact, by the hour, with those of us carrying on the work at PTL. It was not unusual for him to call a division or department head and talk to them for as long as two hours.

Prior to the broadcast of the program, Jim would phone, and we would go over the telecast for the day. As the primary host, I needed his advice. He developed the fund raising ideas, and I looked to him to know what to present to our viewers.

During the telecast, Jim would call at anytime — while we were live on the air, on a break, or while the PTL singers were singing. I would receive a message to move my right knee or push the book that was on the table a little to the left. He'd direct the show by phone, positioning guests and telling them which way to turn or where to place their coffee cups. His suggestions were always appreciated.

Jim Bakker saw everything, not as the average person would see things, but photogenically through the eyes of a television lens.

In hotels, I have watched him move from one side of the room to another.

"Are you looking for someone, Jim?" I would ask. Then I'd realize, he was analyzing the room.

"This post should not have been put here. It should have

been put over there because then the room would photo-graph much better," Jim would say.

Once, while boating on the Mississippi River, Jim was lying down near the front of the vessel. Along the riverbank at that point, there were no telephone lines or signs of modernization.

When he lifted up his head, Jim remarked, "You know, we could shoot this as the Amazon River." His mind assimilated everything in the form of a picture.

After Jim had been in Palm Springs, California for about a week, he called one day and said, "Pastor Dortch, I can't do it. I just can't be here and run the program and PTL in Charlotte. Tammy is very sick. She has entered a lengthy treatment program, and I'm required to go through part of it with her."

Jim had often mentioned to me that he had been preaching out of town when Tammy Sue was born. He'd carried that guilt for years.

On the phone that day he again said, "I've been away from Tammy so much in the important times of her life. I'm not going to do it this time. Tammy needs me now, and I don't care what the consequences are, I'm going to stay here with her until she completes this program. It is going to take a couple of months."

Then he told me, "Pastor Dortch, you go ahead with the ministry, and I'm trying not to watch the program. I'll let you do what you have to do, and I will do my best not to interfere."

I believe Jim sincerely meant that. Still I was dependent on him because he was the television professional. Acting as a TV host was not my area of expertise, and I did not consider myself to be his equal. But I tried to do my best under the circumstances, especially now that the daily telecast and being its host, had become my responsibility.

The full administration of PTL operations, along with the television program and the church — with one telephone call — fell into my lap. Make it or break it — the responsibility was now mine. But I didn't have a Richard Dortch to help me. I felt alone, like a man on an iceberg, drifting who knows where in the cold, dark waters.

I immediately called the management staff together. "We are going to stop all building programs, except the Heritage Grand Towers," I told them.

"That's the project we need to focus on. It has to be finished," I said, and they all agreed.

At the time we were also building a huge, new Wendy's fastfood restaurant. It was going to be the largest Wendy's in the world. We slowed that project down and called a halt to all other construction. All that mattered now was housing people and fulfilling our commitments to the Lifetime Partnership Program.

We decided to have a special telethon to raise funds. A certain percentage was to go directly to Roe Messner to keep the Towers project going. In fact, Roe and I had an agreement stating that fact.

It didn't take long for people to start asking why Jim and Tammy were not on the daily telecast.

I didn't hold back. I candidly told the viewers and the people. We tried to create good will and give reasons why they were gone.

After a month or so, the questions increased.

Carrying the full load of responsibility for PTL began to take its toll on me physically and mentally. Thankfully, people I had worked with for many years did everything they could to lift the burden. Jim and I called each other frequently, and he offered suggestions and advice for us to follow. I sensed he was trying to pull back, but I needed him, especially in the area of fund raising. For Jim to cut all ties to the ministry would have resulted in financial disaster.

As time went on and the Bakker's absence became more obvious, subversive forces started to undermine our efforts. The rumors concerning Jim Bakker's alleged affair were released by friends and enemies alike. It reminded me of the old saying, "While the cat's away, the mice will play."

As long as Jim had held a microphone and stood before the cameras, he presented a powerful figure who controlled events, people, and circumstances. That was now lost. His disappearance from the telecast left him without a visible identity, making him vulnerable to attack.

Although Jim Bakker had a loving and kind nature, he could also be forceful and assertive. That's how he maintained his authority at PTL. Without him, I felt powerless to control the situation. Confrontations with people had never come easily for me, and I avoided them whenever possible. My ministry has always been one of reconciliation, restoring broken relationships and bringing people back together. When situations demanded it, I would stand.

God hadn't called me to run PTL. That wasn't my gift or my ministry. I knew that from the beginning, and my feelings never changed. I did not have a messianic mantle upon me, nor did that concept cross my mind. I did feel called to be a blessing to people and to assist Jim and Tammy Bakker. That's why I came to PTL.

Running the show and presiding over the telecast often made me uncomfortable. I felt out of place.

I never verbalized my feelings, but I often thought to myself, *I belong behind a desk in an office or before a congregation preaching instead of in front of the cameras.*

But I had never refused a challenge.

I did my best and interestingly, during the months of the Bakkers' absence, partner giving increased fifteen percent over the previous year. The PTL family of supporters pulled together to show Jim and Tammy how much they loved them. It was the viewers' way of responding to a crisis situation. They knew my commitment to Jim Bakker and sensed I was acting on his behalf and for the good of the ministry.

The staff at PTL, however, reacted differently. During that time, long standing jealousies emerged among some key personnel. Underlying problems surfaced and exploded. Because Jim wasn't there and I was in charge, their venom spewed out on me.

It was my responsibility to deal with these people, which in some cases meant removing them from their positions. I knew I had the Bakkers' backing because they had made it clear to me that the attitudes of some staff people were out of line and should no longer be tolerated.

We were also trying to cut back on expenses, and a number of people were laid off from their jobs at PTL. After returning from the unemployment office who do you think appeared at their doorstep? Charles Shepard, *The Charlotte Observer's* investigative reporter. By catching former PTL employees at a time when their feelings about the ministry were most negative, he gathered his evidence, writing stories told by people who had been either fired or laid off from PTL.

For years, *The Charlotte Observer* had been writing story after story about PTL and the personal lives of the Bakkers. Our staff was becoming so paranoid about all the negative material that I decided to have a complete study done on these articles.

Summary of PTL/*The Charlotte Observer* and *Charlotte News* Coverage From 1974 to 1986.

After reviewing 593 stories/articles and 36 editorials spanning from 1974 to May 1986 (as well as some 372 letters to the editor), each was graded according to the following criteria:

Negative bias against PTL

Neutral reporting (balance of positive statements and quotes)

Positive or pro-PTL impact

Each story was judged according to four categories:

Placement: Did the section, page, or crease positioning reflect a bias? For example, burying a very important story would show a negative bias, or placing an extremely volatile article on the front page, top crease, would reflect a negative bias, and vice-versa.

Headline: Did the headline accurately reflect the story? Did letter size of the "kicker" or sub-head show a positive or negative bias?

Opening Statement: Did the first and second paragraph reveal the primary text of the article, or did it seek to sensationalize a thought or theory that was not integral to the story as a whole?

Overall Story: In total, did the article show a bias or a balance in all of the various aspects of the information and statements given?

(See charts on pages 124 and 125.)

It was such a complicated time. I had been on staff at PTL for three years, but the complexities of this organization still confounded me.

In any given week, I wore several different hats. I was the pastor of the Heritage church attended by about three thousand people, the administrator of all facets of the PTL operation, host of the daily television program, and overseer of eighty services and events a week at Heritage USA. No wonder I was confused.

The stress began to take its toll on me physically. To get relief, I tried to get away every three to four weeks. During my brief absences, reruns of the program replaced the live broadcasts.

To make matters worse, rumors about Jim heightened, and I was personally receiving more and more questioning calls. About that time, my integrity was put to a crucial test.

At the end of January, the National Religious Broadcasters held their 1987 national convention in Washington, DC. I led the PTL contingency to the NRB, as it is called.

As one of the principal displays at the convention, the immense PTL booth created a lot of excitement, but without Jim and Tammy, our exhibit didn't generate the usual fanfare. We did, however, spawn a great deal of speculation from convention attendees. Because of the rumors and Jim's month-long absence from the television program, the religious community was trying to figure out what was happening at PTL.

In spite of the gossip, I arrived at the convention hoping to make a valuable contribution to the broadcasting commu-

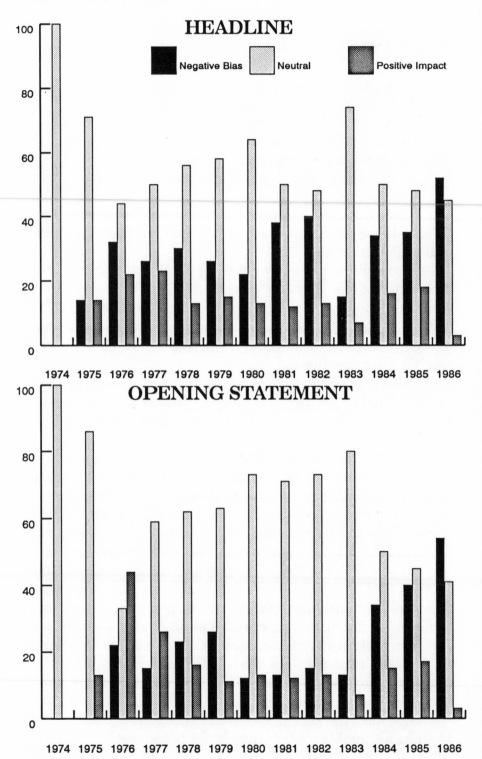

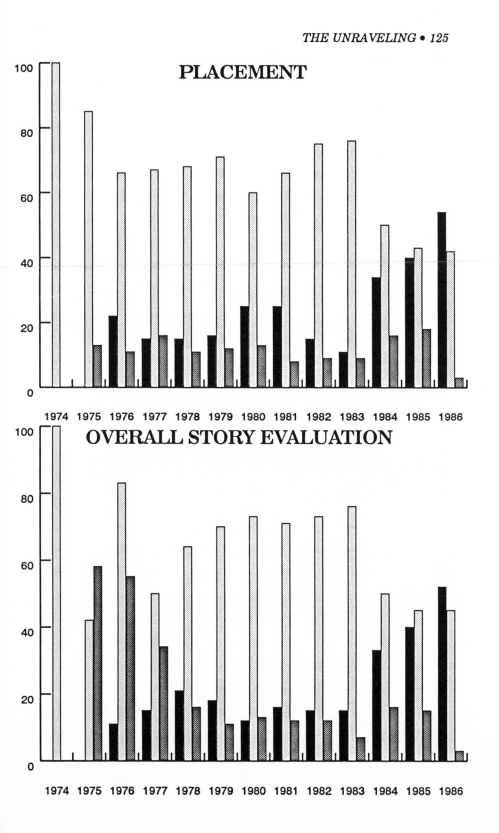

nity at large. The then president of the NRB, Ben Armstrong, received me graciously, and I was gratified to be elected as a director of the broadcasting organization. Sitting on the platform with Jerry Falwell, Charles Stanley, and a host of other "big" names in religious broadcasting left me feeling honored and humbled me at the same time.

The then vice president of the United States, George Bush, had been invited to address the convention. A mutual friend of the Bush family introduced me to the vice president. I had the opportunity to spend a few moments with him and his wife, Barbara. The official photographer captured the moment, and it remains one of my life's memorable experiences.

Also attending the convention was a dear and respected friend, an officer of the Assemblies of God. We greeted each other warmly and renewed our friendship.

Then he pulled me aside in the hallway and in very serious tones told me that a story had surfaced at a meeting of the executives of our church. He wanted to know if Jim Bakker had an affair with someone, and was she paid off?

I was beginning to answer when he asked his next question.

"Did PTL pay her $250,000?"

I almost choked.

My friend noted with a troubled look on his face, "There were serious questions about Jim Bakker."

I looked away, hoping he hadn't noticed the panicked expression on my face.

Envisioning the matter being discussed at the highest level of the denomination overwhelmed me with fear. As a recent member of that group, I knew that these men did not deal with just rumors or gossip. They wanted facts. The executives must have felt it best to have my dear friend ask me about the situation.

"Is it true?" he probed. "Are you aware of it?"

At that point, my integrity faltered as I saw the whole Jessica Hahn incident unraveling before me.

"An affair? Jim Bakker? Well, it's not the way they think

it is," I replied, acting like they were off base.

"What about the money?" he quizzed, hoping for a clue.

"No one has been paid $250,000 to my knowledge."

That's an honest answer, I thought. But my conscience told me I was getting myself into deeper and deeper trouble. I let my friend believe that PTL was high and dry and above the rumors, when I, more than anyone, knew that was not true. In my heart I knew I had not been totally forthcoming. It was clear I had violated my own integrity.

Since then, I've reflected. My response should have been: "If the brethren have a problem or a question about Jim Bakker, I would really appreciate it if they would ask him." After that encounter with my friend, I knew that the light was beginning to shine in PTL's darkest corners. We were headed for disaster. Truth always brings light.

The jig is up, I told myself. *But why should I be worried? It's not me they're asking about.*

I tried to push the incident out of my mind, but my thoughts and spirit remained sullen and downcast. The NRB convention lost all meaning for me. In reaction to the pressure and depression, the Crohn's disease ripped at my insides. But I put on a good front and carried on for the rest of the convention.

Every time I saw my friend, my heart sank and I wondered, *What will he ask next?*

Ashamed and brokenhearted, I left Washington and flew back to Charlotte.

Bewildered, my mind shot in every direction.

I didn't have an affair with Jessica Hahn, I told myself again. *I wasn't involved in any immoral activity. I haven't stolen any money. Here I am in the middle of what could explode into a national disgrace. How did I get myself into this mess?*

I returned home and threw myself across the bed, weeping. That was the first of many episodes of utter brokenness. The net was pulling tighter and closing in on us. I could sense it more day by day. It was not now the Jessica Hahn issue, it was my own integrity.

I knew that the willingness to confront yourself is one of the keys to walking in integrity. I had to confront myself about what I was doing. Was it ever right to stretch the truth, to slant it, to make it serve some pre-determined goal? Is it ever judicious to tell a lie to protect someone? Objectivity and credibility are important issues in today's world. Does the end justify the means? The famed evangelist and lover of people, Dr. C.M. Ward, talked about lying. I heard him speak about it, trying to awaken the church world. Now I was questioning whether or not we had listened. I sincerely doubt that we have learned very much about integrity since he spoke those words. In relationships, in the workplace, at home, or at church, we have become so concerned about success, bigness, and its related issues. Producing character and knowing how to live seems not to be too essential in our society. Here's a part of what Dr. Ward had to say when I heard him talk about truth:

> There are times that truth is, in its primary sense, not a quality of character, but a quality of statements. A statement is either true or false: it does or does not accord with the facts of the case. Even if it's false, the man speaking it can believe it's true. Sometimes people want the truth, but we are in error. We are mistaken. He tells the truth as he understands it. I have no right to blame a man merely because his statements are not true. I blame him for his want of veracity. Does he, or does he not, want to know and speak the truth? We must go beyond the statement to the person speaking. It's quite human to accept things at face value. We would be a strained community if we were all members of the FBI. Our faults consist, often, in hasty judgments and self esteem, in mistaking a love of novelty as a pursuit of truth, in not taking sufficient care to guard against the turn of our minds. There are people who believe what they say, just as much as we believe what we say. The fault doesn't consist in saying what they do not believe, but in believing on insufficient grounds, and under wrong biases which they believe. The weakness of all weaknesses is to suspect everybody who differs from us is insincere. I believe there is a vast amount of lying in the small way. There is a disposition everywhere to justify it, on the grounds that though these are lies, they're just little ones. We

must not be misled by tags! It's obvious to all of us, and we have all experienced it, that lying harms others, but it harms the liar more. It wrongs my soul. Every lie warps the soul. It makes us live in condemnation.

"Lying lips are an abomination to the Lord." "Put away lying, speak every man truth with his neighbor." "He shall not steal, neither deal falsely, neither lie one to another." "Knowing this that the law is not made for a righteous man, but for the lawless and disobedient, for the ungodly and for sinners, for unholy and profane, for murderers of fathers and murderers of mothers, for mainsayers . . . for men stealers, for liars, for perjured persons, and if there be any other thing that is contrary . . . "

It's pretty obvious that this association shows that lying is a crime before the Almighty. There isn't a trace in these biblical words that guilt depends on circumstances, or the end sought. Nothing is said about small lies. We are told never to lie — it doesn't say, except when we think a lie will be harmless, or do more good than harm. The significance that is stated here is that lying is a sin as much as murder, slavery, and theft are sins. If we are going to qualify lies, then we must qualify murder and theft, and say that sometimes it may be all right to kill and steal — that there are small murders and small thefts. It is said sometimes that in some professions, and in some kinds of work, a strict adherance to truth is not expected. It is not meant that it is not required or that it is not necessary. There is integrity and honor in truth! So, whether we expect it or not, doctors should be straight about their diagnoses, their presentation of facts to the patient, and submitting their bills for services rendered, the mail man delivering a letter, or someone weighing, packaging, and pricing a product. Lawyers should keep accurate track of their time, and a pastor never to tell a confidence. If he's committed to confidentiality, so should it be. The journalist is not to make up a part of the story. They are all lies. When we practice deceit, we lie. The problem is that there is a general suspicion and distrust accumulating in society, and now we find ourselves in a state of affairs where hardly anyone believes what they hear.

The laws of God act together in perfect harmony. Always let your heart, your head, and your conscience form a straight line. The moment we begin to allow our notions of policy, or even humanity, to modify or rule our notions of right and wrong, of sincerity and deceit, we open a door to abuses which no man can shut.

That's the rule for football and baseball officials, and bank examiners, and a rule for all of us. Our motive may be altruistic. It may be tender and humane. We may feel the deceit is justified. But we are wrong.

History is a teacher. History teaches us that some of the worst evils and crimes to which we are libel spring from perversion and abuse of the best feelings. "I just didn't have the heart to tell him." Long afterward we wish we had! No pressure of necessity authorizes a conscious departure from the truth.

God responds to truth.

We must be slow to judge another person. I know this! I dishonor the character of God to suppose that God made it expedient or necessary that we should deceive.

I know that people can be good, and not be perfect. That's the difference between Jesus and the rest of us. It is unthinkable that Jesus, in any case or under any provocation, should have resorted to subterfuge. He did it neither to save His own life or the lives of His friends. He might have been more popular — he might have enlarged his cause — he might have gained more financial or social backing — had he been more discreet, diplomatic, and elastic. But the spotless character that underwrites my salvation would be missing. I need a Saviour, not a suave Master of Ceremonies. We need never lie to further God's kingdom. Omnipotence can accomplish its eternal purpose without my help, and certainly without the help of my sins. I am asked to place my trust in God. That is always better than my lie. Apart from the Bible, there is nothing so universally regarded as the point of honor among us all. There's nothing which men and women who think at all of reputation, resent so quickly and so indignantly, as the questioning of their word. Lying is a disgrace — here and in eternity. It betrays a lack of courage. It says, "I don't have the muscle to stand for what is right."

Dr. Ward was right!

We had scheduled the International Church Growth Convention at Heritage USA to coincide with the ending of the NRB convention. This special event had been planned for over a year, and we had invited some of the world's renowned church leaders to come.

Dr. Paul Cho, the pastor of the Full Gospel Church in

Seoul, Korea, the largest church in the world, was the principle speaker. Oral Roberts, Robert Schmidgall, and some of the nation's great Christian leaders were also participating.

Thousands of people jammed the auditorium. Others packed out the studio when these great men of God appeared as guests on the daily PTL program.

What we called the *first* International Growth Convention was highly successful. I was greatly encouraged by the support even though Jim Bakker was absent.

It especially thrilled me to know that Dr. Ross Rhoades, a local minister in Charlotte and a Wheaton College graduate, would be attending. Through my own contact with Dr. Rhoades and by others' intervention, he had agreed to speak at the International Growth Convention. Dr. Rhoades was the epitome of the kind of Christian leader I wanted to see emulated at PTL.

I had another reason for my delight at having Dr. Rhoades speak at Heritage USA. He was a local pastor, and I longed for the church community in Charlotte to accept us and the ministry of PTL. During my three years at PTL, I had focused on developing relationships with some of the Christian leaders in the area.

The late Dr. Thomas Zimmerman, former general superintendent of the Assemblies of God and a good friend of mine, held a position in a Christian outreach organization based in Charlotte. This organization was headed by Dr. Leighton Ford, the brother-in-law of Billy Graham and one of the most conscientious, righteous, spiritual leaders I have ever met.

Several times, when Dr. Zimmerman came to Charlotte, we enjoyed a meal and fellowship together with Dr. Ford. Later, when everything fell apart at PTL, Leighton Ford was one of the few local residents who reached out to me in Christian love and showed his concern.

As we approached the end of the week, when Dr. Rhoades was to come for the first time and minister at Heritage USA, disaster struck.

Charles Shepard, the investigative reporter who covered PTL exclusively for *The Charlotte Observer*, had been snooping around the conference for days. Some of the guests told us he was leaving phone messages for them to return his calls. Those who did contact Shepard were asked questions about every facet of life at PTL. He was openly pursuing his investigation, hoping to uncover any kind of dirt.

The heat was on.

I had enough presence of mind to know that in that environment, anything could happen. The disclosure of the Jim Bakker and Jessica Hahn tryst could be *The Charlotte Observer's* next headline.

Then it hit me.

I cannot let Dr. Ross Rhoades come, I told myself.

I did the right thing.

The day before he was to speak at the conference, I phoned him and asked for his confidence. Without sharing explicit details, I simply said, "Shortly, disclosures are going to be made that could hurt PTL. They might have some carryover effect upon you, and I feel it's best if you do not appear at the conference."

As painful as it was, on this occasion, I kept my integrity intact. I was trying to protect this godly man from any kind of criticism from his own church. I did not want my brother hurt.

For a few moments during that phone call, Dr. Rhoades became my father confessor. I knew I could trust him.

He wasn't the only one who provided spiritual solace at that time.

One night on the way back from the auditorium to the Heritage Grand Hotel after the close of the church growth seminar, Oral Roberts asked me to stop the car.

He said, "Let's get outside."

As the two of us stood there alone, he suggested, "Let's pray."

He sensed the distress in my spirit and knew something wasn't right, yet he was honorable enough not to ask for the details. Not knowing exactly what was going to ensue, he realized I needed God's help.

In the chilly night air, Oral Roberts laid his hands on me and prayed, "Lord God, give my dear brother the guidance he needs. Help him through these troubled times. And Father, if by Your grace, You could spare this ministry and spare all of us the pain of what is happening, I will be grateful."

That moment in time is fixed in my memory. I'll never forget that night when a true brother reached out to me as a friend. Few men have been attacked and misunderstood more than Oral Roberts, but this incident revealed to me his true character.

Since 1976, when Jim and Tammy came to Charlotte, *The Charlotte Observer* had printed hundreds of articles about PTL. The central focus of *The Charlotte Observer's* investigations for the past ten years had been the PTL ministry. Everyone in Charlotte knew that. In my opinion they had a vendetta against charismatic and evangelical Christians. The paper constantly highlighted PTL.

A lot of people in the Nixon administration suffered, rightfully so, because they tried to steal documents about Daniel Ellsberg. The press can take stolen documents, knowing that the person who gave them to the reporter knowingly and fraudulently took them. In any other circumstance knowingly accepting stolen property brings a felony conviction. The press can accept stolen property, "for the greater good." Stealing is theft! The eternal editorial policy is made in Heaven, not in the newsroom.

I recently read an interesting article in one of America's great newspapers, *The St. Petersburg Times.* It was written by one of their editors, Bill Stevens. He stated, "It is not a newspaper's place to keep secrets, especially when the information is about somebody in a powerful position to affect public policy. They are held to the highest of standards, personally and professionally." He further states, "Although the press is powerful, so is the public's right to know." The public does have a right to know what was going on in the personal life of powerful people that affect public policy at *The Charlotte Observer.* From an outsider's perspective, when I first came on the board of PTL in 1978, I quickly learned that *The Charlotte Observer* was obsessed to rid Charlotte of Jim and Tammy Bakker. Here were two young evangelists who did not fit the mold of *The Charlotte Observer*. This was the newspaper that, approximately ten years before, had heralded to the world that there was a, "Billy Graham slush fund." Nobody believed that. *The Observer* did! Even when the facts stated otherwise, *The Observer* never let up. With the power of the Knight-Ridder press empire, they tried to make their move to discredit Billy Graham. They failed miserably. This was another opportunity to bash an evangelical.

During the time that I was at PTL I was firm in my sense of what *The Observer* was doing. Editor Rich Oppel, in a moment of reflection in his office, told me that I was effective in stating my case about *The Observer*. A time occurred when I really didn't know whether or not I was being set up, but here is what happened. In the closing days of the revelation of the Jessica Hahn out of court settlement, I was talking to the then managing editor of *The Charlotte Observer*, Mark Etheridge. I liked Mark. I trusted him, even though I was warned not to. He promised me that our conversation would be off the record, never reported, or printed. He was trying to pin me down as to the facts of the Jessica Hahn case. I would not tell him, and I tried to lead him astray from the facts. I did tell him that I was not alone in dealing with the PTL problem. I stated that other PTL people were involved in the decision, and that I was not present at the settlement. That was true. Investigative reporters at *The Observer* reported on their version of those events. The covenant made by *The Charlotte Observer* was broken. Mark Etheridge had left *The Observer* by then. He was not a part of the decision. The world was told that I had been speaking to *The Observer* off the record during those troubled times, and what I had said. Lying was all right if it benefited *The Observer*. When they heralded the stories of PTL they were quick to point out those who were not forthcoming in telling the truth. But they had a special relationship with the Almighty. Selective integrity was in full operation during much of the PTL revelations. They departmentalized the truth. I pled guilty in this case. I have admitted failure to be forthcoming and up front. I participated in an attempt to withhold confidential information about Jim Bakker. That is a matter of record. What I, and others, have waited for is an admission by those who were "cleaning up the mess." They withheld information. Only parts of the story were told, to confirm what they already believed. Why is it so hard for institutions to simply say, "We have made mistakes, even in trying to help. We didn't tell it as it really was." Humbling oneself is good, not only good for the offender, but for the offended.

When the Jim Bakker/Jessica Hahn story began to unravel in the press, two highly regarded Charlotte businessmen came to me and said, "You need to know something. But if we are ever asked, we will probably deny it."

What's this all about? I wondered.

These men told me a very sad story about what had happened in the life of a child of one of the management people at *The Observer*. They said that there had been offences, and that *The Observer* had been hypocrital in their pursual of PTL. Their allegations were specific as to who did what. The men questioned why there had not been equal publicity of the failures of those who *The Observer* wanted to protect. In writing this book I could not bring myself to hurt a family. I would not treat people the way *The Observer* so relentlessly came after us. I want to bring hope and healing to people, not hurts. I leave to the Great Judge of the universe these matters. I bear hurt and pain because of *The Observer*, but I state my case and leave the rest to God.

These two men were not, to my knowledge, PTL supporters.

It's always easy to alter our integrity to meet our own set of circumstances. This is selective integrity.

How many times have we said, "My sin is okay, but your sin stinks!"

Jesus said, "Let him who is without sin, cast the first stone."

C.M. Ward, Richard Dortch, and James Watt.

8

Ankerberg, Swaggart, and Falwell

The Church Growth Convention ended, and we returned to our normal schedule of events at Heritage USA. Because it was February and Jim Bakker was still gone, the crowds had declined somewhat. But the remainder of the winter season looked promising, with planned appearances by outstanding musicians and nationally-known speakers.

The "real" story hadn't yet broken. But rumors were flying and building in intensity day by day. The whole world seemed to be looking at us, and they were! We were living a day at a time, hoping and praying to grab hold of some lifeline that would rescue us from the turbulence swirling around PTL.

I knew *The Charlotte Observer* had put together a story that would probably include the Jessica Hahn incident. We believed that the story was going to be in the newspaper very soon. Unless something was done, and done quickly, everything was going to break loose.

More telephone calls and constant inquiries indicated that the approaching doomsday was near. Several close friends, who wanted nothing from me but who simply cared, called during those days to extend their love. A few came to Heritage USA just to be with me.

Three kindred spirits, Dr. Richard Dobbins from Ohio, Rev. Allen Groff from Texas, and Rev. Dick Foth from California, merged at Heritage USA just to spend the day and be a source of encouragement to me. I failed these friends by not fully disclosing the full nature of PTL's problems. It was difficult to legitimately keep a confidence and at the same time be forthcoming.

Stories about PTL and Jim Bakker were rampant by then. A lot of people in high places knew something tragic had happened, and some were trying to sort things out. My desire to shield the ministry and Jim Bakker got confused with my desire to be open with my friends. I tried to paint the situation in its best light and my conduct in highest terms. I failed at both.

About the first week of March, at the conclusion of the daily telecast, I decided to re-broadcast several shows. I needed time off to get away from Heritage USA. The pressure was taking its toll on me physically, and my body and mind required rest. The crowds at Heritage USA were encouraging, and we had well-known seminar speakers scheduled who, I knew, could keep interest alive.

I decided to spend the greater part of the second week of March in Florida. My administrative assistant, Gene Shelton, planned to accompany me. Wherever I was, work came along, too. It never stopped.

"I know where we're going," I said to Gene.

"Where?"

"The Cardinals are in spring training in the Tampa Bay area, and I know some people in the Cardinal organization. We can catch a few games and still be near the water," I explained, pleased with myself for coming up with such a great idea.

I've been a baseball fan all my life. Having been raised in the St. Louis metropolitan area, the Cardinals were my favorite team. I could spend some time with my family, relax near the water, and enjoy some baseball all at the same time.

One afternoon, as Gene and I returned from a ball game, my secretary, Leslie Jones, called from PTL.

"Several representatives from Jerry Falwell's ministry are trying to reach you. They want you to call them." She gave me their phone number.

I knew one of them, Warren Marcus, because he had worked at the Christian Broadcasting Network as a producer. We had talked to him about coming to PTL. The other two were Mark DeMoss, of the DeMoss insurance family, and Jerry Nims.

When I reached Warren by phone, he sounded concerned. "Mark and Jerry Nims and I are representing Jerry Falwell. We've learned there's a problem at PTL, and we want to help if we can."

At that point, when PTL's ship was sinking, I was ready to listen to anyone who said they wanted to help, especially someone associated with a ministry as prestigious as the Falwell organization.

"Can you meet us in Tampa at the Tampa Airport on the executive aircraft side at 11:00 tonight?" they asked, giving no indication as to what the nature of the meeting was.

In spite of the late hour, I agreed.

My wife, daughter, grandson, and my administrative assistant drove with me to the Tampa Airport. We waited for a long time because the plane was late. When Jerry Nims and Mark DeMoss arrived on the Jerry Falwell jet, we went into the administration building to a conference room upstairs.

"John Ankerberg called and told us that he and Jimmy Swaggart know about the Jessica Hahn incident," Jerry Nims explained bluntly.

My heart nearly stopped.

"Ankerberg wanted Jerry Falwell to join him and Swaggart in confronting Bakker," Mark interjected. "But we don't trust Jimmy Swaggart."

"We wanted to know what Jimmy Swaggart knew, so we sucked him in to believing we would help them out," Jerry Nims continued.

"John Ankerberg faxed us this letter," he said, handing it over to me.

Still too stunned to speak, I read the fax. John Ankerberg had written the letter to Jerry Falwell saying that Jim Bakker needed to be confronted with his sin. "Are you willing to help us?" is what Ankerberg wanted to know of Falwell in the letter:

> According to biblical admonition and the spirit of Christian love, we come to you as representatives of the Body of Christ and of Christian media. We are aware of certain well-documented facts, plus additional allegations involving Jim Bakker, PTL, and an unmarried woman from New York state . . .
>
> Given the serious nature of the above mentioned offenses, given the high profile of Jim Bakker, we come to you urgently requesting a meeting to discuss the matter. Our purpose is to seek a biblical solution. We trust you'll allow us to meet with you.

Ankerberg seemed determined to meet with Jim and I, and he wanted Jerry Falwell to join him and Jimmy Swaggart in that confrontation.

"Here's the letter that Jimmy Swaggart faxed back to Ankerberg," Mark commented as he laid it on the table.

The letter follows:

> John, I know how the minds of Bakker and Dortch work. They will take that letter and show it over television, deleting the part they do not want read. They will say, "We had to take these two men off television, and then they went on a 'witch hunt' to hurt us."

Furthermore, I have already approached

Dortch, gave him the evidence, and he lied to me about the situation. I even told him I would like to meet with Bakker, but all to no avail.

As far as I am concerned, Matthew 18 has been satisfied with these people.

Last of all, if any of this should ever go to trial, they would use that letter in any way they could. *The Charlotte Observer* will do its part. The Assemblies of God has finally started to move on this, and they will do their part.

Please believe me there is absolutely no chance of Bakker and Dortch stepping down for any type of rehabilitation. First, they will try to lie their way out of it, but the documentation should be irrefutable. Then they will pull out of the Assemblies of God. Their last step will be to institute a barrage, which has already begun, to elicit sympathy from the general public. That will be their modus operandi.

If there are severe difficulties and problems I will bear the brunt of it, not anyone else.

I realize that your course of action is correct. However, you do not know these people as I know them . . . it really will not work, and I will be surprised if Falwell will allow his name to be used for obvious reasons.

I picked it up slowly, hoping somehow this was all a bad dream.

Jimmy Swaggart had written that he wanted no part of an encounter with us. He said he knew of Jim Bakker's sin with Jessica Hahn, but he feared that Jim Bakker and I might involve him in the issue and then deny everything. He didn't want any problems created for him. Swaggart indicated to Ankerberg that they did not need to worry about the problem because, in his judgment, Jim Bakker and Richard Dortch would be brought down.

Shock waves coursed through my system as I read

Jimmy Swaggart's final comments: *"The Charlotte Observer will do its part, the Assemblies of God will do their part, and I will do my part to bring about PTL's downfall!"*

I couldn't believe what I was reading.

"Why are you bringing these things to me?" I asked the two Falwell representatives.

Nims answered, "Jerry Falwell is convinced, and we're convinced, that if Jimmy Swaggart brings you down, he would certainly bring us down, too. He's probably out to get us also. We need to stand with you to stop Jimmy Swaggart from trying to tear up your ministry."

I tried to find the reasoning behind their statement, but by then I was too tired and too confused to think straight.

"Jimmy Swaggart has obtained a minimum of eleven people who are prepared, willing, and ready to file a class action suit against PTL for the lifetime partnership program," Nims said solemnly.

Then he asked me, "Do you know what a class action suit is?"

"I have a general idea, but no specific knowledge," I replied.

"Eleven people is a sufficient number to go to a judge and say that they want to file a class action suit. If that happens, PTL would probably be put into receivership. That would tie up the ministry and effectively put PTL out of business."

If they were trying to frighten me, they were doing a great job.

Then Jerry Nims asked me if PTL had written a check to a certain organization in the last couple of weeks for a certain amount of money.

My response was, "Yes, how do you know that?"

He said, "We got that information through Jimmy Swaggart. He has a plant, a spy, in your organization who keeps him informed of everything going on at PTL. We've talked to John Ankerberg, and he says he's talked to Swaggart, and he also knows everything. He is determined to bring you down."

All this was quite shocking, especially the fact that

Jerry Falwell's people were the ones bringing us this account. The fact, however, that Ankerberg and Swaggart were involved came as no surprise.

A member of Swaggart's organization had recently told us, "Frances Swaggart is sending one of her employees to Heritage USA to learn what she could about what's happening there. They heard that Jim Bakker is going to resign momentarily, and they want to be there to hear the announcement."

When we received this tip that a certain lady was coming to PTL, we were also told when she was going to arrive on the premises. A member of our security staff was assigned to follow her the entire time she was at Heritage USA. We knew the phone calls that she made and where she went. We knew if and when she did anything.

That Sunday morning this woman came to the church service. Before I preached, I went to the control room of the television studio and had the director pan the audience with the camera to find her. She was sitting in the congregation in the middle section near the front — an ideal place for her to cover everything.

I pointed the woman out to the director and told him, "At least thirty times while I'm preaching, I want you to bring her face up on the screen." And he did!

Jimmy and Frances Swaggart had told me in a meeting some months before that they watched all our programs. I knew they were perceptive enough to know that if we put the face of this woman who worked for them up on the screen thirty times, they would know we knew why she was there.

As the two representatives from Jerry Falwell's ministry presented their case, it was not hard to believe that Jimmy Swaggart had involved himself in trying to bring PTL down.

For over a year Jimmy Swaggart's magazine, *The Evangelist*, had consistently, from month to month, attacked the PTL ministry. It was public knowledge that the Swaggarts despised Jim Bakker. Anyone who read their literature or watched their television programs knew that for a fact.

Several months before, I made the decision to take one of Swaggart's programs off the PTL network. I didn't want Jim Bakker blamed for it. Jimmy Swaggart had continued his venomous attacks on us on a regular basis each month, and I felt enough is enough.

Dr. Charles Cookman, superintendent of the Assemblies of God of North Carolina, took note of Swaggart's attacks against Heritage Village Church and the Assemblies of God in North Carolina. These onslaughts were so persistent that Dr. Cookman decided he should go to Swaggart's headquarters and have Jimmy Swaggart tell him in person what it was that he knew about PTL.

Dr. Cookman contacted the superintendent of the Assemblies of God in Louisiana, Rev. Cecil Janway, asking him to arrange a meeting for the two of them with Jimmy Swaggart to solve any difficulties that Swaggart had with PTL. When Rev. Janway, Jimmy Swaggart's superintendent, contacted him about the meeting, Jimmy Swaggart said, "Yes," he would meet with Dr. Cookman. But he also wanted me to be present.

Dr. Cookman then contacted me and asked if I would be willing to come to Batan Rouge, Louisiana and attend such a meeting. I concurred, concluding it would be good for us to get things out in the open, and a date was set.

A few days before the date of our proposed meeting, the director of our television network told Jimmy Swaggart's ministry that we were taking his daily 9:00 a.m. teaching program off the air.

Jimmy Swaggart's program aired fifteen times a week. Five of those programs were at 9:00 a.m., Monday through Friday. The "Jim and Tammy" program aired live at 11:00 a.m., two hours later.

Foolishly, Jim Bakker and I were watching Jimmy Swaggart attack us each morning at 9:00 a.m. Then, at eleven, we got on the air and fired back at Jimmy Swaggart.

Without consulting Jim Bakker, I told Walter Richardson, the head of our television network, that I would begin broadcasting my own program at 9:00 each morning from the Upper Room. It was to be a call-in prayer program and would accomplish two purposes. It would give me the program I had long wanted, and it would remove Swaggart from the 9:00 a.m. time slot.

We gave Swaggart's ministry the customary twenty-eight day notice required by their contract, telling him he would lose his 9:00 a.m. slot. The other ten programs were permitted to continue to run. When we sent that notice, I did not know that within the twenty-eight day period, I would be going to Louisiana to meet with the Swaggarts.

Dr. Cookman and I flew to Baton Rouge with one pre-condition. My general superintendent, Dr. Thomas F. Zimmerman, had advised us to keep the meeting with Jimmy Swaggart only.

"Make sure you have a clear and thorough understanding as to who's going to be in the meeting when you meet with them," Dr. Zimmerman had counseled me.

I told Dr. Cookman I would go if we met only with Jimmy. He contacted Rev. Janway, and assured me that would be the case. I sought that assurance a second time, to be positive. I was assured once again that we would be meeting with Jimmy Swaggart only. That was it.

Dr. Cookman and I flew to Baton Rouge, arriving in time for the 11:00 a.m. meeting at the Hilton Hotel. Soon Rev. Janway joined us, and we waited for Jimmy Swaggart to appear.

A few moments after eleven, Rev. Janway answered a knock on the door. We were all shocked to discover Jimmy and Frances Swaggart, Donnie Swaggart, and Jim Rentz, Jimmy Swaggart's top assistant standing in the hallway.

By the grace of God, I kept my mouth shut, but I knew already we had been violated and lied to. Rev. Janway led us in prayer, and then Rev. Cookman, who had called the meeting, prepared to ask some questions.

Before anybody had a chance to say a word, Jimmy Swaggart looked at me and asked, "What are you going to do about Marvin Gorman?"

This was the Marvin Gorman who was awarded a $10

million judgment in 1991 against Jimmy Swaggart's continued slanderous allegations.

I was taken back. What was I going to do about Marvin
Gorman? I was no longer an official of the Assemblies of God.
I did administrate the PTL Television Network, and we did
carry Marvin Gorman's program. I guessed that Jimmy
Swaggart wanted to know what I was going to do about
taking Marvin Gorman off the air.

"That's a matter between Marvin Gorman and the
television network," I explained. "I'm not going to discuss
that with you."

He wouldn't stop there. Again he asked, "Well, I wanna
know. What are you going to do with Marvin Gorman?"

I said, "Jimmy, if we were taking an action," (which at
the time we were), "about you, I would not be discussing it
with Marvin Gorman. So I'm certainly not going to discuss
anything about Marvin Gorman with you."

He quickly turned and looked at Dr. Cookman and said,
"What are you gonna do about Marvin Gorman?"

Dr. Cookman was overwhelmed and stammered, "I
don't know what you mean."

He said to him again, "Well, I want to know. What are
you going to do about Marvin Gorman?"

He said, "I'm the superintendent of North Carolina. I'm
not the superintendent of Louisiana. Your superintendent
is sitting beside you. Ask him, don't ask me."

He began to attack Dr. Cookman because neither he nor
I would give him an answer. He was hostile, raising his voice,
and dogmatically demanding an answer.

When he finally slowed down, Dr. Cookman stood to his
feet and walked over and stood in front of Jimmy Swaggart.

In prophetic fashion, he pointed his finger at him and
said, "Jimmy Swaggart, you are discourteous, you are rude,
you are mean-spirited, and unless you get a hold of your
spirit, you will not stand. You are going to be brought down
if you don't get control of your spirit."

That, I believe, began the process of the purging of
Jimmy Swaggart.

Jimmy Swaggart looked up at him and said, "I MEANT to be rude, and I MEANT to be discourteous. That was my choice."

Dr. Cookman sat down and wept. Profusely wept. It was an awesome sight, etched clearly in my mind.

Jimmy Swaggart looked at me with nastiness and said, "What about Jim Bakker with the boys?"

I truthfully said, "I don't know what you're talking about."

Once again, the question was asked, "What are YOU going to do about Jim Bakker with the boys?"

I said, "I have no idea." I had never heard such a question or allegation. I had no knowledge of such improprieties.

He quickly said, "Well, what about Jim Bakker with the girls?"

To such a broad-based, vicious question, my response was, "What are you talking about?"

Once again he said, "Well, what about Jim Bakker with the girls? I understand that Jim Bakker has paid off a woman for a sexual encounter for $250,000."

I looked at Jimmy and said, "If Jim Bakker paid off a woman with $250,000, I don't know about it."

Did I tell the truth? In my spirit, I knew I wasn't giving all the facts. I questioned whether I owed Jimmy Swaggart an explanation at all. My response should have been: "I won't discuss that matter."

Technically, I told him the truth. I probably sought justification in the climate and environment in which I found myself. I gave him an honest answer, and yet I knew it was not the ethical kind of a response I should have given.

The heated discussion continued, and Donnie Swaggart began his attack.

But before he got too far, Jimmy told his son, "You be quiet. I've already made a fool of myself." He then turned to Cookman and said, "Brother Cookman, I owe you an apology. The Bible says not to rebuke an elder, and I've already violated that, and I'm sorry Brother Cookman."

Dr. Cookman replied, "You were forgiven before you asked."

The dramatic conclusion of that meeting passed through my mind as I studied the faxed letter Jimmy Swaggart had sent to John Ankerberg. John's involvement against Jim Bakker didn't surprise me either because we had also removed his program from the PTL Network.

John Ankerberg's "Talk Back" show thrived on debating controversial and divisive issues affecting the church. The more argumentative and objectionable his guests, the more John seemed to like it. His format turned most people off. Someone once described him as "the blond-headed guy who encourages people from different denominations to dislike each other."

At one point, John Ankerberg came to Heritage USA to talk me into keeping him on the air. Actually, Jim Bakker had made the decision to remove John's show, and I had agreed with him. John Ankerberg's program was divisive, and his spirit and attitude, to me, were anything but Christian.

We had been warned previously, and told by a leader in the evangelical movement, that John Ankerberg's reputation was suspect. When a reporter from the national media contacted us and asked if we knew the nature of John Ankerberg's problems, I decided to address John myself.

On several occasions I wrote John Ankerberg, telling him I felt he needed to come forward and confess what it was that the media was trying to find out. I felt he needed to clear his soul and his conscience and admit his need for help. It's my prayer that the time will come when John will confess and receive the cleansing power of forgiveness that many of us have found.

When I met with Ankerberg that day, he appeared to be an angry, self-centered man concerned only about promoting his own interests. He didn't come across to me as a minister of the gospel desiring to build the kingdom of God.

"The PTL network is my largest outlet. If you take me off, it will ruin my ministry," he argued, hoping I would change my mind.

I knew he didn't want to lose our fifteen-million home cable system, but I refused to back down. As far as I, and many other leaders, were concerned, Ankerberg's program was doing nothing more than damaging Christian unity.

John Ankerberg's faxed letter to Jerry Falwell sounded very self-righteous, but I knew John had no interest in restoring Jim Bakker from a sin of moral failure. It wasn't restoration Ankerberg wanted; it was revenge. He was angry because we would not air his program on the PTL Television Network. His motive to me, was revenge, pure and simple! Ankerberg had no other compelling interest in PTL and no love lost on Jimmy Swaggart. In fact, they were on opposite sides of the theological fence. He and Swaggart were drawn together because of their mutual hatred for Jim Bakker and PTL.

After listening to the Falwell representatives' two-hour presentation, I knew I was out of options. I had no where else to turn.

"The Jessica Hahn story is true," I admitted finally, giving them only sketchy details as to how she had been compensated for the out of court settlement. I didn't feel that was their business, but I did acknowledge the fact that there was a problem.

"Dr. Falwell has helped others in this situation," Nims explained. "There was a church in Maine whose pastor had a moral failure. Jerry Falwell took the church over for a period of time and helped them. Then he returned the church to its pastor."

They never specifically told me that Jerry Falwell planned to use that same method with PTL. I thought by "help" they meant Jerry Falwell wanted to offer Jim spiritual support and counsel.

"That's a decision Jim Bakker will have to make," I commented. "It's not my call. All I can do is tell Jim about your visit. If he wants to meet with Jerry Falwell, I will set up the meeting."

Long into the night, the representatives of Jerry Falwell

continued to tell me they had a solution to the problem. As they talked, I thought about what Neil Eskelin, our director of press and public relations, had told me right before I had left for Tampa.

"Charles Shepard has submitted a list of questions that *The Charlotte Observer* wants us to answer," he had said.

I had looked over the list Neal handed me. "Looks like the seven deadly questions," I had joked, wishing I could laugh about the whole situation. But, as I read them, I almost cried. I could tell Charles Shepard had the story down pat.

1. When did you first learn of allegations of a sexual encounter between Jessica Hahn and Jim Bakker?

2. What, specifically, did Miss Hahn accuse Rev. Bakker of doing?

3. Did Rev. Bakker have sexual relations with Miss Hahn?

4. What is Rev. Bakker's response to Miss Hahn's allegations?

5. How much money have you, PTL, or PTL associates spent to resolve this matter? Please specify the source of money paid, the amount of money paid, and the recipients of money paid.

6. Please explain the terms of the Jessica Hahn trust.

7. Who at PTL made, or has approved, the decision to spend PTL money to resolve this matter?

How did he get this information? I wondered. The only people who really knew the exact story were Jim Bakker, Roe Messner, and myself.

I had said to Roe Messner, back when he sent the money to the lawyer in California, "Roe, we must keep this in confidence. If this matter ever comes to a court, we are both released . . . Other than that we're to keep it confidential."

That was my understanding, which I maintained. It was evident to me, from the questions asked by Charles Shepard, that someone had spilled their guts.

"It's going to explode any day now," I said to Mark DeMoss and Jerry Nims, explaining that Charles Shepard had told Neil Eskelin a story was in the works.

After hearing and knowing what Jerry Falwell, John Ankerberg, and Jimmy Swaggart knew, I realized it was just a matter of time before everything became public.

"We know a lawyer, Roy Grutman," Jerry Nims said. "He can prevent *The Charlotte Observer* from releasing its impending story."

That was the best news I'd heard so far.

"Roy Grutman is a first amendment lawyer, and he works with the press in protecting first amendment rights," Nims clarified. "If you call him, he will get the story stopped."

"By all means," I agreed. "Let's contact Roy Grutman and try to keep the story out of the press. I will also talk to Jim Bakker about setting up a meeting with Jerry Falwell."

The meeting concluded on those two notes.

"You realize," I pointed out before leaving, "that the final decision on both matters rests with Jim Bakker."

I left the meeting at 2:00 a.m. and called Jim Bakker, supplying all the details of the night's events. I faxed him a copy of the letters they had left with me and explained to Jim the whole situation.

"They've advised us to call Roy Grutman," I told him.

Jim Bakker inquired, "Do you know anything about the man?"

"No," I answered, "I've never met him, but they say he can help us."

Put yourself in our situation. You know *The Charlotte Observer* is going to come out with a story that can ruin not only your ministry but your life. Then somebody says, "This man can stop it."

I called Jerry Nims, who phoned Roy Grutman, and we had a three-way conference call.

On the phone that day Roy Grutman said, "Yes, I believe

I can get the story stopped."

He faxed a letter telling *The Charlotte Observer* what he would do if they published an article about Jim Bakker and Jessica Hahn. Grutman then sent a copy of that letter to me.

The Charlotte Observer agreed to withhold the story from being published that weekend. He told them we would take legal action if they went ahead with the story. In return Roy Grutman promised he would produce me the following week for an interview. But I refused to do it.

The story did not appear in Sunday's paper.

When I had asked Jim about meeting with Jerry Falwell, he told me, "I'm not going to leave Tammy. I haven't left Tammy for the ministry of PTL for the last three months, and I'm not going to leave her now for anyone! If Jerry Falwell wants to see me, he can fly out here."

I conveyed that message back to Jerry Nims and Mark DeMoss.

Monday afternoon, I flew with our son, Rich, and Mark Burgund to Lynchburg, Virginia. As soon as our plane landed, I immediately boarded Falwell's waiting jet. Roy Grutman greeted us, and I met him for the first time in person. Then Jerry Falwell got aboard, and we took off for Palm Springs, California for our meeting with Jim Bakker.

The seats on this corporate jet faced each other. Roy Grutman sat across the aisle, Jerry Nims had the seat beside Grutman, and Jerry Falwell's was next to me. Mark DeMoss was at the back of the plane working on something.

Before the plane took flight, the quiz began. Jerry Falwell questioned me at great length about the whole Jessica Hahn matter, the state of PTL, asking everything anyone ever wanted to know about PTL but was afraid to ask. During the extensive two hour conversation, I avoided telling him the details of the out of court settlement to Jessica Hahn. That didn't seem to be the wise thing to do at that point.

After Falwell and Nims saw they were getting nowhere with me, we had our evening meal.

I then asked Roy Grutman if he would go to the front of

the plane. Privately, I wanted a client-lawyer relationship, where I could tell him something in confidence.

The previous Friday, in a phone conversation with Roy Grutman, I realized I'm not a lawyer. I don't understand the law.

Roy Grutman had said to me, "I will be your lawyer."

I was assuming, he would be my lawyer. What else would a layman in the law take that to mean?

That's the reason I asked him specifically: "Will you be my attorney? I can then tell you some things confidentially."

He said, "Yes."

That evening on the plane, I told Roy Grutman explicitly about the out of court settlement, the money, and how it was paid.

"After Roe Messner had received compensation of about eight million dollars for the building projects at PTL," I told Grutman, trying to explain the situation with Roe.

"He would stop in to visit with Jim Bakker and me constantly," I continued. "In fact, Roe spent most of his time at PTL, even though he had some twenty other projects going on at that time all across America. Roe told me there were a great number of things he had done at PTL for which he would never bill us. That didn't surprise me. Roe and I had been friends for years, and I knew of his generosity. In fact, Roe tended to get himself into financial difficulties because he was too nice for his own good."

Roy Grutman listened intently, asking few questions.

In explaining my conversation with Roe about paying the money for Jessica Hahn, I told Grutman, "I cautioned Roe not do anything to jeopardize his family. I advised him to be sure that he got a twenty percent down payment before he started the project. Roe is a good man, not a perfect man, but hopefully well-meaning.

"Roe would stop by my office occasionally and say to me, 'Here's what is happening. The money is coming in a little slow. I've gotten eight million, but I've done a hundred thousand dollars worth of work that I will never bill you for. I'm just going to give a lot of work to PTL.'

"He seemingly kept a running account of that. I don't think he was keeping an accurate account. But I do remember when he said, 'There is about $200,000 that I have done for PTL which I will never ask you to pay.'

"I remember specifically asking him, 'What is that?' That much money interested me as to what he was doing.

"He told me, 'My costs for one of your projects was about $1,500,000. You will never get a $150,000 bill for the architectural services.' Commercial architectural services usually run around ten percent. He had said that he had done other things, too.

"I had the answer to my question as to what he was doing. Roe Messner at the time had over fifteen full time architects on staff. Obviously those people had to be paid so, when he said he was doing things like this for us, I didn't question him. It was very logical that when you make drawings and plans as he did, that it would cost a great deal of money.

"Periodically he would tell me he had done work for us that we would never get a bill for. I didn't keep any audit of it. Toward the end of his work at PTL, when I left, he mentioned that he had given over $800,000 worth of free work and services to PTL. We would never receive a bill for it. About the time that he was nearing the $200,000 level, that's when the Jessica Hahn matter surfaced.

"Roy, I wanted to get the Jessica Hahn matter settled. I did believe that Roe Messner was going to get back the $265,000 he had wired to our attorney in California.

"At that time Roe Messner had already given us $200,000 or more in work. Even though I didn't say this to him — I'm relating to you what was going on in my mind — I felt if, in fact, he had done a couple of hundred thousand dollars worth of work, then he could bill us. We wouldn't be losing anything because he had given us that much work.

"I admit that it was a stupid, foolish thing to do, but I thought we were getting value for the dollars that we spent. In my mind, right or wrong is not the point. I found some justification for Roe's giving the $265,000 for the settlement because he said that he already donated that much."

When I finished, Roy Grutman responded, "What you really did is — you simply said to Roe Messner . . . "

"I didn't *say* it." I corrected him.

"Well, the implication for Roe to pick up on was," Roy Grutman began, trying to put the incident in his own words, " 'You have already given us several hundred thousand dollars of services, so go ahead and bill us for what work you have done. Here is a discreet obligation, a bill, a payment we want to make. Go ahead pay that. Bill us for the legitimate work that you have done. What work you have done here we will pay you for it. If you want to do something to help us, rather than taking it off the bill, pay this discreet payment.' "

"Yes," I replied. "That's how I meant it, and that's what I thought Roe Messner understood me to mean."

At that point Roy Grutman knew, the night we flew to Palm Springs, everything I knew about Jim Bakker's indiscretion, the out of court settlement — everything.

I figured it was foolish not to tell my lawyer everything. *How can he help if he knows only half the story?* I thought. So I spilled my guts to Grutman.

When our airplane pulled into its parking spot at Palm Springs, we climbed out of the plane. To my horror, shock, and amazement, I looked to one side and saw Jimmy Swaggart's jet. I looked to the other side and there sat Oral Roberts' jet. Jimmy Swaggart's, Jerry Falwell's, and Oral Roberts' jets were parked side by side.

I knew then that Jimmy Swaggart and Oral Roberts were also in Palm Springs, which made me wonder what was going on.

That fact jolted the Falwell people, too.

We later learned there was no significance other than the fact that both televangelists had come to the resort town for a rest.

The Falwell people went to a hotel. Jim Bakker's security man picked me up and took me immediately to Jim and Tammy's home. I had not seen them in two months.

Richard Dortch, James Watt, and Rex Humbard.

9

Jim Gives PTL
To Falwell

On my arrival at their Palm Springs home, Jim and
Tammy warmly greeted me. Our visit that evening was
pleasant but very serious. Jim asked me a lot of questions
about my conversations with the Falwell people and what I
thought.

For the next two hours, I repeated to Jim and Tammy
what I had already discussed with them on the telephone,
fully disclosing everything I knew to that point.

Tammy went to bed, and I spent more time talking to
Jim.

"Can you give me an overview of what's happening at
PTL?" he asked.

"Well," I began, "the finances are up over 15% from the
previous year. But we had to stop all the major construction."
I hated to have to tell him that, I knew the buildings were his
pet projects. "We're just trying to keep our heads above
water," I explained.

At the same time, we were also trying to obtain a

$50,000,000 long term loan. I believed if we stopped the projects and got a loan amortized over fifteen years, we could make it. By doing that we would cut our debt service dramatically. Then we'd have no surprises. We could budget ourselves accordingly and live within that budget. That's the way I liked to operate.

I stopped talking, noticing the far away look in Jim's eyes. It didn't seem the time to burden him with too many details. Besides, Jim was obviously preoccupied with the fact that Ankerberg, Swaggart, and Falwell were aware of his tryst with Jessica Hahn. I could tell he dreaded facing the renowned Baptist televangelist the next day.

Jim and Tammy's meeting with Falwell and his people was set for nine o'clock in the morning. We didn't think our meeting would shock the press if they discovered we were all there. The media had widely reported about Tammy's stay in California and that she was now in the Betty Ford Clinic after her release from the Eisenhower Hospital. Besides, Palm Springs was accustomed to visits from high profile people.

Jim and Tammy arrived at my hotel room about 8:30 a.m. We then went to the lobby where Jerry Falwell met us with his entourage. Someone had taken care of getting a suite in the hotel that included a large sitting room with a dining area and another room off to the side.

As soon as we entered the suite, Jim and Tammy went into the side room with Jerry Falwell. After about fifteen or twenty minutes, Tammy opened the door. I could hear Jerry Falwell telling her that he would pray for her, and then she left the hotel.

Jerry Falwell and Jim Bakker stayed in the room.

Jim told me a month later, it was the biggest mistake of his life. In the years that I had known Jim Bakker, as a friend, board member, or associate, I had never known him to meet with anyone on an important matter alone.

I assumed Jim was talking to Jerry Falwell about the Jessica Hahn incident. Because of the emotional way Jim had reacted when I first discussed Jessica Hahn with him,

I didn't want to press my presence in his personal conference with Falwell. It was such a private matter. Jim Bakker had not asked me to come into the room, and I didn't push my way in. That was not my style. Besides I wanted to be discreet.

Little did I know what else they were talking about.

Meanwhile, out in the sitting room, Roy Grutman — Falwell's attorney and ours — conversed with me about the Jessica Hahn matter. Then he became very impatient.

"We'd better hurry this session along," he suddenly commented. For some reason he was concerned about the time.

Getting edgy, he remarked, "If they take all of their time doing this, I won't be able to talk to Jim Bakker about the story we are trying to stop."

"You're right," I said. *After all that's what we're here to do,* I thought — *to find out how Falwell can help us.*

Finally Roy Grutman said, "If they don't come out in another ten minutes, I'll knock on the door."

Within moments, Jerry Falwell walked out and said to Roy Grutman, "Roy, Jim wants to talk to you."

Then Jerry Falwell moved his towering frame across the room to where I was sitting. Standing over me and peering down, he began to speak, using a very deliberate tone of voice.

"Jim has just turned the PTL ministry over to me, provided that you are the president and the host of the show."

Scrambled signals whizzed around inside my head. I tried to sort them out and comprehend the significance of his words.

With the message still ringing in my ears, Falwell continued, "I've agreed to that. So you and I need to get to work to decide who we want on the new board of directors because Jim wants to approve who the new board will be."

I couldn't move. I sat there stunned, in shock.

I had anticipated some action on Jim Bakker's part to get help from the Falwells. Getting help, to me, however, did not mean turning the ministry over to Jerry Falwell. We hardly knew the man and what his plans were!

Recently Jim and I had talked extensively about turning PTL over to another prominent evangelist we both knew very well. His integrity and reputation were outstanding. This other ministry could provide an umbrella for us, and for six months our friend could manage PTL. That's the amount of time we thought it would take for the Jessica Hahn storm to blow over.

Three weeks before we were ready to approach this person and ask him about the possibility of managing PTL temporarily, complications developed. Something unfortunate happened, not of his making, and the evangelist's name surfaced in the press for a period of time.

That day Jim came into the dressing room and told me, "We can't ask him because of this negative publicity. We just can't do it."

Our strategy had to be re-evaluated. At that point we had no where else to turn.

Now Jerry Falwell had offered to fulfill the same purpose Jim and I had planned for our friend. I can only assume that's why Jim Bakker so readily accepted Falwell's proposal. Within hours Jim had turned the ministry over to Jerry Falwell.

Falwell repeated his plan, "Pastor Dortch, you are going to be the president of PTL, and the host of the show. Then, within six months to a year, we'll give the ministry back to Jim."

Falwell then described in compassionate tones how he had previously helped the fallen pastor of a large Baptist church in Maine. I later realized this was his way of baiting us for the final catch.

There's no question in my mind now that we were being intentionally drawn into a premeditated scheme. During the coming months, as the drama unfolded, Jerry Falwell's true nature emerged, revealing him as a master of deception.

Falwell looked at me and said, "Don't you think James Watt would be a wonderful person to be on our board?"

James Watt, the former Secretary of the Interior, was

an Assemblies of God layman, whose son had worked with me for two years. *With James Watt involved,* I thought, *there's nothing to worry about.* He was an honorable man, and had been a former cabinet member of President Ronald Reagan, who was still in office.

More bait, and I grabbed for it!

Falwell then mentioned the names of several other prominent charismatic leaders, all of whom I knew would bring their character and integrity to the operation of PTL. That was important to me.

They won't permit any harm to come to Jim Bakker, I told myself. *They'll try to help him. With these people on the board, we're in good hands.*

This might work out after all, I thought.

After about a half an hour, Roy Grutman came out with Jim Bakker. "Jim and I are going over to the Bakker's house to find Tammy," he reported. "We want to tell her about the decision to turn the ministry over to Jerry Falwell."

A short time later, they returned, telling us of Tammy's fears, her anxiety, and her reluctance to hand PTL over to Jerry Falwell. Tammy's common sense and perceptive spirit saw through the scam. She was right, and we were wrong. But no one took her hesitancy seriously.

For several hours, the four of us sat around a table and began to talk about the mechanics of making the transition.

During this planning session, Jim mentioned again that he would like to approve the new board of directors. He assumed this was the board he would have to work with in another few months when he returned to PTL. Jerry Falwell also implied that Jim would be accountable to this new board of directors.

Jim and I trusted Jerry Falwell, unaware of his hidden agenda. I did, however, feel that Roy Grutman had a plan he was already attempting to set in motion. At the time I couldn't put my finger on his motives. I wanted to trust him. After all, he now knew everything. My future was in his hands.

"You and I will fly back to Lynchburg," he told me,

meaning Falwell's headquarters. "Then I'll accompany you to Charlotte and stay at Heritage USA. I can check the constitution and bylaws of the Heritage Village Church and see that everything is done legally in the transition period."

Still reeling from the dramatic events of the morning, my mind had difficulty assimilating Roy's rapid-fire details. But one thing was obvious to me — there were too many cooks in the kitchen.

As Roy and I prepared to leave, we were all together in the room for a few moments.

I turned to Jim Bakker and said, "Jim, I take this responsibility only until you can come back." It never crossed my mind that Jim Bakker would not be returning to PTL. Not in six months, not in one year. Never!

"Jim," I continued, hoping to drive my point home, "when I was the state secretary of our church, our superintendent, Dr. E.M. Clark, lost his voice. Effectively, for several months, I had to serve in his role of leadership. When Dr. Clark recovered, I no longer accepted the invitations from churches. Those were the responsibility of the superintendent, I felt, and gracefully backed out quickly.

"I'll never forget the day that Dr. Clark called my wife and me into my office and shut the door. He looked at us, and said, 'Thank you for being an honorable friend. You had to more or less serve as my replacement during my illness, but you were honorable and stepped aside, encouraging me to go on and do my job.'

"That meant a lot to me, Jim. I knew it was better to be an honest state secretary than for me to become a dishonest office seeker, or even attempt to do anything to hurt my superior."

I hoped Jim Bakker would get the message I was trying to convey: "I've been through this before, and I'm going to do the same thing for you. I don't want this job. I don't believe I am called to do your task. But I'll do it if I can help you."

We said our goodbyes. I hugged Jim, not knowing I wouldn't see him again until our indictment before the grand jury.

I said, "Jim, I need your help. I don't know how to do this job like you do."

He hugged me and said, "Don't worry. I'll talk to you on the phone."

On the way back to Charlotte, I finally had time to assemble my thoughts. My world had changed dramatically. Responsibilities I had not bargained for when I came to PTL were suddenly heaped upon my shoulders. But most difficult was adjusting to the fact that my friend, Jim Bakker, was resigning as president of the ministry.

Other facts hit me like bricks, each striking a blow to my consciousness.

I'm going to have to face a staff of about 1,500 people! I said to myself. *I'm going to be thrust out in front of the whole world to face the press and give explanations.*

The weight of these obligations overwhelmed my already burdened soul. One thought gave me some comfort: *I'm still going to lean on Jim and keep him abreast as I always have.*

How I wish Jim were here now, I mused, looking toward the back of the plane where the Falwell people were seated and maneuvering their plans. I could hear them discussing who was going to be appointed to PTL's new board of directors.

Jerry Nims mentioned people like Bailey Smith, the former president of the Southern Baptist Convention; Dr. Charles Stanley; Sam Moore; and others. The charismatics who had been named in Palm Springs appeared forgotten as the Falwell camp maneuvered their own kind into place.

Just as we landed in Lynchburg, Jerry Falwell was talking about trying to get Bill and Gloria Gaither to come to Heritage USA. Using the language of television he said, "Let's keep up the hype for the first couple of months." That was his ploy to draw attention away from the Bakker disaster and his sinister plan of action.

A special meeting of the present board of directors of PTL was called for. Roy Grutman was to explain to PTL's group of faithful and capable directors why they were being asked to resign. After doing so, one by one, they were replaced by the new people Jerry Falwell had selected.

That Thursday, the day Jerry Falwell was supposed to present me as the new president of PTL, we were to have a telephone conference call with Jim Bakker in Palm Springs, and Jerry Falwell in Lynchburg, Virginia.

At that time, Jim Bakker would read a letter of resignation to the editors and reporters of *The Charlotte Observer* over a speaker phone in the newspaper office. Then the press could ask Roy Grutman questions. This would make it possible to accomplish the disclosure of Jim Bakker's resignation and Jerry Falwell's appointment as the chairman of the board of PTL at the same time.

For days I held my breath, waiting for the bomb to drop. I had no idea that when it came, it would destroy much more than I ever anticipated.

The Charlotte Observer, on March 20, heralded the story in the headlines: "JIM BAKKER RESIGNS FROM PTL, JERRY FALWELL ASSUMES LEADERSHIP." A story followed describing the transfer of control of the PTL ministry.

March 20, 1987, marked the day the Jessica Hahn indiscretion became known to the world. On that date, Jim Bakker resigned, and Jerry Falwell assumed control of PTL.

Roy Grutman made a statement to the press, saying simply, "Mr. Bakker has resigned. He no longer holds the positions he had before. This is an absolute resignation, and there are no secret agendas."

Nobody knew what kind of a role Jim Bakker was going to play in the future, if any. I was appointed to replace Jim as the president and host of PTL. In addition, I was the only member of the former board of directors appointed to serve on the new board.

As usual, there was a great deal of confusion in the press. Some newspaper reports stated I had worked at PTL for seventeen years. A South Carolina paper reported I had served as Jim Bakker's right hand man for ten years and was "one of PTL's staunchest defenders." Some said I was from Missouri, others indicated North Carolina. I had never read or heard so many distortions of the facts.

Television reporters interviewed visitors in the lobby of the Heritage Grand Hotel and asked, "What's your reaction to Jim Bakker's resignation?"

People simply said, "He'll be back." Many of our partners didn't believe that Jim Bakker could leave PTL. No one did!

What shocked PTL partners even more was the fact that Jerry Falwell had taken over. When Doug Oldham heard the news that Jerry Falwell was coming he cried out, "Jerry Falwell blaming Jim Bakker, give me a break, Jerry has permitted some of his own staff to stay on for years after they've had sexual problems. Some of them have been caught more than once."

Some partners responded, "Jerry Falwell isn't even of the same faith. He's a fundamental Baptist and most of us are charismatics."

"I don't know who dreamed this up," others said, finding the situation too farfetched to believe. Christendom was stunned, dazed, and outraged.

Jerry Falwell announced that the new board of directors would include, as he had promised, former Secretary of the Interior James Watt and evangelist Rex Humbard. Others appointed were Ben Armstrong, the director of the National Religious Broadcasters; Sam Moore, the president of Thomas Nelson Publishing Company; and several who were called "Jerry Falwell people." Initially Dr. Charles Stanley of First Baptist Church in Atlanta was asked to be on the board, but he later declined.

The media hung onto Roy Gruttman's every word. At that time, he was acting as PTL's spokesman and holding press conferences.

On the airplane going to California, I had told Roy the whole story about Jessica Hahn. He initially interpreted her actions to be blackmail, which in fact they were, and he said so publicly. His statement to the press was, "Payment was made which was characterized as blackmail by Pastor Bakker."

From that point on, the media went crazy.

The three major networks, ABC, CBS, and NBC parked their tractor trailer satellite uplinks in front of Heritage USA and made daily broadcasts from the site. At least 150 to 200 reporters swarmed over Heritage USA at any given time of the night or day. It was something to behold.

America's leading newspapers and news magazines, TV and radio stations, sent staff to cover the story. Reporters from the *Washington Post*, the *New York Times*, *Time Magazine*, *Newsweek*, *US News and World Report*, and *USA Today*, took up residence at Heritage USA, staying in the hotel and eating at the restaurants.

The week following Jim's resignation, Jim and Tammy's picture appeared on the covers of *Newsweek*, *Time*, and *US News and World Report*. Who would have thought two Bible school students from Minnesota could send shock waves throughout America and around the world? ABC's "Nightline" had the largest rating in their history the night Ted Koppel interviewed Jim and Tammy Bakker.

At every telecast of the PTL daily program, there were probably a hundred news reporters snapping pictures and taking notes.

To get from the studio back to my office or to the hotel required tactical logistics of which the CIA would have been proud. Our security people devised a system using four cars at different locations outside the studio. One was in the garage, one in front of the church, one was on one side of the studio, and the other outside the school building exit adjoining the church. Drivers waited in each car, and two security men stayed with me. They would say, "You pick the car."

The reporters covered the garage and the front of the church where the car usually emerged. Located in the back of the studio, the garage provided more privacy since I could get in the car and shut the doors without dozens of microphones and cameras being stuck in my face.

When no reporters were around, I usually went out one of the side doors, got into an old vehicle, and laid down in the back seat so no one could see me. I lived and worked under the strain of those conditions for about two months.

Television and newspaper reporters waited out in front of our house night and day. Some walked right up the sidewalk and knocked on the doors or windows trying to get inside. Finally security people had to be stationed at our house, and a mobile home installed for them to stay in.

In spite of all that was happening, we tried to go on living. It was difficult, if not impossible, at times.

David Maines of "100 Huntley Street," a TV program broadcast throughout the United States from Canada, happened to be at Heritage USA the week that Jim Bakker resigned. He was a gift from God and brought great stability to the situation. I was so grateful for David's presence.

On the 22nd of March, just two days after the resignation, *The Charlotte Observer* started focusing on me with the headlines: "DORTCH MAY FACE SCRUTINY OVER ROLE IN BAKKER CASE."

The sub-title read: "Jerry Falwell Says New PTL President Needed Partly As Transition Person."

Charles Shepherd's story on the front page of *The Observer* that day stated that I was likely to face scrutiny over my role in the ministry's handling of allegations of sexual misconduct against my former boss, Jim Bakker. He wrote that I was personally involved in PTL's responses to the church secretary from New York who accused Bakker of having sexual relations with her in Florida in 1980.

Jerry Falwell was quoted as saying, "We clearly need a transition person in such a traumatic change." It wasn't until later that the true meaning behind that statement became obvious.

In addition to the constant badgering by the media and the many new responsibilities placed on my shoulders, I also had to continue my role as the spiritual leader of the Heritage Church.

Try to understand, from a pastor's heart, standing in front of a shocked, bewildered congregation of over 2,500 people that first Sunday. A great part of that crowd were employees of PTL — people whose futures had turned uncertain overnight. Preaching to that group on Sunday, with my own basket of mixed emotions, took every ounce of spiritual strength I could muster.

Of course, many newscasters and reporters attended, hoping to catch some phrase to use against me the next day in the press. They weren't disappointed.

The Charlotte Observer carried a comment I made during the church service that Sunday. "The real story as to what happened in the last few weeks has not been told. In God's time it will all come out," I had told my congregation.

It didn't take long.

Jessica Hahn publicly admitted the incident. Still few people would acknowledge that we had been blackmailed over this sexual encounter between Jessica Hahn and Jim Bakker. No one seemed concerned about getting at the real truth.

It was stupid and dumb to have given Jessica Hahn a cent. The first time I received a letter from her representatives asking for money, I should have taken it to the FBI. It was blackmail. But in spite of that, I went along with it. What a fool I was.

Dr. Fred Gross, a clinical psychologist and founder of a Christian therapy program at Palmdale Hospital Medical Center in Palmdale, California was invited to appear on PTL's daily telecast. On the air, he stated that Jim Bakker had met with him for over three and a half hours shortly after Jim had the extramarital encounter.

Dr. Gross said on the program that I hosted, "Jim Bakker was shaking so violently that I had to hold him. He was totally distraught, out of control. He was racked with pain and guilt from his head to his toes."

I believed him. Knowing Jim as I did, it was possible to imagine such a severe reaction on his part. My heart broke for my dear brother.

During this time, Jim Bakker continued living in Palm Springs, California. His house was staked out by the media, and the Bakkers were virtually held hostage for days. From time to time, either he or Tammy would appear and speak to the host of waiting reporters and camera crews.

Before long, rumors of an attempted takeover of PTL by Jimmy Swaggart flooded the media, but this was not an accurate report. The truth was — as the Falwell people had indicated to us — that Jimmy Swaggart was trying to bring about the downfall of PTL, not take it over.

Jim Bakker talked to the press on March 23 saying that PTL attorneys had documents by a well-known individual, detailing Jimmy Swaggart's plot. But anyone who had read Jimmy Swaggart's monthly publications for the past two years knew his intentions. Swaggart had stated numerous times on his television programs, "PTL is a cancer eating at the heart of the church."

The newspapers began to herald the infighting of Jimmy Swaggart, Jerry Falwell, Jim Bakker, as the "Holy War." That caption, highlighted in the media, reflects a misnomer. At no point was there any indication that the warfare was holy.

On Friday, March 20, the day everything broke loose, Jimmy Swaggart said to the Associated Press, "Richard Dortch should resign. He was involved in a coverup. It is impossible for him to continue."

I was used to Jimmy Swaggart's public attacks and didn't think anyone would take him seriously, especially those of my own denomination who were aware of Swaggart's constant haranguing against PTL.

Our denomination, the Assemblies of God, began an investigation.

During those last few days prior to Jim's resignation, people called me saying they had been contacted by several national leaders of the Assemblies of God asking questions about my conduct.

I immediately called our state superintendent, Dr. Cookman, and asked if there was an investigation going on about me. His response was quick, "No. I am not aware of anything at all."

I couldn't understand why the North Carolina church leaders weren't aware of an investigation. If North Carolina had not carried out their responsibilities, then the rules state that the national office has a responsibility to step in. But the state officers had not been informed of any failure on their part. I had never spoken to Dr. Cookman about the Jessica Hahn settlement, ever! The week before the bomb hit, when Jerry Falwell was about to take over I told Dr. Cookman there was a problem, who was involved, but he never knew that a financial settlement was made with Jessica Hahn. As far as I know he heard about it the first time when he read about it in the paper. He never heard it from me. A fair question that we need to respond to is the question of confidentiality. How much is right for a pastor to know about the sins of a brother minister? The secrecy of this investigation bothered me. Was an unofficial investigation taking place?

That question was the primary reason I had resigned from the Assemblies of God. I knew the resignation would have to be approved for acceptance, but I didn't see any problem with that. I knew they would ignore the resignation and make their own determination. However, my resignation was submitted as was Jim Bakker's. When I told Jerry Falwell I was going to resign from the Assemblies of God, his response was, "It's none of their business whether you resign. PTL is bigger than the Assemblies of God. Just tell them to paddle their own canoe."

I made a terrible mistake by going on national television and announcing my resignation as an ordained minister of our denomination. That was wrong and my attitude was not what it should have been. But I felt I had been forsaken by the very people who should have stood by me during this most trying time in my life.

During this time, the media had a heyday speculating about what the Assemblies of God was going to do with Jim Bakker and Richard Dortch.

On April 1, leaders of the Assemblies of God announced they would consider Jim Bakker's and my resignations. When the leaders met to consider the PTL problem and our credentials, they met with a group of our accusers, most of whom had no connection with the Assemblies of God.

My accusers included John Ankerberg, an avowed anti-charismatic. He had no first hand information about PTL, Jessica Hahn, Jim Bakker, or any of the allegations against us. Probably the most unlikely individual to attend the meeting was Bill Treeby, the attorney for Jimmy Swaggart. Another person present was Walter Martin, known as the "Bible answer man," who is since deceased. Paul Roper, Jessica Hahn's California representative, was also in the meeting.

John Ankerberg, Jimmy Swaggart's attorney Bill Treeby, and Walter Martin were there to accuse Jim Bakker and me behind closed doors. These three people, had no first-hand knowledge of the incident, and only Treeby was a member of our church.

After listening to the accusations brought by this group of outsiders, a statement was given to the press.

First they acknowledged an investigation had been conducted.

"We have no indication of either a takeover attempt or blackmail. On the contrary, the evidence seemed to indicate that effort and money had been extended to cover moral failure," they stated.

I was bewildered and stunned to learn that prior to us meeting with them, a public announcement was made about their inquiry.

When I realized what had happened, my heart broke. To me it seemed I was being publicly rejected by my church. The pain and humiliation was almost more than I could bear.

In the months ahead, I would take many personal and emotional beatings. I had never felt so forsaken. Prison was easy put along side this.

Reflecting back after four years, I acknowledge that I did not handle my relationship with the church very well at all. I did not respond like I should have in a kind way. I wanted out, and quickly. I was wrong in the way I went about it. My attitude was not right. I later met with my church leaders and apologized and asked for forgiveness. If I didn't handle things right, how could I be angry at them? We were all broadsided by the press, by the national attention. We all weren't prepared for this. I've often said that if I took a course in Grudges 303 at a university, I would flunk the course. Nothing is worth losing a relationship with God, and a friend. I knew those leaders were my friends. In my opinion, they just didn't know what to do with me.

I learned another lesson in integrity the day a friend told me, "You have taken more blame than you should have for the events that took place at PTL." My response was immediate, "I want to cleanse my soul, and for my part be right with everyone." When you tell about some things that took place within the PTL family, it is tough. It hurts because these are people that I have loved. In recounting this story I have tried to be careful to protect the identity of people who I felt were "victims" of the system. They were there, and got caught up in it. They did not, in my judgment, "set out" to hurt anyone. For them, it "just happened." There are others, very few, who were "on a mission." Their intent, clear and plain, was to destroy. These are people who were, in my opinion, "given over to the flesh." Some had a passion, a focus. Nothing would stop them. They did not hide it. How did we know that? They told us! Regretably, Al Cress fit into that plan. There is a reason he is so important in this story. I believe that he was a key person who wanted to bring damage to PTL. At that time my heart, mind, and life was in its most grievous crisis. I was hurting so bad, and I couldn't believe what he was doing. All I know is what he told me. He admitted to me before the unraveling that he was "on a mission." Al was, in my opinion, one of the key players in the public disclosure of these sad events.

I chose Al to be my administrative assistant. He was a college student with keen administrative skills, who would soon complete his studies. Albert Cress became a co-worker, trusted colleague, able helper, and friend. We took him into our family as one of our own. One of the primary reasons that I hired him was to travel with me and assist me in my visits to the churches and pastors. That required about fifty percent of my time. It wasn't long before he told me he did not want to travel. That was the purpose of his being brought on board. He gained a great deal of recognition for his outstanding work. He enjoyed the power of the office I held. His work was outstanding. He built a reputation as a hard working, efficient professional. When the decision was made to go to PTL, I encouraged him to come with me. He told me he would not go, but I believe my persuasion changed his mind. I asked him to come with me, even if it were for only six months to a year. He reluctantly decided to come, but he was never happy about it.

PTL was a different world for Al. As my top assistant in Illinois he told me he felt he was "number 2" when I was out of the office in Illinois. He wasn't, but he considered himself to be the "number 2" person. At PTL he lost that power. He encouraged me repeatedly to assert my authority at Heritage USA/PTL. I wasn't worried about my authority. I knew who I was. I was exhausted. I didn't want any more responsibility than I had.

After the Jessica Hahn calls began, Al came alive. He had an avid desire to be at the center of things. His problem was that I wasn't talking. I told him what I wanted him to know, and I was steering him away from something that was none of his business. He had to have more. Even if he had to create it.

He became a critic of the leadership of our church. He told me once he had seen one of our top executives drinking. I did not believe it. He became as focused in his bitterness as any minister I have ever observed. He was a very angry man. His best and dearest friends became greatly concerned about his attitude. I asked him to go to the bank and wire $25,000 for our West Coast attorney's retainer. About the time the Jessica Hahn matter was being resolved, he immediately began to tell people that we had paid $25,000 to "the woman" with whom Jim Bakker had an affair. He "knew" it; he had sent the money. He was sure. The $25,000 was never a part of the payment to Jessica Hahn. It was for legal fees for services that involved more than the Jessica Hahn settlement. When he didn't know the facts, he appeared to leap over them and created his own story. That money wire was the "certification" for him that someone was being paid off. Because he did not really know what the whole story was, it only whet his appetite for more. In my opinion, he believed he was God's special messenger to clean up PTL. He never told me about his feelings; he just ran amuck.

He was creating problems for my leadership. I finally told him his attitude was wrong and it reflected in his job. He was much more angry after that. What I had brought him to do at PTL wasn't being done. I was going home late at night with my work not done, and Al was presiding over his anger. Among the many very good qualities about Al was his love and commitment to his family. In the spring of 1985 he was deeply concerned about his mother. She was very ill. He had made trips home, and all of us understood and encouraged him in his concern for his mother. He came to me during this time and asked me to have the ministry pay his way home and also financially help in his mother's needs. I told him that was impossible. He was from a wonderful, large family. He was earning over $75,000 a year, driving a new Cadillac, and living in his own luxurious home. I felt that was his responsibility, not PTL's. We appreciated him, but were not prepared to deliver his every financial request. The financial demands continued. In June his dear mother passed away. All of us were saddened by her death. My wife, our daughter Deanna, and several couples (executives from PTL) attended her funeral in Colorado. PTL was always generous in giving employees time off for these kinds of things. He was shown every courtesy.

Several weeks after his mother passed away, I decided I must have help. I asked a committee of our church administrators, Eric Watt, our business administrator, Mark Burgund, and our son, Rich, to study my duties and my time constraints, and develop a plan for me to get the most out of my time. With over two thousand employees to administrate, and my involvement in the church and in television, I needed to maximize the value of my time each day. I believed that two MBA's and a Yale graduate could do a better job than I to get my day organized. Their recommendation was to have someone stay with me during the day who could feed things back to Al at the office to follow through.

Al and I had communicated by memo for years. That was not unusual. He gave me a long list of memos every day. After the decision was made to move forward with the new work plan, I gave him a memo explaining to him that our office would now have Brad Bacon with me during the day, and Al would run my office as he had always done. He was out of the office the day I wrote the memo. I put it on his desk. When he came back and read the memo, he walked out. He quit. He was finished. To this day he tells people I fired him, and the press has reported that "fact!" Jim Bakker's assistants told me he had threatened them with the news, "I have documents that I will use someday." Several pastors from Illinois told me that he had made the same threat to them.

Al Cress had become for me a person trying to destroy us. He took important personal correspondence of mine that did not affect him, and showed them to other PTL staff members. That was a breach of trust. He became so obsessed with trying to "get" us that he called denominational officers, and in my opinion, took documents from my file, or copies of them, to show them.

In 1987 *The Charlotte Observer* obtained a letter written to Paul Roper, Jessica Hahn's representative. The letter included the bank statement showing that $10,000 in interest had been paid to trustees for a "Jessica Hahn" escrow account, on a principal of $150,000. It is my opinion that a copy of the letter was wrongfully taken by Al Cress. I was the only person receiving any documents from our California attorney who had negotiated the Jessica Hahn settlement. He was the only person with access to the files. He had threatened me several times personally, and now, to me, he was carrying out his threat. The documents that were taken became a part of his quest to do what he could to damage all of us.

I have often wondered how he feels having been a key

player in the PTL events. He joined with Jimmy Swaggart to destroy PTL. His arrogance led him to contact church officials, and give them over fifty questions he wanted them to ask me. Did he not believe they could do an adequate job? Would his questions be better? To clean up PTL he was willing to take things that did not belong to him, and do what he believed was necessary to bring PTL down. When I later confronted him, he denied that he took the documents. He did acknowledge that he had made copies of them. Finger pointing has always scared me. It did Jesus, also. "Why do you point to the mote in your brother's eye, when you can't see the beam in your own eye?" Jesus asks.

We must all face our sins and wrongs. All of us must. Even though it is painful. There is something wonderfully redemptive about it. That is what I want for all of us. Integrity has to do with seeing ourselves as we are. In my opinion, the most disappointing thing about this episode is that the Bible was used so little. At no time, to my knowledge, was the scriptural process used, thus mass confusion reigned.

10

Forty Days and Forty Nights

The week following Jim Bakker's resignation, the staff and the leadership team walked around like zombies. Everyone existed in a state of confusion and uncertainty, asking questions that had no answers. The people who attended the church, the partners, and the viewers across the nation wanted to know what was going on at PTL.

So did I. The whole ordeal had left me badly shaken. The first weekend after everything became public, it seemed all I could do was cry.

In fact, how I kept up a front before the cameras or went about my duties, I don't know. Every night after working very late, I would go home and lie in bed and sob. A fountain of tears flowed uncontrollably. All I could do was constantly weep.

On Thursday, March 26, *USA Today* ran the headline, "JERRY FALWELL REVEALS PTL PLAN TODAY."

Jerry Falwell held his first board meeting and appointed me as president of PTL. Finally, I had some idea of what to expect in the days to come.

Falwell also announced to the public that Jim and Tammy Bakker would continue to draw their salaries, but there were no plans for their return. "PTL would not be here without Jim and Tammy Bakker," he said. "It would be less than Christian to terminate and cut off the life supply for the persons responsible for this ministry. Such action was never even considered."

In the meantime, Charles Shepard continued to probe for information about the Jessica Hahn payment. Soon an article appeared in *The Charlotte Observer* questioning the amount of money that Jessica Hahn got, how she got it, and who was involved. The spotlight turned on me. In fact, the story focused more on me than it did Jessica Hahn who received the money or Jim Bakker for whom it had been paid.

As the initial shock of the first few days wore off, I faced the reality that I had a TV program to put on the air, a staff of 1,500 people to manage, and a church to pastor. In my mind, our church had a television ministry, not the television ministry that happened to have a church.

I went to work, but it wasn't easy. Living under the constant strain and tension of public scrutiny and fearful uncertainty, night and day, stirred up concealed hostilities all over Heritage USA. People began to openly unleash their emotions on one another. The media, the staff, the management — the whole climate became antagonistic, mean, and cruel.

Sitting in the dressing room preparing for the TV program, I simply prayed, "Lord, help us to create an environment here where people are loving and considerate of each other."

For many years, I had been called the "forgiveness preacher." As I prayed that day, I was made to know that "forgiven" ought to be PTL's theme. That concept resulted from a sincere desire to create a charitable, loving, forgiving atmosphere for myself and among the staff and guests at PTL.

The press, particularly Charles Shepard of *The Char-*

lotte Observer, and other media, picked up on the word and convoluted the whole concept to mean "let's create a forgiving environment to get Jim and Tammy Bakker back."

Jim and Tammy were in my prayers — that was true — but they were not in my mind at the time I decided to make "forgiven" PTL's theme. I was trying to solve day-to-day problems resulting from people living and working together in a stressful setting. I was not projecting six months down the road. I was trying to create an environment of forgiveness that would generate more understanding and compassion in our present situation.

How could I expect the press or Charles Shepard to understand that?

While hosting the TV show one day, I asked our viewers across America to let forgiveness flood their hearts and be the attitude with which they approached all their relationships.

I suggested to the staff, "Write 'forgiven' on the wall of your office. When you pray, start forgiving each other. All over this facility let our byword be 'forgiven'."

To my delight and amazement, within a couple of days the grounds crew had cut out, in the shrubbery, the word "forgiven." Anyone entering Heritage USA immediately saw the word "forgiven" spelled out in large, living, green letters.

The press picked up on the unusual statement. In fact, Charles Shepard admitted to me that his Pulitzer Prize winning stories that culminated in his book, *Forgiven*, were named after my "forgiveness" theme.

I was not trying to push at that point for Jim and Tammy Bakker to come back. My main objective was to create an environment of Christian love, and if not love, then at least civility. After a while, the theme did contribute to a more conciliatory spirit at Heritage USA.

Charles Stanley, the esteemed pastor of the First Baptist Church in Atlanta, Georgia, preached a sermon that first Sunday after Jim's resignation that I will never forget. He held up a large stone in his hand and simply said, "Does anybody want to use this on Jim Bakker?"

Later, I told our television viewing audience that we ought to use a stone as a premium and send them out to our critics. Then they would have plenty of ammunition for their attacks.

Billy Graham is the only person who remained silent during that time. Billy Graham, godly man that he is, said nothing. What a wonderful thing it would have been if people would have followed his example. But everybody seemingly wanted to get in the act and to respond.

Little did I know that our worst critics were camped right in the executive offices down the hall. I soon realized that Jerry Falwell was a man of many faces.

The Jerry Falwell who had talked to me on his jet and in the Palm Springs hotel suite was now playing a different tune.

In the beginning Falwell and Jerry Nims told me repeatedly that Jimmy Swaggart was trying to bring PTL down, bring Falwell down, take over the ministry, and start a class action suit against PTL. "Jimmy Swaggart and all of his people are out to get Jim Bakker and my ministry, too," Falwell said, leading me to believe that Swaggart was our common opponent.

Then the first time Jerry Falwell was interviewed at PTL, reporters asked him about Swaggart's intentions. Falwell said, "No, he's not trying to get PTL. I don't believe Jimmy Swaggart would do anything like that."

I sensed from that moment forward, PTL was headed for trouble.

During the next six weeks, Falwell called a number of board meetings.

Anybody who understands corporate law knows that it is wrong to call for a board meeting and only invite certain members of the board. Such action is immoral, and in some cases illegal. Anytime that group or body is meeting in session and making decisions, it's a board meeting. Whether it's called that or not.

Falwell, on a number of occasions, called the non-charismatic board members together to make decisions that were later imposed on the uninvited members.

At one point, Falwell called a meeting of the board of directors of PTL to be held in Nashville, Tennessee, on a given date. When that date approached James Watt, Rex Humbard, and myself were told the meeting had been canceled. But, in fact, the meeting took place as planned with all the other members of the board present except the three of us.

Obviously, they didn't want us there.

Members of the board who knew such proceedings were out of order would describe to James Watt and me what had transpired at the closed sessions.

Of even greater concern to me was the fact that Jimmy and Frances Swaggart had also met with the Falwell component of the PTL board. We were told by members present that a heated discussion had transpired concerning the involvement of Jimmy Swaggart and PTL.

At one point in this meeting, Jerry Falwell reportedly looked at Jimmy Swaggart and said, "Jimmy, it seems to me that you want Heritage USA, that you want PTL, and if you do, I'll give you the keys to it. You can have it!"

We were told that Jimmy Swaggart had replied, "No. No. I don't want it." Then he apparently stood up and began to prance around. Sitting in the room was Ben Armstrong, the top man of the National Religious Broadcasters; Bailey Smith; Jerry Falwell; and Jerry Nims.

First Jimmy Swaggart walked up to Jerry Nims, put his finger in his face, and shouted, "Do you believe I was trying to steal PTL, take it over?" Jerry Nims prior to that time had told me Jimmy Swaggart was trying to do just that.

Jerry piously answered, "No, I don't believe that at all."

Then Jimmy Swaggart pranced down in front of Jerry Falwell and put his finger in his face and barked, "Do YOU believe that I'm trying to take over PTL, trying to steal PTL?"

"No, I don't believe that," Jerry Falwell replied cautiously.

Turning to Ben Armstrong, he repeated his question and received the same reply, "No, I don't believe that."

Coming to Bailey Smith, Swaggart arrogantly asked, "Do you believe I was trying to take over PTL?"

Bailey Smith answered, "Yes! And I still think you're trying to take it!"

Finally Jerry Falwell asked Jimmy Swaggart, "What is it you want?"

Jimmy Swaggart looked at Frances, "You tell him."

Frances said, "No, you tell him."

Jimmy then tried again, "No, you tell him."

"No," she replied, "you tell him."

Jimmy Swaggart then turned to Jerry Falwell. "Can Frances and I step outside for a few minutes and talk?" he requested.

"Of course," Falwell answered.

The Swaggarts stood in the hallway for about ten minutes and then returned.

"Now, Brother Swaggart, what is it you want?" Jerry Falwell pleaded.

"Frances, you tell him."

"No, Jimmy, you tell him."

Finally Swaggart said, "Well, we've made up our minds. We want Richard Dortch's resignation."

When I heard that, I was floored. Not so much that Jimmy wanted me to step down, but that Jerry Falwell had brought Swaggart to a meeting and asked what it would take to appease him.

Why was Swaggart so hostile toward me? The irony is for many years, Jimmy and Frances Swaggart and Mildred and I had been very dear and close friends. In fact, Mildred and I had flown to Baton Rouge, Louisiana, and for several days helped organize the Swaggarts' twenty-fifth wedding anniversary celebration. Together with Donnie Swaggart, we planned the program, and I hosted the evening.

Later, when I went to PTL, we were actually closer friends of the Swaggarts at that time than we were of the Bakkers. For many years Jimmy Swaggart came to Illinois, where I was the state superintendent, and at my invitation preached in our churches and conventions. On several occasions I visited Swaggart's operation in Baton Rouge and ministered at various functions. We had been friends for thirty years.

In 1983, when I made my decision to go to Heritage USA, it surprised many people in our denomination. The Swaggarts apparently, in light of our close friendship with them, could not accept my decision to join Jim Bakker's ministry. A former executive of the Jimmy Swaggart Evangelistic Association later told me that the Swaggarts couldn't handle the fact that I did not consult with them about going to PTL. That explained one reason for their recent vindictiveness toward me.

It was also clear to me that Jimmy Swaggart wanted to bring down Jim Bakker, PTL, and me. His own letter to John Ankerberg had stated that fact, and his actions since then had proven his intentions.

Jimmy Swaggart called for my resignation both in Falwell's private meeting and publicly at a news conference. One of his motives, I believe, was revenge. Jimmy Swaggart felt I had lied to him about the Jessica Hahn incident when I met with him and Dr. Cookman in Baton Rouge. This was his way of getting even.

At the time I could understand Jimmy's bitterness. Then I discovered he was in no position to judge me because he had tried to cover his tracks in precisely the same way I had — by making a statement that absolved him of wrongdoing.

Jimmy Swaggart, in my judgment, does not need anybody to beat on him now that he is down. However, a look at the PTL incidents where he interjected himself is a fair matter.

In the midst of Jimmy Swaggart's outrage over Jim Bakker's sin and my supposed "lie," a former member of the Swaggart band who had sung, played guitar, and accompanied Jimmy Swaggart for years showed up at my office at Heritage USA. He told me about his sexual involvement with a member of Jimmy Swaggart's family. I had heard these allegations many times before but had discounted them. Now it appeared they were true. I was stunned.

This former band member explained to me that when Jimmy Swaggart learned of his indiscretions, Swaggart tried to force him out of town. The man had refused to leave explaining he was in the process of buying a home owned by the Swaggart ministry. Jimmy Swaggart then proposed paying off the man's house if he agreed to move away and keep quiet about the situation.

That's the story that was told to me.

Not long after the band member's visit to my office, Jimmy Swaggart appeared on the "Larry King Live" show. A caller asked the question, "Is it true that a member of Jimmy Swaggart's family was sexually involved with a drummer in his band?"

Jimmy Swaggart quickly responded and said, "I don't know of anybody in my family that's ever been involved with a drummer in my band."

He answered truthfully, but he didn't clarify his answer since the man was not the drummer but the guitarist. Did that make his statement a lie?

Actually, I was grateful that the man asked Jimmy Swaggart if it was the drummer rather than the guitar player. That gave Swaggart a way out. I wouldn't want a member of his family to suffer the agony of public ridicule the way we have. That's why I have not disclosed the person involved. I wish Jimmy Swaggart had been as compassionate with me.

We do reap what we sow. I hope Jimmy Swaggart has learned the same hard lessons I have: The means do not justify the end, and integrity cannot be selective. Integrity involves the whole individual and requires full disclosures.

Jerry Falwell in his efforts to oust me continued his unofficial meetings with groups and individuals. At the same time, *The Charlotte Observer* attempted to sniff out the Jessica Hahn money trail.

To accomplish his purposes, Charles Shepard relentlessly pursued Roe Messner.

On a daily basis, Roe repeated to me, "Don't worry. I'll

never tell *The Observer* anything." But it was obvious from the information contained in Shepherd's articles that he was getting enough bits and pieces out of Roe Messner to put the story together.

Who else could be talking to Shepard? Roe and I were the only two who knew the story. That is, except for Roy Grutman.

On Saturday, April 18, *The Charlotte Observer,* using information intentionally leaked by one of Falwell's staff, printed the salaries of PTL's top officials. I was told this was done to make it impossible for Jim Bakker to return to PTL and to eliminate those of us still in leadership roles. Conveniently, one of Falwell's long time employees who was presently on our staff, Doug Oldham, was left off the list. His approximate $150,000 a year salary wasn't mentioned.

I wasn't surprised when told that Jerry Nims was the informant who leaked the salary list to *The Observer.* His reputation in the South was not exactly spotless. He had been sued on a number of occasions and his hometown newspaper, *The Atlanta Constitution* had closely monitored his actions for years.

Why was Jerry Nims' past never mentioned in *The Charlotte Observer*? Many observers believe that the Charlotte newspaper and Jerry Nims had a deal: "I'll provide you with information, and you lay off of me." That's what we were told, and the facts speak for themselves.

About this same time, Jerry Falwell appointed a committee comprised of Roy Grutman and two board members to compile a report for the board of directors meeting on April 28. They were to investigate the settlement with Jessica Hahn — where the money came from and how the payment was made.

When I heard about this committee, I thought: But Roy Grutman knows everything. I told him the whole story on the plane to California. He's my attorney. How can he pretend not to know? What kind of an attorney is he?

The next morning my questions were answered. I could tell by Jerry Falwell's conversation and the questions he asked me that Grutman had violated our client/attorney relationship. Now Falwell knew about Roe Messner and the out of court settlement with Jessica Hahn.

At the same time, a story had surfaced around the country suggesting that Jerry Falwell might resign as the leader of PTL at the next board of directors meeting. That item along with the Jessica Hahn settlement report had captured the attention not only of the board members but of the nation as well.

Poised for the latest news, the media set up their microphones and cameras at Heritage USA. As usual, when the press doesn't have any facts to present, they speculated daily on the outcome of the April 28 board meeting.

Sunday morning, April 26, I preached my last message at the Heritage Village Church. How could I continue to pastor in the wake of the havoc over the disclosure of the PTL salaries and the heightened interest of the press in the Jessica Hahn disaster? Those dear people in our congregation deserved better.

The day before the meeting, James Watt and Rex Humbard arrived at the Heritage Grand Hotel by 4:00 in the afternoon. Later, when James Watt, his son Eric, our son Rich, and I sat down for dinner at 6:30, one of us said, "I wonder where all the other board members are?"

At least seven other board members were supposed to attend the meeting, and none of them were yet on the premises.

"Isn't the meeting scheduled to begin at eight o'clock in the morning?" Eric asked.

"Yes, and there aren't many more flights due in tonight or early in the morning," I replied. Having traveled as much as I did, I knew few flights came into the Charlotte Airport after 7:00 in the evening.

As we sat there discussing the matter, the reality of what was happening hit me!

"The other board members are meeting with Jerry Falwell in Lynchburg, Virginia, and they're flying down on his private jet tomorrow morning!" I announced.

James Watt quickly responded, "My wife, Leilani, knows Sam Moore's wife very well. Let me call my wife and see if she can find out where Sam is."

James Watt went to the phone and quickly called his wife, who called Mrs. Moore, who exclaimed, "Sam isn't here. He's in Lynchburg for a PTL meeting before they go to Heritage USA."

That was it. An illegal meeting was again being held without the charismatic members of the board. Obviously plans were being laid and rehearsed that would, in fact, be implemented in the next day's meeting.

The four of us began our own series of speculations.

"Perhaps Jerry Falwell is going to resign," Eric Watt commented.

"It must be something they don't want us to know," James Watt added.

"Nothing would surprise me," I said, having no idea that my job was at stake. In fact, the thought never crossed my mind.

"Falwell probably just wants to make sure things are going his way," I concluded. I may have been sarcastic, but I never imagined that at that very moment a cruel and sinister plan was being scripted and rehearsed in Lynchburg.

The four of us said good night. My wife and I had checked into the hotel to avoid contending with the media throng outside our house in the morning.

At 8:00 a.m., the scheduled time of the board meeting, no one from Falwell's ministry had yet arrived. At approximately 8:30 a.m., Jerry Falwell and the other board members entered.

Also accompanying Falwell was what the PTL staff called his "goon squad" of heavyweight, personal bodyguards. They looked somewhat like a Mafia entourage hired to protect "the boss."

Jerry Falwell surveyed the room we normally used for board meetings and said, "This is too open, let's go upstairs to the Presidential Suite."

We made our way into the suite, and doors were left open

to the living room, where the meeting was being held. That way members of the "goon squad" could easily monitor what was happening.

After a brief, opening prayer, Jerry Falwell immediately announced that he was staying in the leadership position of PTL. "I am here for the duration, and I have no intentions of leaving," he commented smugly. Within ten or fifteen minutes that matter was finished and put to rest.

He then turned toward Roy Grutman and said, "Now, give us the report of the Jessica Hahn matter."

At that moment, Roy Grutman stopped acting as my attorney and took on the role of prosecutor, making outrageous accusations against me. He said I knew the lifetime partnerships were timeshares and that I did nothing to stop it. Then he accused me of funneling the money to Jessica Hahn and using PTL funds to make the payment.

Grutman asserted that by such conduct I had contaminated myself with the events. I was guilty by association for the whole Jim Bakker episode. That was his report.

Roy Grutman in essence told the board everything I had disclosed to him within two hours of the first time I met him, almost forty days before. But he never once mentioned that I was his client or that I had openly shared that information with him.

It was a charade of the highest order, scripted by Jerry Falwell and performed by players well rehearsed and on cue.

Before I could offer any explanation, Bailey Smith looked at me and harshly stated, "I move, Mr. Chairman, that Richard Dortch be terminated as the president of PTL, and that he be given the opportunity to resign if he chooses."

One of Jerry Falwell's cronies seconded it.

"Let's take a vote," Falwell ordered.

At that point, Rex Humbard picked up on what was happening. He stood and remarked, "I will not be part of what is taking place here. I am tired and weary of the whole thing." He then stepped outside the room.

Several people heard him say, "I've heard of lynchings before, and I'm sure not going to attend this one."

A poll was taken of the vote. Ben Armstrong, Sam Moore, and James Watt would not agree with the vote.

I was in total shock and could not believe what was happening. I had been in the ministry for thirty-six years, and at no time had any area of my life come into question. No one had ever accused me of any kind of improper behavior or financial mismanagement.

A feeling of nausea swept over me.

For over twenty years, I had been involved in the discipline of ministers. I knew how to soften the blow when evidence was presented and a vote was taken. I knew how such a devastating experience could affect a man's spiritual relationship, his self-esteem, and his health.

Now I was being treated like a common criminal. What was my crime I had participated in? I had never before seen such cruelty and anger and malicious intent demonstrated by Christians toward another brother in the Lord.

Stunned beyond belief, I sat frozen in my chair listening to Jerry Falwell confirm my firing.

Then he said, "Richard Dortch, a few days ago on national television, said, 'There are some who feel those of us in leadership in PTL were overpaid, and I want to be submissive so this next year I will take no salary for my services at PTL. None. I will simply trust the Lord. Obviously, I'm going to need to live in the house in which I'm living. I'm going to need a car to drive, and I'm going to need hospitalization insurance. But other than those three things I will live from whatever God provides, and will not accept any salary from PTL.'"

Jerry Falwell explained that I had done that, and in his opinion, with good intentions. He respected that. But he stated, "Pastor Dortch is in different circumstances now. When he made that statement he believed he would have a house, a car, hospitalization, and a job when this year was over."

He then looked at me and said, "Pastor Dortch, we forgive you and release you from your statement. It is the only honorable thing we can do. So on behalf of the board, we release you from that promise, and we must do something in the way of compensation for you."

Sam Moore spoke up and said, "If we don't give him six months salary, I'll resign from this board."

Some discussion ensued, with the general understanding that I would be kept on the payroll at my normal salary until a final conclusion could be made.

I put my head in my hands and bawled like a baby.

I was too embarrassed to walk out and too scared to stay. Finally, I asked someone to go get our son, Rich, and Eric Watt. I eased out of the room as quietly as I could, taking a back way to avoid the reporters.

Weak from the encounter, I crawled into the back seat of my car that was parked in the private garage. The security people were already waiting for me. When the garage door opened, a host of television and other reporters crowded around trying to see who was inside. I bowed down my head, and we made our way toward my home.

As I was being driven home that awful day, the cruel planning behind what had taken place in the meeting finally dawned on me. Nothing could have devastated me more had I been shot with a pistol.

It didn't take long for people to find out what had happened. Staff members started to arrive at the house to give their support. That was about ten thirty or eleven o'clock in the morning.

After the meeting ended, Jerry Falwell held a press conference. Those of us who were watching the live news report could not believe what we were hearing and seeing.

Jerry Falwell stood before 150 or more national media and local press and said most piously, "In the meeting this morning I prayed and waited upon God for an answer. After the board had been in much prayer, they discussed the possibility of my leaving. Then a verse of Scripture came to me, 'He that putteth his hand to the plow and looks back is not fit for the Kingdom.' And after much discussion and prayer, (implying that it had been over an hour or so into the meeting), I was finally persuaded to make the decision that

I should stay."

Later in the evening James Watt and others came to our home and watched the replay of the news conference.

James exclaimed loudly, "Which board meeting did he attend? It wasn't the meeting I was in!"

Jerry Falwell also, continuing his acting role, told how badly he felt that a very good man, Richard Dortch, had resigned today, and how sorry he was because of the resignation.

Was I angry? No.

Was I bitter? No.

Was I beaten down, dejected, and utterly broken? Yes!

When Rich arrived at our house, he lovingly put his arm around me and said, "Dad, life isn't like you think it is. Everybody doesn't love you. Everybody is not as trusting and sincere as you. They don't believe everything they hear like you do.

"Dad, this is the real world, and you're being treated like the world treats its people!"

It had taken me fifty-six years to grow up. Now my world of innocence had evaporated. I had simply believed that loving and trusting people meant everything. If people made mistakes, you forgave and you hugged them. You showed them the way.

That was the way I treated any pastor I ever disciplined. I had never, in the scores of people I'd dealt with, ever left them broken by the experience. I showed them the way back, how to reverse the action we had just taken, and how to overcome their failures and mistakes.

But "my religious brothers" left me with hopelessness, condemnation, and fear.

Never before in my life had I ever been fearful of anyone for any reason. I didn't have any reason to be. My life up to that point had been filled with joy and anticipation of what life would bring. Some said I had a winsome disposition. I loved being around people.

I still faced a confused public, overnight I became fearful of outsiders — afraid people would try to physically hurt me.

I acted like a scared, hunted animal, cringing with terror at the slightest unexpected move. Every time I pulled out of my driveway or crossed the street, a sense of dreaded apprehension overwhelmed me. In my mind's eye I saw myself being struck by a car and killed. I lived with that feeling day to day. In fact, I still experience many of those fears, even after four years.

The remorse, shame, and humiliation I was walking through touched every facet of my life — my thought process, attitude, and relationships. I was especially concerned about our children. Deanna had already gone through enough. The load Rich was carrying really got my attention. He was in his late twenties, had attended several great colleges, Wheaton, Evangel, and had earned his Master's in Business Administration from Duke University. He is bright, articulate, and a person of impeccable integrity and character. His problem was his name, Richard William Dortch II. He was living in Charlotte, North Carolina, and planned to live there the rest of his life, where all of this was happening! Was there anyone in Charlotte who had not heard of Richard Dortch? Through my shame and hurt for a son who bore my name, I sat down and did the most hurtful thing I have ever done. "I understand, Rich, you must do what is best for you," I began. "With all that has happened I would understand if you want to change your name. Please do it if it will help you," I said through my tears.

Rich wrapped his arms around me. "I love you, Dad. I would never do that."

Even though I hurt for him so much, I sensed the love of our son for me. That was greater than the pain.

Later, when I studied the calendar and counted out the number of days since my appointment as the president of PTL, I discovered I had held that position for two days shy of six weeks.

Forty days and forty nights.

11

Confessions
Of Failure

It's tough to admit it, but there comes a time when we must acknowledge failure. It didn't happen because the enemy of our souls broke through and overpowered us and took us as prisoners, it wasn't because someone struck us down from behind in the dark. It wasn't that we committed any aggressive crime. It wasn't because we had stolen anything. For the most part, as I have walked through this experience, I'm convinced that my problem was what I failed to do. The thing that I must speak to my heart about, is that it is just as dangerous and treacherous to not do something as it is to be involved in a positive and aggressive sin. With my background, it was easy for me to believe, and how foolish, to think that if we're simply pious, and do no wrong, everything will be alright. It's absurd to get into our minds that we are Christians by what we do not do, instead of by what we do. Obviously, there are certain sins that are damaging and damning. But, when we fail in our duty, and know to do good and do it not, that is sin. The Greatest Man who ever lived taught us again and again that truth. What was wrong with the fig tree that Jesus spoke to in the Bible? Why did He curse it? It was not loaded with poison. It simply had nothing but leaves. What charge is brought against many of us? We're simply made to see the neglect that we have had in our own personal lives. We have left some situations and people alone when we should have become involved.

What was wrong with the five foolish virgins? It was not that they had water in their lamps. It was simply the fact that they had no oil. What was the matter with those to whom the judge said, "Depart from me?" Only that they had failed in their duty.

Often when we fail it is not through ignorance. It is not because we did not know what we were supposed to do. Usually we understand perfectly well what we are to do, and we understand the importance of why we should do it. We are in a life and death situation as it concerns our destiny, and yet we fail and fail miserably. But it is not because of our ignorance. Our greatest need today in the moral realm is not for more knowledge. My greatest need is simply to have the will to live up to what I already know. Oftentimes we are unwilling to do better.

I am confident that God has a particular task for every single person, and I am equally confident that He will let us know what that task is if we make it possible for Him to do so. When we see something that isn't right, we must listen to our hearts, and in a loving, kind way, move into people's lives and affirm what is right. "In all thy ways acknowledge Him and He will direct thy path."

I didn't experience failure because of a lack of ability. I had superior numbers most of my life. The problem is that I didn't make a fight of standing for what I knew was the best. I didn't have my place of failure because of idleness. It wasn't because I or anyone else at PTL was lazy. We worked, and hard, but we failed not from ignorance or inability or from idleness, but because we were too busy. We cannot deny it. The secondary so absorbed us that we neglected the primary.

The trouble with having so much that is good is that it robs us of the privilege of doing the best. The prodigal's problems in the far country was not simply the fact that he was in a hog pen. He might have been in a palace and been just as bad off. It was the fact that he was missing the privilege of being in his father's house.

The sin that we must fear the most is not the sin of vicious wrong-doing, it is the sin of choosing the second-best. And that's where our integrity fails. If we spend most of our time doing trivial things, we rob ourselves of doing something better. So much of our time is spent in good things, but perhaps not the best. Often we were engaged in great, stressful, straining trivialities. Perhaps they were not especially harmful, but the calamity of it all is that they so absorbed us, we didn't have time left for the highest. It is so easy to become passionately involved in amusing ourselves. We were doing a thousand and one decent and good things; but while we were busy here and there, something of God slipped out of our lives and we didn't have the keen interest we should have in simply "knowing God," which should be our highest goal.

Through all of this experience, I've learned a simple lesson. To maintain integrity we must put first things first. Listen to the voice of the Greatest Man who ever lived. This is His message: "But seek ye first the kingdom of God, and his righteousness; and all these things shall be added unto you" (Matt. 6:33). That verse pounded in my spirit from the day the bubble began to burst and the castle tumbled. When we fail to seek the Kingdom first, even though the task be noble and we toil hard, we will not taste in the end the joy of victory we so desperately sought.

Yes, disillusionment is a part of life. Oftentimes during what was happening after the fall of PTL, I asked the question, "Why should it happen to me?" In some ways we had been living in an "Alice in Wonderland" world. I had lived in moments of innocence for so long, but I quickly came into an age of accountability and things were never the same again. We had been in a kind of honeymoon at PTL, but it dissipated in a few days. I was awakened from my dreams. For so many years I had been writing the script for triumphs, but I had left out the testings. I had been ill on several occasions. I was used to sickness and weariness. But now I faced failure, financial pressure, desertion by friends, closed doors. I had been ready to conquer the world, but now the mirage had vanished.

Imagination is one thing, but God's schedule is another. I learned that I would survive, and in doing so I would grow stronger. Often the biblical character, Joseph, came to my mind. All of his dreams seemed to mock him. David's trials came to my mind frequently. Their reverses made them the people that God wanted them to become. Being spoon-fed in life has its miseries. It was obvious it was time for me to grow up. The sorrows are what deepened my life and ministry. I had been baffled by what was going on around me, but it made me search further until I made the necessary new discoveries of faith. I certainly didn't plan it that way, but when I look back, I wouldn't want to change a thing. I wouldn't have it any other way. Only the great heart of a God who loves us allows us the moments in our lives when we can dream, and I had been dreaming for a long time. I had never deserved the positions, the accolades, and the recognition that I had. God helped me to understand that maybe I didn't "deserve" what I was getting now. But I was in school and I must learn well. The stern realities of life were going to take care of making me the person God wanted me to be.

During the very darkened hours when I had to speak to myself, I had to come to grips with the things I had learned during the daylight hours. Would they work now? Would they work in the darkness? I began to recall those great Bible stories that I had learned as a child, that God was not only the Lord of the hilltop experiences, but also the valleys. And I remember how I got the integrity that I had for those many years.

BenHadad was on the throne of Syria. Ahab was king of Israel. God was with Israel. His blessing had been poured out upon the king in a wonderful way. Divine protection had been given them and their enemies had been defeated on the field of battle. One of the victories was so wonderful that no explanation could possibly be given, other than "the might and the power of the Lord." They had been hopelessly outnumbered. The children of Israel had arrayed themselves in a battle formation against the Syrians. The fight occurred on top of the mountains. The Syrians were defeated. Once more, God had vindicated His promise. It seemed that the host of heaven had been fighting on the side of the people of the Lord. Perhaps it had come to the ears of the king of Syria that so many of the songs of Israel had to do with the eternal hills. Their country was hilly, mountainous, and many of their cities were built upon the mountain tops. They were a hill people, while the Syrians were children of the plains. Woven like a thread through all of their customs, culture, and religious literature was the story of the mountains and the glory of the hills.

Perhaps BenHadad thought about this. He couldn't understand defeat. How could such a little army defeat a force like this? In his heart he knew that the God of Israel had brought about the victory. He arrived at a decision. God was a God of the mountains, and he was not a God of the valleys. He decided to go to battle once again. The cry to arms rang throughout all of Syria. He was going to prove that he was right. The bugle call sounded through the countryside summoning an army exactly the size of the one that had been defeated. The king insisted that there must be man for man, horse for horse, and chariot for chariot. He must have felt sure of his ground. He would prove to the whole world that the God of Israel might be a God of the mountain top, but certainly not the God of the valleys.

The day of battle came. On one side were the armies of Syria. It was a tremendous group of soldiers that assembled under BenHadad that day. Confidence was in the air. They felt certain of their victory. On the other side was the army of Israel. In comparison to the size of the Syrian army, the Scriptures tell us the men under Ahab were like two small herds of goats. When the battle was over, Syria was broken and defeated. Thousands of their young soldiers had fled in dismay, taking refuge beneath the city wall. Further disaster awaited them there. The wall fell and crumbled upon them, and thousands and thousands perished at the hand of the Lord. God had proven that He was not only the God of the mountains, but He was also the God of the valleys.

All of this is history. I have learned so much through this experience. I now have the opportunity to assimilate into my spirit all that I had learned and walked through during my life. I want to write upon your minds truths that time will never take away. In days to come, when you're in the midst of battles, as I have been, I pray that some guardian angel will reach into the chambers of your memory and hold before your eyes what I'm going to tell you now.

We know that God is the God of the mountains. We love to live on the mountain top. I do! I had gone to church all of my life, and love to have joy and let the hallelujahs ring. Because most of my life I have had mountain peak experiences, I was quick to praise God for victory. It was great to shout for joy, because most of my life I had nothing but triumphs. I was glorying in the fact that my head was above the clouds. Most of the testimonies and sermons that I have given were about the mountain top experiences.

As a general rule, when I lived in the valley, I forgot to praise, and looked with envious eyes at the people who had come out of the valley to the peaks of the mountains of victory.

Nothing is more legitimate than the song of the victory. To be thankful and have praise to God for triumph is something we should never forget or neglect. But I must tell you that to a marked extent, we have been wrong in our method of giving praise to God. The valley is really the place of blessing. I know. I've walked in it. Through this five year experience, I have learned so much more in those low places, far more than the mountain top. The experiences from which I would shrink often proved to be the portals through which I was to go to the richest and sweetest experiences of life. The trials that had beset me were now a benediction in disguise.

I was developing strength by testing, and I knew that my character and integrity would be attained by overcoming in this valley. Valleys are much more important than mountains. There is far more danger in victory and conquests than there is in the valley. I could learn very little while I was on the mountain top, both as a well-known denominational executive and TV personality. Now, in defeat and failure, the lessons were going to be made real.

Do you know what it is that we learn in the testing and trials of life that develops strength to each of us? There is not half the danger of forgetting God in our heartaches and trials as there is when we are living beneath the cloudless sky and on the pinnacles of the mountains. I was experiencing tears of sorrow, but then I felt the need of Jesus. Cares were surrounding me and difficulties had me on my knees, and I was longing for strength and an arm that would not fail me. I had looked to others to keep things going. Now the winds of adversity had struck and the hurricanes of life were whirling around me, and I looked to "the Rock that was higher than I." I learned that what I had been taught at my mother's knee was true. It's in the time of storm that you feel the need of a shelter, and when the heart is breaking, I long for the oil of joy. To me, this experience was somewhat like standing beside an open grave. Often my wife and I would talk about it. The similarities of death is what we were walking through. It was as if there was a death in the family. I was waiting for the angels to sing an anthem of resurrection. I was lonely and longed for companionship, the kind the disciples found on the road to Emmaus. I made so many discoveries.

We are far more likely to forget Jesus on the mountain than we are in the valley. It's so easy to backslide in church and doing the Lord's work. There is a great, grave danger of losing our relationship to God in the place of seeming security. Integrity can be lost so easily in the place where we're most secure. Jesus' mother lost Him in church, and thousands of us have lost Him in the same place. Momentarily, we did!

Have you noticed how people skip along the pathway with a spring in their step and a song in their heart? You can get by with as little prayer as you can. There isn't a cloud in the sky. We accept God's blessing as a matter of fact, it's just the normal course. God's blessings become common place, and we neglect the altars in our hearts because seemingly there's no special need to pray. If we only knew it was there that we had the greatest need in our lives. This is a point of danger. The valley with its heartaches, trials, tears, and sorrows is the place where we grow, far more than when we seem at ease on the mountain top.

Something wonderful occurred to me and I hope we will all learn from it. The majority of us constantly indulge in a foolish practice. I did it. I blamed *The Charlotte Observer*, Jerry Falwell, Jessica Hahn, and sometimes Jim Bakker, for my problems. Because everything was going wrong in my life. Sometimes I even said it was the devil that was bringing these trials to my life. I shared that thought with others, certainly the enemy of our souls must be after me. It must have been a monotonous, repetitious thing that I was asserting, that the devil was testing me. I learned that when I felt happy, I would say it was the Lord's goodness, and when I felt pain, I said it was the devil. I was confident that all my afflictions came from the pit. I am not at all convinced of that today. I hold no brief for the adversary of our souls. I do not like him, and he does not like me. My eyes have been opened during these troubled times to the truth of what I am saying. I have stopped my foolish whimpering about my testings and trials coming from Satan. I am absolutely convinced that the vast majority of my lowest moments have been sent by the Lord.

I believe the apostle Paul discovered the secret. How many times do we find in his letters that he rejoiced and gloried in his victories? I cannot. Every time he starts to have a praiseful heart and sing songs of gratitude, it was because of his trials and testings. Did he not rejoice in his infirmities? Did he not glory in a cross? Did he not have praise for his afflictions? Had he not arrived at the conclusion that these were the things that were working out for him a far more exceeding glory? I am forced to an inevitable conclusion. Paul came to a place in his experience where he knew that his trials and testings were far more important than his victories on the mountain. The secret of growing in grace is to be in a place where you need grace. The secret of leaning hard on God is to get into the circumstance where you have to. You can only know of God's companionship when He has brought you through your heartache and sorrow. Why does He do it? To make us better, of course. To make us nobler, sweeter, to show us that we are completely and totally dependent upon Him.

God is not trying to get even with us when we lose our integrity and when we've come through the valleys. He loves us too much for that. Ofttimes we imagine that the heartache we've come through was a punishment because of our shortcomings. I don't believe so. The tears that were falling and the sorrows that beset me were not punitive, they were remedial. If they were punitive, then I would be atoning for my wrongs. That could never be. Our Saviour atoned for our sins by what He suffered. I cannot say that God is punishing me, but He has been trying to bring all of us back. His chastisements will make us better. When we view them in the light of the future and not to give us a whipping for tomorrow, we can understand that hidden somewhere in them is God's care for us. The burden I bear, the heartache and sorrow that is mine, will prove to be a blessing and bring light to my tomorrows. The beauty of character shines all the more against the dark background of difficulty and trial. It was in the Phillipian jail that the Apostle went on record of giving hallelujahs. The songs that sound the sweetest are the ones that ring through the darkness of the night. I experienced that.

We all should learn that the song in the night is sweeter by far than the song in the day. We must come to the place where we can have total honesty and sincerely believe that the things that happen in our lives do not happen by chance. "The steps of a good person are ordered by the Lord" (Ps.

37:23). We say that we believe that "all things work together for good to them that love God" (Rom. 8:28). Then as soon as some of the "all things" happen, we begin to whimper and cry and say that the devil is attacking us. That is not consistent. Let me repeat that I am absolutely and thoroughly convinced that the majority of difficulties and testings in our lives are sent by the Lord to strengthen us in faith and make us grow in grace. Why would there be grace unless it was needed? Why would there be strength unless it was required? Why would there be power unless there was some victory to be won? Dormant faith will never make an impression, but active, alive faith will bring honor and glory to the One who deserves it. We need God, both on the mountain top and in the valley, but we are more likely to feel that we need Him when we experience the need so manifest in the valley experiences of life.

The supreme lesson in the life of Abraham was the valley through which he went on the way to Mount Moriah. He was trudging along with the sticks for the sacrifice. By his side walks his boy. We hear his son's cry: "Daddy, where is the sacrifice? We have the wood for the fire, but what are we going to offer for the sacrifice when we get there?" Can you not see Abraham swallow that which keeps rising in his throat? Can you not see the lines of anguish that wrinkle his grief-stricken face? What a valley experience that was! What a trial and testing for the old man to go through! But how can you know how strong faith is unless you put it to the test? How can you know how much you trust the Lord until you are tried and tested? I presume that if you had stopped Abraham in the midst of the valley experience he would have said to you, "This is the hardest thing I've ever done in my life. I am perplexed and bewildered. I cannot understand, but I know my confidence and trust is in the Lord." It was as if he walked through the deep, dark valley on his way to Mount Moriah and no one cared. Do you know what transpired there? Do you know how wonderfully he was brought through that experience? Victory came out of defeat!

The story of his faith was so glorious and beautiful that

angels must have looked at it and wondered, and all of us mortals stand in contemplation. Down the mountainside came Abraham and his boy. I assume the old man's heart was so filled with God's presence and glory that it overflowed. It was more wonderful than words could tell. The thing that seemed to be grievous today will shine like a jewel in the sunlight of another morning. Our God is truly the God of the mountains, but He is also the God of the valleys, and I have walked through them. Yes, He is the Lord of the mountains and the valleys. We must learn, like Paul, to rejoice in our infirmities. There is more blessing in the battle than there is in the victory that follows it. When the trials of life hurt us, we can rest in the sublime consciousness of His abiding presence — His never-failing care — and His undying love. Then the light will shine in the darkness, and faith will sing in the night, and you will know the truth of pure integrity. Wholeness has come. The God whom you love and adore is the God of your mountains. But the richer and sweeter lessons in life will be those when you lift your tear-stained eyes heavenward and raise your hearts towards the skies and declare that He is the God of the valleys, too.

Richard Dortch and evangelist James Robinson.

12

Under Siege

"This building is now secured and under the control of Pinkerton armed guards. No one is permitted to leave without being searched!" a guard bellowed through the megaphone.

People standing in the atrium lobby of the Administration Building at Heritage USA froze in their tracks, shocked by this sudden announcement. Staff and office workers poured out from the three stories of offices surrounding the central atrium and looked down to the main floor below. Pinkerton armed guards stood guarding all the entrances and exits.

A former member of then Vice President George Bush's staff happened to be in the building at the time and recounted the unusual event. As visitors and employees left the building, women had their purses searched and men had to open their briefcases. He couldn't believe this was happening at Heritage USA.

Bewildered employees wondered, "What's going on? What are they looking for?"

It didn't take long for them to realize this overt act of control demonstrated Jerry Falwell's feelings toward other

Christians. Most of PTL's staff were born-again believers, but they were not disciples of Jerry Falwell. That made them his enemies.

PTL, in its worst moments, had never experienced such uncivilized treatment of its staff and employees. Hundreds of them were handled like common criminals. In a moment's time, the authoritarian command post set up by Jerry Falwell changed the cooperative atmosphere and spirit of Heritage USA to one of suspicion and hostility.

This premeditated maneuver also revealed something else about Jerry Falwell — he did not tell the truth when he later told reporters at the press conference that after prayer and discussion he was persuaded to stay at PTL for the duration. If Jerry Falwell had not known he was going to stay at the helm of PTL, why were guards employed before-hand for the permanent takeover immediately upon my dismissal as PTL president?

Was Jerry Falwell trying to protect himself from Jim Bakker, who, as everyone knew, was in California with Tammy? At that point, Jim posed no threat.

Maybe Falwell thought I was going to steal important PTL documents. Why would I do that when it had never crossed my mind that I was going to be removed? In fact, I did not even go to my office the morning I was fired.

Why were people being searched if no one in the administration knew I was going to be dismissed? What was Jerry Falwell's real purpose in securing the Administration Building? The answer went beyond the obvious, but before long, most of us realized: It wasn't Jimmy Swaggart who was trying to take over PTL — it was Jerry Falwell.

The day of my dismissal people came to our home bringing food and offering condolences. There were hugs and kisses and crying, just as if there had been a death in the family. We were experiencing a wake.

A pall hung over the evening, interspersed by visits from beloved friends. Their presence indicated more than their feelings of sorrow for me and my family. I knew they were saying, "We know what's really happening, and we will stand with you."

James Watt, with his son, Eric, and Eric's wife, Becky, bravely identified themselves with our suffering. As the former Secretary of the Interior in the Reagan administration, James Watt had lived under intense media criticism during his service as a cabinet member. He and his family understood our pain probably better than anyone else.

My colleagues, Mark and Wanda Burgund, and Russell and Sandy Hosey, our beloved friends from Illinois, stood by our side every moment. Business people such as Bob and Trish Ragsdale, who were not even employees of PTL, came and showed their support. Esther and Brian Boone were there ministering to us. Leslie Jones, my secretary, who herself had gone through much adversity, understood. She was an angel of light. Our house filled with people reaching out to us.

The Heritage Village Church which I had co-pastored had a staff of thirty-one ministers. Two of them came to express their concern before we left the next evening.

Those who didn't come also made a statement. Some people, whom we considered close friends, were conspicuous by their absence. Evidently, they were staking their claim in the Falwell regime as quickly as possible, negotiating a place of prominence.

In fact, I later learned some staff members in the hierarchy of PTL had contacted Jerry Falwell prior to my dismissal. They wanted Falwell to know they were ready to strike a deal if any changes took place in the administrative or pastoral leadership. Immediately upon my removal as president, a few PTL employees took positions at Jerry Falwell's headquarters in Lynchburg, Virginia.

The change of command at PTL served as a proving ground for many people — a test of character that revealed their true motives. Integrity, like 1 Corinthians 13 says: "Does not flaunt itself. Is not puffed up, does not seek its own."

In one instance, a top management person had told me he was leaving town for the weekend to rest. Later, in conversation with another department chief, I mentioned how sorry I was this person was out of town. He looked at me totally amazed and said, "No, he's not resting. He's made other arrangements. He went to Lynchburg." I later learned that he made the trip to try to get my job.

By the evening of my firing, sides had been chosen, and lines had been drawn. I marveled and grieved over the mutiny.

The view from our window brought further distress. Throngs of media people were lined up in our driveway like vultures waiting to scratch and pick at a rotting carcass. Television station helicopters were flying over our house.

With constant radio and television reports trumpeting my ouster, it was impossible to escape the publicity. All day long, the TV networks had broadcast the latest turn of events at PTL. My dismissal captivated the media, and I watched with the rest of America as my own personal history unfolded on the nightly news.

After our friends had gone and darkness had fallen, Mildred and I had to face the future alone. Instead of sleeping, we laid on the bed and wept. It was tough to control our emotions. I look back now and wonder how I made it without having a heart attack, a stroke, or going into shock. It's amazing what the human system can endure.

Seeing my wife so upset and my family struggling to comprehend what had happened troubled me greatly. I was concerned about my wife, and both of us were concerned about our children, even though they were adults. *How would this affect my grandchildren?* I wondered.

Actually, the people who showed their love most during this time were our daughter Deanna and our grandson Michael, both of whom had been living with us, and our son Rich, his wife Rhonda, their daughter Ivory, and Uriah, their son. They provided a bulwark of strength and brought us great joy and comfort.

Mildred and I had spent a lifetime nourishing our son and daughter both spiritually and physically. Now the blessings had come full circle, and our children were meeting our needs. It was wonderful to behold, and probably the most rewarding thing that happened within our family.

Even though our house was filled with people, and many friends were standing alongside me, I felt very much alone. It was facing myself that I feared the most. I knew I was going to have to pass my own personal challenge.

Adversity like I had never known it before gripped my heart. It almost strangled me with its monstrous tentacles. *How would I handle this kind of test?* I wondered. *Do I have the spiritual strength to endure this blow?* I examined my heart for the answer.

I felt like the biblical character, Job, in his suffering. Job had ten fresh graves on a windswept hill not far from his home. They were the burial sites of his children, who one by one had tragically been killed. His livestock, servants, and finally, his health vanished. Job's friends came to comfort him and give him counsel. At first, they tiptoed gingerly around the ash heap where he mournfully sat. But as time wore on, they started pointing accusing fingers at their friend.

Job searched his heart for the reasons for his suffering. Had he failed God or had God failed him? His integrity was tested to the limit. Whom would he blame? Job's wife expressed it best when she said to him, "Do you still hold to your integrity? Why don't you curse God and die?"

Like Job, my patience soon wore thin under the abrasive rub of adversity. It happens even to the most godly people. If the scraping is hard enough, coarse enough, and lasts long enough, dismay sets in, deteriorating the very fabric of our lives.

The words of the Scottish essayist, Thomas Carlisle, spoke to me. "Adversity is sometimes hard upon a man, but for one man who can stand prosperity, there are a hundred that will stand adversity."

As a mover and a shaker on a vertical climb up the ladder, I had experienced success and prosperity. I realized that adversity tests one's ability to survive; prosperity tests one's integrity. Adversity simplifies life by reducing it to the basics; prosperity complicates it.

Whether on the mountaintop or the valley, whether prosperity or adversity prevails, one thing I knew for sure — the tilt of my neck should be the same. I had to look up to see God. He is the judge over all the earth. He's the one who gives or takes away, who raises us up or brings us down.

Arrogance had spread its cancerous roots throughout my life, and now the scalpel had to cut it away. Jerry Falwell had hit me where it hurt — in the core of my heart — my life. I had been humbled. Exposed, I finally saw what I had become.

Before PTL, I had walked in integrity. Now I searched my heart to see if it still remained. *Who am I?*

Since the days of youthful ministry, I had a pastor's heart, desiring only to serve and help others. But another side of me had taken over in the past two years. Now separation time had come. Was I a huckster or a true shepherd?

I wanted to prove to myself and others that I was still a man of integrity. Could I regain what I had lost?

The true test of integrity comes when no one is looking, when the cameras are turned off and the audience has gone home. How I acted in the shadows of obscurity would reveal my true character. *Can I measure up?* I asked myself.

The words of Edgar A. Guest came to mind: "I'd rather see a sermon than hear one any day; I'd rather one should walk with me, than merely tell the way . . . And, the best of all preachers are the men who live their creed. For to see good put in action is what everybody needs."

In the past, I had been known for my integrity. Not because I was always a righteous person, but because I continually searched myself for any signs of impure motives or ungodly actions. I knew the positions I held in my denomination demanded constant scrutiny and an open heart before God and man.

In light of Roy Grutman's accusations, I tried to apply the same search light to myself. At that point I believed my behavior had been above reproach. Only the Jessica Hahn matter troubled me. My integrity had been called into question because of another person's sin and my willingness to help him keep his sin hidden.

The loss of my previously spotless reputation brought shock and panic, followed by denial. I knew my reaction would only lead to anger and disillusionment. Depression set in. I had to escape.

Because of the media blitz, I wanted to get out of town as quickly as possible. The bombshell had hit Tuesday morning, April 28, about ten o'clock. By that evening I had made up my mind to leave Charlotte before Wednesday night.

Gene Shelton, my administrative assistant, stayed by my side during that time. He was my sounding board, my brother, and my trusted friend. If anybody deserves accolades for his loyalty, Gene certainly does. He bore my sorrows with a maturity beyond his age. Not knowing what his own future held, Gene made a deliberate decision to stay with me for the next several weeks.

The next morning the security people allowed a reporter from *The Charlotte Observer,* Elizabeth Leyland, to get beyond the gate and knock on the door. My wife told her that we weren't talking. She left. I stayed at home the whole day unwilling to face the myriad of media people waiting for me at the end of the driveway.

The one reporter that stood out from all the others was Jack Kelley of *USA Today.* When the Jessica Hahn/Jim Bakker story began to surface Mr. Kelley came to Heritage USA. He asked me if I would tell him what the facts were about the alleged payoff. I had a commitment of confidentiality. I told him that if I revealed the facts, I would have to lie to do it. "No story is worth a lie," was his response. Jack Kelley was always a person of impeccable integrity—he was the most accurate and best recorder of the events of PTL.

In the past, the press had followed us to restaurants and chased us when we left the house. "This time it isn't going to happen," I told Mildred, and we developed a plan. We decided to pack my clothes and the other things I was taking with me to Florida in the car. Someone else would drive the car out. I didn't want to be seen leaving the house.

Our house faced a large lake seventeen miles long. About five o'clock Wednesday evening I got in a boat and crossed the lake to a state park. Several people accompanied me so I wouldn't be noticed. At the same time, three cars were driven out of our driveway, including the car I was going to drive to Florida.

At the time I didn't know I would only return to our home one more time, and that would be after it was empty and before Falwell changed the locks. After that day, our lives would never be the same.

The trip to Florida was one of the most painful experiences of my life. Gene Shelton, my assistant, made the trip with me. As we were driving through Columbia, South Carolina, a city ninety miles south of Charlotte, I began to weep, wailing with near violence. I couldn't come to grips with what had happened. Gene tried unsuccessfully to comfort me.

Each time we stopped, I bought a newspaper. The same story covered the front page of every paper. In Columbia, South Carolina; Savannah, Georgia; Jacksonville and Orlando, Florida; the headlines read the same. When I saw the April 29 edition of *USA Today* with my picture on the front page, it all hit me. *This is for real*, I thought. *I'm gone from PTL! What about my integrity?*

To make matters worse, I had to deal with the fact that I was still under investigation by the Assemblies of God. I had lost the friendship of associates I had known for years. I believed I had lost my ministry. And now I was about to be ousted from the denomination that I loved so much. My heart broke with deep grief.

After going through the torment of being humiliated before the nation and the manner in which it was done by Jerry Falwell, I began to question this man's methods. What kind of Christian would knowingly, with premeditation, subject another brother to such shame and disgrace?

I began to think back over recent events and the way

they had happened. The day Jerry Falwell came out of his first meeting with Jim Bakker he told me Jim had asked him to take over the ministry, providing that PTL's current leadership remained intact.

From that day until the Saturday before I was dismissed, for thirty-seven days, I talked with Jerry Falwell almost every day. I called him at night at home, and he called me. I phoned him in his pickup truck, or he called me in my car. He repeatedly said to me, "I'm only at PTL as long as you are, Richard. If you leave, I'm gone too. I must have you as a transition person, and I'm only here as long as you are."

From the first day he named me president until the day he fired me, Jerry Falwell knew as much as I did about the Jessica Hahn matter. The report Roy Grutman gave to the board of directors came as no surprise to Jerry Falwell. Nothing was revealed that he and Roy Grutman didn't already know. They went through the charade of an investigation that wasn't any investigation at all because they already knew the details of the Jessica Hahn arrangement!

To present to the press this hoax of an investigation was a smoke screen. It was a cover for their scheme to eliminate the leadership of PTL so that they could have the network. Falwell and his men knew as long as I was there, PTL would remain intact under leadership other than their own. They were merely waiting for the opportune time to get complete control. Jerry Falwell and his team had one objective from the very beginning: To seize a network that wasn't theirs.

It's true Jim Bakker gave Jerry Falwell the opportunity he needed. But, when Falwell realized he couldn't manage the operation with me as president, he decided to gain control by firing me and discrediting Jim Bakker. Rather than return the ministry to Jim Bakker, Jerry Falwell decided if he couldn't make it work, he would take PTL into bankruptcy.

Jim Bakker and I talked almost every day. I was surprised when he told me that he had discovered that one of Jerry Falwell's former employees, an associate pastor, had gotten the word to Jim that he had attended a staff session several years before when PTL was discussed. Jim was shocked when the former Falwell employee stated, "Jerry Falwell told us that someday Jim Bakker is going to blow it. When he does, I am going to be there to get the network."

Dr. Bob Gray of Trinity Baptist Church, a close friend of Jerry Falwell's, made some very interesting remarks to his congregation the Sunday before I was fired. The following was transcribed from a tape of the March 15, 1987, Sunday morning service:

> While I was in Germany for the month of March doing missionary work, the news broke on the immorality of the sponsor and emcee of the PTL television club. When I got back, I tried to read as much I could on the news magazines and the papers to find out exactly what happened. It's a tragic mess, and, of course, the thing that perhaps shocks you and shocked me the most was that Dr. Jerry Falwell, who is a very dear personal friend and has been a friend of our church down through the years, took over this ministry and became the chairman of its board.
>
> I have always believed in giving every person an opportunity to speak for himself or to at least explain himself. I don't jump to conclusions and I've always tried to be consistent in my ministry and go as closely as I could by the Bible in handling problems like these.
>
> Let me say, first of all, that Dr. Falwell has been a friend to this ministry like few other preachers of our acquaintance. We love him; we thank God for him. That doesn't mean we always agree with what he does or his position on certain issues. But we do appreciate the fact that he has been a dear and a devoted and dedicated friend and, as far as I'm concerned, he still is.
>
> However, when I learned that he had taken over the chairmanship of this board, I was, frankly, shocked. I could not comprehend what was going on. Then I guess I got one, as you did — I've often recommended to people, if you're lonely send Dr. Falwell a gift and you'll never be lonely again. You'll get more mail than you can keep up with. So, I got one of the letters that he sent out to everybody on his mailing list, asking for money to save the PTL club.
>
> Several of you had told me that you had seen a televised news conference where he was answering questions from the

press. I did not see it, but I take your word for it. You said that on that news conference he said that there would be no change in the format of the PTL club, which meant that the charismatic influence and program would go right on. Well, that shocked me also. So then when I got this letter pleading for money, I felt like that was just absolutely as far as I could go without making an inquiry. I flew to Lynchburg on Thursday. Dr. Falwell gave me an appointment, and I met with him, and I will give you the essence of our conversation.

I started by reminding him of my love for him and my friendship for him personally and thanking him for his interest and help in our church at a time when very few were willing to assist us a few years ago, and I will always be eternally grateful for that.

I said, "Realize that I am only saying this as your friend, I'm not trying to tell you what to do, and I'm not trying to tell you how to conduct your ministry, but as your friend, I think you've made the biggest mistake you've ever made in your life and your ministry by identifying favorably with the PTL format." I said, "I know that you're not charismatic, and unless you've changed since the last time we've talked, in your doctrine, I know that you certainly have not changed to embrace the charismatic position."

He said, "You're absolutely right. I haven't changed one iota. I've always been against it, and I still am. Let me explain to you what my motive is and where I am going.

"When I received word that this was about to happen, I determined that if at all possible I would try to get the PTL network for the 'Old Time Gospel Hour,' and this is the only way that I felt like I could do it."

I said, "Well, I personally don't agree with your methods, and I don't agree with your philosophy. But that's between you and the Lord. But, I do feel that it was wrong for you to identify with this movement."

He said, "My whole purpose — I don't care what happens to the country club down at Charlotte and all of the jamboree stuff that goes on there. I'm only interested in the PTL cable network. It's the largest Christian cable network in the nation, and I'd like to get that for the 'Old Time Gospel Hour.' "

I said, "Well, I feel that you have placed your friends in an indefensible position, and I'm one of them. I am 100% opposed to PTL, and when I got your letter asking for money to save it, my first reaction was, why not go ahead and bury it, and everybody would be a lot better off. I've never felt that

God was in it from the beginning. If that offends you I'm sorry, but that's my honest convictions. I think it's been the biggest religious charade on television that's ever been telecast, and I've been 100% against the charismatic movement. I think it's the devil's counterfeit for the fullness of the Holy Spirit in our generation. I believe that as a matter of strong Bible conviction."

Then he said, "I think that you would also like to know that this coming Tuesday I'm having a press conference, and at that time we plan to expose Jim Bakker, not only for immorality with a woman, but homosexual immorality. Not only him, but Dortch, and all of those in a leadership position on PTL. I plan to fire 1,600 workers on Tuesday, and probably it will be in bankruptcy before too long, and the sooner the better. All I want out of it is the cable network for the Lord."

I said, "Well, that's between you and the Lord, but again, I do not agree with your philosophy of getting it. I do not agree with what you had to do to get it. Millions of people across this nation are confused and wonder what in the world is going on, and why would you suddenly identify with a movement that you've always been in opposition to." And he has. For example, on the application blanks for Liberty University, this question is clearly asked: Do you believe in speaking in tongues, and have you ever spoken in tongues? And if a person says "yes" they don't get enrolled in Liberty University. That's how strong of a stand he's taken in the past. And that stand, he says, will continue.

He also said that he thinks the sooner the organization goes bankrupt, the better off it will be because the assets will then be auctioned and disposed and the network will then be free for purchase, and they hope to purchase it and go on from there.

Well, again, I do not agree with his approach and his philosophy, but I do love him. I am his friend. I was scheduled to be in a conference there in August. But I said, "In all fairness to you and to me, I do not want to be identified in a pro-charismatic position, so I'm canceling the invitation to speak here in August. I could not go back and speak for you until you've taken a clear-cut stand publicly against the charismatic movement per se, and divorced yourself from any association with the present format with PTL."

I feel like I've done the right thing. You may or may not agree with it. I'm just simply telling you what I've done and where I stand on this issue. Only God knows what the outcome of all of this is going to be. I'm just simply saying that I cannot endorse something that I know to be wrong. I cannot be misleading to God's people as far as my position on this is concerned. I've tried, through the years, to be very plain spoken and outspoken as far as where I stand, what I believe, and the issues of the day, and deal with them as scripturally and objectively as I know how.

I want to close by saying this. I love Dr. Falwell. He's still my dear friend. I trust you'll love him and pray for him. But until this issue is clear I hope you'll not send money. I mean that. Until this issue is clear I believe you'll answer to God if you put a dime in PTL or any other charismatic ministry. I believe you'll have to answer to God for it at the judgment seat of Christ. Now that's nothing new. That's a stand I've always taken. But I felt that you needed to know, and I wanted you to know. I appreciate him giving me the time.

I thought this was interesting. He thanked me for asking for the appointment. He thanked me for coming to see him. He said, "I've had a lot of letters from preachers who have written me off, but you're the first preacher of my friends who has come to me and asked to talk to me about this, face to face. I appreciate it more than I can tell you."

I said, "Well, that's the way I've always tried to be, and that's the way I'll continue to be in the future."

So I wanted you to know the full scope of what's happening there. Don't be shocked by what happens in the next few days. It's going to get worse; it's not going to get better, but pray that God will give him wisdom and direction. I was encouraged. I noticed just a little excerpt on the news last night at eleven o'clock that they mentioned this forthcoming news conference on Tuesday and some of the possible developments out of that. Then the commentator made this observation. He said, "Rev. Falwell is having second thoughts about his identification with the PTL because of pressure that he is receiving from preacher friends."

I was glad to hear that. Maybe my voice will count just a little bit to help him at a time when perhaps he needs help as never before. No man is perfect. Keep your eyes on the Lord Jesus, not on people. Keep your convictions on the basis of the Word of God, not on which way people go. That way you'll never have to worry about getting off track spiritually; you'll always be moving in the right direction.

Thank you for your confidence in me and for bearing patiently. A lot of people called as soon as I got home and said,

"What do you think? What do you think?"

I just simply said, "I don't know what I think, and I won't know until I talk to him personally." And I think that's the right way to handle it, and that's the fair way and the scriptural way.

(END OF DR. GRAY'S REMARKS)

How many evangelical leaders knew what was going on and closed their eyes, refusing to take action? Consensual integrity takes place when people know what is going on and do nothing. How does their sin compare to the act Jerry Falwell committed?

Every evangelical leader I have talked to about this matter in the past four and a half years, without exception, has told me they believe Jerry Falwell was trying to grab the PTL network. He really didn't care about Heritage USA, but it was the network he had planned to take all along.

Executive committee members of the National Religious Broadcasters and council members of the Evangelical Council of Fiscal Accountability told me unanimously, "Jerry Falwell was trying to get the network." Yet, not one evangelical leader has ever had the integrity to confront Jerry Falwell about his manipulative plan.

Did Jerry Falwell deceive his own supporters, all of Christendom, and the entire nation with his plot to get control of the PTL network? All the while, Jerry Falwell was pointing an accusing finger at Jim Bakker and me. Is scheming and deceiving as bad as immorality and making secret out of court settlements? Tell me who has paid the greater price for their sin? Are there little sins and big sins?

When I was dismissed from the Assemblies of God because of my involvement in arranging for the out of court settlement for Jessica Hahn, my dismissal letter stated that I was dismissed because of "the non-disclosure of the sins of a brother minister." Many times Christians are disposed to tell things that they shouldn't be talking about. Then, when we try to fashion the facts to protect someone, it can be devastating to our own integrity. That is where the breakdown came between me and my church.

Protestant theology, supposedly, doesn't differentiate between little sins and big sins. Most evangelicals teach that all sin is transgression against the Law of God. Sin is missing the mark. Sin is saying one thing and doing the other. There are no big ones or little ones; they're all the same.

Our Roman Catholic friends, however, believe in venial sins and mortal sins. Perhaps Catholics are more honest and forthright in their theology. They admit the fact they believe in little sins and big sins. Evangelical Protestants say there is no such thing, but we practice it regularly, by our actions and our conduct.

If we're pointing the finger at someone and at the same time doing something as bad or worse ourselves, does that make my sin any better or less significant? Absolutely not.

But it does mean that the significance of a life of integrity is its wholeness — its completeness. What's dirty on one side is dirty on the other. What's clean on one side is clean on the other. There can't be a two-faced, double meaning to the things we do. Our lives are complete in detail, without duplicity. Integrity brings us through adversity whole.

Confused, betrayed, and broken I knew I needed a fresh start.

When Gene and I arrived in Florida, we decided to look for a condo to rent on the beach in Clearwater. A real estate agent showed us an apartment on the eighteenth floor of a gulf-front building.

As we were looking around from room to room, the agent said, "I think I recognize you." I didn't say anything. We went out on the balcony and looked at the gulf.

Then she pointed to a large building on the right and said, "That's where it all happened."

I responded, "Where what happened?"

She said, "That's where Jessica Hahn and Jim Bakker had their rendezvous." I couldn't believe my ears or my eyes. The second building from our condo was the Sheraton Hotel where the infamous events had occurred that brought about this move to Clearwater. I pondered the coincidence many times after we moved into the apartment.

The highrise Sheraton constantly reminded me of something else — the Heritage Grand Towers that I left behind still under construction. Little did I know at the time that the criminal investigation would not center around the Jessica Hahn incident but focus on the availability of lifetime partnerships at Heritage USA.

Eric Watt and his wife, Becky, joined Mildred and me in the same condo building in Clearwater. Here were dear friends helping us to get back on our feet emotionally and spiritually.

Soon we began to integrate into life in Clearwater. Something amazing began to happen. When we would go shopping or walk out on the street, people would stop us and begin to share their broken hearts and buried dreams. Because we were hurting, they knew we would understand their problems. They felt free to share their concerns and burdens with us.

We marveled at the number of professional people, politicians, lawyers, doctors, and ministers who desperately needed someone to whom they could unburden their loss. Although these people knew about my association with PTL, for some reason they disconnected me from the tempest they saw presented on the news. I had been a part of the establishment, and now I wasn't. They felt they could confide in me and I would understand without being judgmental.

I've never considered myself, nor do I now, a professional counselor. My training and experience are not in that area. In the art of human behavior, however, I do view myself, as do others, as a person who cares. I genuinely love people and will listen to their problems and try to help them as effectively as I can.

Some people who came to us needed a job; others needed health care; some needed a lawyer; and most just needed someone to pray with them. All of them needed to be loved, and I can do that as well as anyone. Most people just need help in the very simple, basic matter of living.

That fact seems especially true of professionals, business people, politicians, and ministers. In a time of need, my experience tells me these people are the most helpless. Why? Because they've never had to ask for help before, and they don't know where to turn in times of crisis. Usually, they just need someone to love them and walk through the experience with them. I can do that, I thought.

I had learned long ago that the best way to heal your hurts is to try to help others in a practical way. It's all part of the wholeness, the completeness, the integrity we must know as believers in Jesus Christ.

Some people, for reasons I can understand — although I don't agree with them — tell me they are reluctant to go to their own churches and share personal needs with the minister. Most people of stature feel the social structure of some local churches makes it an unsuitable place to take their problems.

I've always believed the church is the place to go for help. If people don't feel comfortable discussing their personal problems there, however, then we, as the body of Christ, must provide a place where they can come and unburden their hearts. If they will go to an office somewhere, share their problems, and feel secure, then let's make that available to them.

Soon it became apparent to Eric and me that we needed a place where we could counsel and minister to these people and get them beyond their crisis. Eric began to look for a facility, and before long people were coming for help from all over the country.

"What will we call this evolving crisis agency?" I asked Eric.

"I don't know, but we should give it an identity," he added. We had talked about a number of names, but no one seemed to like them.

"I think it would be good if we found a name that had the word 'challenge' in it," I suggested. "I also like the word 'life.' "

Our then nine-year-old grandson looked at me and said, "Pop, why don't you call it Life Challenge?"

"That's it," we all agreed.

When we went to the attorney to tell him our decision, he said, "You've got a winner." He was right. Life Challenge has been operating for approximately three and a half years, caring for people in crisis.

It was a new beginning. I had experienced a life challenge and believed I could help others.

Little did I know that my greatest challenge lay ahead of me.

Dr. Paul Yonggi Cho and Richard Dortch.

13

After Midnight

During the summer of 1988, I went to Robert D'Andrea, the president and chief executive officer of the Christian Television Corporation in Clearwater, Florida, and proposed the format for a late-night call-in program.

"Do you think there's a need for a program where people can call in from all over the nation and request prayer for their spiritual, physical, and material needs?" I asked Bob. "There seem to be a lot of hurting people we could minister to after midnight."

To my surprise and joy, this spiritual leader and businessman replied, "Actually, I have been praying about developing such a program for many years," Robert answered, "and the time has come. What I needed was someone to do it live, late at night."

We began a one-hour television program, five nights a week, on satellite throughout the United States that was simultaneously broadcast by the Christian Radio Network. Using an intimate studio setting, we had only myself and our pianist, Mark Moody, under the lights, on camera.

Although the media continued to flood the airwaves with stories of PTL, Jim Bakker, and Richard Dortch, it did not affect our ministry at CTN. In fact, an average of only about two or three callers a month even brought up the subject of PTL. In almost fifteen months of broadcasting, I do not remember any embarrassing moments on the program. People, in their mercy and kindness, had separated me from PTL and the events that had taken place.

Mercy overshadowed me. I knew that I was not walking alone, and I had the consciousness that everything was going to turn out all right. A higher plan and purpose was in operation.

Did the Almighty want this tragedy to happen? I think not. Did God let it happen? Of course. But I do not confuse my own failures with the perfect plan of a compassionate God. He doesn't throw us away because we have failed, but He does heal our hurts and forgives our sins.

During my appearances on "Larry King Live," the "Geraldo Show," the Ted Koppel program, "Nightline," on television programs all over the nation, and in newspaper articles, I repeatedly said, "Please forgive me. Please, forgive me. I am sorry." I meant it because I was truly sorry.

When I pled guilty to the charges against me in federal court, it was because I *was* guilty of what the government said. How could I look at hundreds of hours of television tapes and say that I did not do what the government alleged? It was an experience which I regret.

I wrote hundreds of letters to friends and associates asking for forgiveness. I spent many nights in tears. Without success, I tried to learn how to set aside what I couldn't change.

One day my wife and I were in a restaurant and, all of a sudden, sorrow gripped me. I started to weep. My wife had to lead me out of the restaurant because I was crying so profusely. People must have thought that I was in pain or that some tragedy had befallen us. They were right.

Fearful that people might hurt me, I was psychologically in a state of trauma. I lived in that condition for months.

One Saturday afternoon, I was so broken and lonely I didn't want to stay in the house. The burden I was carrying had become so heavy, I had to get some relief. At that time, the prospect of the grand jury had just surfaced, and the thought of prison was more than I could handle.

After driving up in the northern part of Pinellas County, near our home, I felt I desperately needed to talk to someone. I didn't dare go to a pastor. In my mind, I could see him calling his friends as soon as I left to tell them, "Guess who was just here?" Having gone through the religious "holy war" at PTL, I didn't trust too many people, especially preachers.

Passing a beautiful Catholic church, I saw a car parked near the rear entrance. Supposing that a priest was there, I stopped and went to the vestry. The priest embraced me with open arms and prayed with me. He touched my broken heart. Finally, I'd found someone whom, I knew, would keep my visit between him and God.

I drove away thinking to myself, *Why did I have to come here? Why can't I feel I can have trust?* At that time, my state of mind and my broken spirit made it impossible for me to believe I wouldn't be bashed again. In my mind, the rejection I had received from my own church crushed me to the point of despair.

Every night near midnight, however, I sensed God's overwhelming presence. Knowing it was time for the telecast and I would be helping others brought me out of my anguish.

Across the atrium from the office where we were operating Life Challenge, Dr. Alfred Fireman, a psychiatrist, had his practice. We got to know one another.

One day, while talking to him outside of his office, I told him, "I think I need to have a professional visit."

It dawned on me that we don't hesitate to go to a medical doctor when our stomach aches or our foot is sore. But when our mind is hurting, we attach all kinds of spiritual ambiguity to being treated by a psychologist or psychiatrist.

From the very beginning, this loving and caring doctor shared his perspective of psychiatric care. "Some psychiatrists may attack the patient's faith," he told me, "but I believe a person needs his faith to build on when going through a crisis."

In consultations or therapy with me, Dr. Fireman did his best to strengthen my faith. During that period of time, I saw him on a regular basis, and he offered me hope and showed me how to manage my emotions. More than a doctor, he was a friend who helped me with my mental and physical needs during this critical time in my life. For that I am deeply grateful to him. He is one of the reasons I made it through my crisis.

Herman Bailey and his wife Sharon, who host a television program "Action Sixties," and Robert D'Andrea and his wife Molly, also ministered to me with their love and encouragement. From day to day, as I spent time with Robert and Herman, I drew strength from them. They were my pals.

Four or five months after coming to the Clearwater/Tampa Bay area, I did not attend church anywhere. In fact, I did not go into a church building except on that one occasion to see the priest. I was so fearful, I wouldn't even go to any community activities. The PTL program had been carried on all the local cable systems, and the extensive coverage of the PTL disaster by *The Tampa Tribune, The St. Petersburg Times*, and the local TV stations kept my name and face in the news.

Although not yet convicted of any crimes, still I felt the public believed I was not an honorable man. What had I done?

Was it so wrong to try to help a friend who needed my help? Was it dishonest of me not to make his sin public — a sin that happened four years before I even knew about it. Was I a liar and a cheat for trying to help arrange an out of court settlement with a lady who was blackmailing him? My sin was not admitting I had helped.

In my mind I could hear people across America shouting, "Yes, you're guilty. You're not a man of integrity!"

I had poured out my heart and soul to God and to people, yet I was still criticized, belittled, and berated. I knew God and a host of people had forgiven me, but the question kept surfacing in my mind and spirit, *What do you do after you have said I'm sorry?*

What do you do after you have confessed everything that you know? What do you do after people have beaten on you for so long and the media won't stop? How do you survive and rise above it all? How do you put your life together again?

Those questions ricochetted through my emotions, ripping at every part of my being. *Oh, God, where are You?*

"Why don't you come to church with Sharon and me this Sunday?" Herman Bailey urged one day.

"Where do you attend?" I asked.

"The Pinellas Park Wesleyan Church," Herman answered.

I had only heard of the Wesleyan church a few times in my life. Sensing my need for fellowship with other Christians after such a long time, Mildred and I decided to accept the Bailey's invitation.

That first Sunday at Pinellas Park, something unusual occurred in the service. After singing several hymns, the pastor, in a very warm and loving way, asked Mindy to come to the platform. This petite, twentyish girl literally ran to the platform. As she approached the front of the church, everyone stood and applauded.

Then, at the same time two ladies each holding a dozen roses stepped out from opposite sides of the platform. While the congregation continued to stand and applaud, the pastor gave Mindy the roses and asked the people to be seated.

He put his arm around her and said, "Mindy, you have been gone for two and a half years, and many of these people don't know who you are. For you friends who do not know, Mindy is one of our own precious girls who has just been released after two and a half years in the Florida Prison for Women. She was involved in a drunk driving accident, and she is a part of our family. Mindy, how many of these people have written to you or come to see you since you went to prison?"

She looked up with a beautiful smile and said, "Pastor, I quit counting after a thousand."

At that point in my own life, I knew a grand jury had

been called and that I could be sentenced to jail if convicted. I touched my wife and said, "Honey, we are at home."

Pastor and Mrs. Larry Freeman became dear friends, along with other members of their staff and church. No one going through the turmoil we were experiencing could have found a more loving and warm group of people. They sheltered, protected, and cared for us without recrimination, finger-pointing, or fault finding. I repeatedly reminded the pastor that he had a church where the people acted like Christians.

Pastor Donald Lunsford, of the First Assembly of God in Clearwater, also expressed his love and kindness. He and his wife Beverly came to our side anytime we needed them. Gordon Matheny, Tommy Waldron, and Glenn Harris reached out to me in genuine love. Rev. J. Foy Johnson, an executive of our church, with his wife, expressed their concern often. Karl and Joyce Strader were faithful, loving friends. Dr. Dale Berkey came to see me, called, and wrote often. He cared.

Still, something within me kept me bound by fear and condemnation. I know now what I was longing for at that time. I was searching for my lost integrity. I wanted to be right with God, and I wanted to be right with men.

When you are a rejected minister, you feel you are of no value to God or man. That's how I felt. I knew I had lost everything. I was dead. They had not as yet removed the articles from my body and buried me. But I knew the time was coming.

I have always tried to walk in integrity. I learned it in a relationship with God, and at the feet of my godly mother and father, from my pastors and churches. Truth and integrity have been my goals as a human being, a Christian, and as a churchman, but most of all, as a person.

Now I had lost it! It seemed that not too many cared.

Musings of PTL days . . . Rather than trying to be a big-time Christian politician, TV evangelist, denominational officer, why not just try to be a simple Christian? . . . "By this shall all men know that ye are my disciples, that ye love one another?" . . . It has always puzzled me why people bash one another. When Christians do it, I am very sad.

The Washington representative of the National Association of Evangelicals, Robert Dugan, was one of the, if not *the*, meanest person in his public comments about PTL. Dugan crucified PTL. He knew only what the press and Jerry Falwell was saying. He had never heard any other side of the story. Yet he joined the chorus to crucify PTL. Whatever happened to 1 Corinthians 13? In some cases the secular press was kind, comforting, loving, and fair.

When the president of the Evangelical Council of Fiscal Accountability, the watchdog of evangelical and TV ministries, had a moral failure several years later, there was no public statement, no condemnation. It was a fine-tuned cover up. To my knowledge, this is the first time it has been told publicly. They had been warned about their president, Arthur Borden, before. I had warned them in 1985. It was easier to cover up ECFA's problems. Dick Chapin, the chairman of ECFA at the time, knew of Borden's lapses. I told him about a conflict of interest in 1985.

At the end of 1985, I contacted Ben Armstrong, the president of the National Association of Religious Broadcasters, to tell him of my concern for our Christian television industry at that time. Not one of the top 10 daily Christian TV programs belonged to the Evangelical Council of Fiscal Accountability. I did not trust Arthur Borden, its president, and my assessment of him proved to be right. I did feel that the National Religious Broadcasters needed their own accountability agency to give credibility to its ministries. Ben and I agreed that we should call the TV ministries together. We did that. A small group of us met in Washington, and it began. I met with Ben Armstrong in 1988 in Clearwater, Florida. Ben encouraged me when he said, "Richard, I know you are going through a lot, but remember, it was your idea that gave birth to the NRB having its own accountability program." That will surprise a lot of people.

Richard Dortch and Efrem Zimbalist, Jr.

14

Pleading Guilty

My television appearances on "Larry King Live," the "Geraldo Show," Ted Koppel's "Nightline," and other national programs gave me an opportunity to talk about Life Challenge. Many local and regional TV programs from Seattle to Miami also interviewed me, asking questions about my involvement at PTL and my views on the electronic church.

The American University in Washington, DC, asked me to give a lecture, as did a symposium of newspaper reporters and editors in Phoenix, Arizona. I was invited to speak at Kiwanis Clubs, Rotary Clubs, and churches. In fact, one church denomination invited me to speak at their national convention.

Florida's Tiger Bay Clubs, noted for their ability to procure well-known politicians and speakers, asked me to participate in one of their tough question and answer lecture programs. At each meeting an award is given to the member who asks the most difficult question of the night, but I was treated kindly and fairly.

In addition to doing radio interviews and talk shows constantly, I was trying to carry on the work of helping people at Life Challenge. It was good to stay busy and not be preoccupied with the events swirling around me.

Every morning I purchased a copy of *USA Today*. That's where I first read that perhaps the government might involve itself in the matters that had transpired at Heritage USA.

Concerned, and wanting to know more, I asked someone who had worked in the highest levels of government in Washington to look into the matter. He was able to find out that the Justice Department and the states of North Carolina and South Carolina did not plan or anticipate any legal action in the PTL matters. My friend assured me that, because it was a church issue, the government did not want to touch it with a ten foot pole.

Not long after I was given this assurance, the Attorney General of the United States, Edwin Meese, gave the commencement address at Liberty University in Lynchburg, Virginia. Jerry Falwell, Liberty's founder and chancellor, then invited Attorney General and Mrs. Meese to spend time with the Falwells. A few weeks later the announcement was made that a grand jury was being called.

I shouldn't have been surprised. Jerry Falwell could get what he wanted in the Reagan administration, and he wanted Jim Bakker and me. Edwin Meese was willing to help.

The events at Heritage USA focused around a 3:00 p.m. news conference held daily by Jerry Falwell or one of his team. Jerry Nims and the key Falwell operative, Harry Hargrave, for weeks had been demanding that the federal government take legal action against the former leadership of PTL.

"Why isn't legal action being taken?" Jerry Nims would ask the press almost daily. "There's an $80,000,000 black hole in the funds. How did that money disappear? We want some answers."

USA Today and other media quickly reported that $80,000,000 was missing at PTL. It was front page news . . . in color. The press coverage along with Jerry Nims and

Harry Hargrave constant haranguing put pressure on the government to take action.

When the black hole story was released, I was too ashamed to even show my face in public. The press and even some televangelists ridiculed and harassed me over the air. Surely, the leadership of the National Religious Broadcasters and the evangelical community will intervene, I thought. They never said a word. Consensual integrity was in operation.

What about the black hole?

While the allegations mentioned in *USA Today's* front page story had the intended effect, no one ever missed the $80,000,000 because it wasn't missing. Few people read the newspapers closely enough to see that two days later, on a page toward the back, they learned that there wasn't any black hole after all. Neither the government investigators, the IRS, nor the postal service ever brought up the subject to me, their so-called principal witness. I participated in four judicial processes — for myself, Jim Bakker, David and James Taggart, and Samuel Johnson — but the United States attorneys and prosecutors didn't question me about the supposed black hole. Not once!

Why? Because Jerry Falwell, Jerry Nims, and Harry Hargrave had orchestrated another falsehood to manipulate circumstances for their proposed takeover of the satellite television network. They knew the black hole was a myth and that $80,000,000 was not missing from PTL funds.

Why then would Jerry Falwell and his men discredit the very organization they were trying to revitalize?

Instead of putting the past behind them and building for the future, Falwell's team had only one objective in mind — to destroy PTL. When it appeared the government was going to take a hands-off approach, Falwell fabricated the story of the black hole and turned up the heat, forcing the Federal government to respond.

The morning I picked up *USA Today* and read that a grand jury was going to be called, chills went up and down my spine and fear gripped me. In shock, I continued to read the report.

If you're not doing anything wrong, why worry? I thought, still believing that truth and justice would prevail. How naive! I chided myself. I hadn't done "anything wrong" in the out of court settlement for Jessica Hahn, but I ended up being fired. That memory jolted me back to reality.

In the early part of May, 1987, I made a trip to Charlotte to contact a businessman friend. He tried to encourage me but also advised that I obtain legal counsel.

The in-house attorney at PTL had already told me what my friend was suggesting, when she said, "Pastor Dortch, you probably need to see a lawyer. If you simply tell the truth," she assured me, "everything will be all right."

"The only attorney you should even think about contacting is Mr. William Diehl," the businessman recommended. I had heard of Bill Diehl and had read about him in the newspapers, but I had never met him. He was a bit of a legend in Charlotte.

When I called his office to make an appointment, I was quite surprised when this brash person came on the phone and said, "This is Bill Diehl. What do you want?"

I said, "This is Richard Dortch, and I would like to talk to you."

His response was, "I've got no use for preachers, much less television preachers."

I said, "Mr. Diehl, I'm not taking a poll. I'm looking for a lawyer. I'd like to come and see you."

He quickly stated, "Are you aware of the fact that I'm one of the meanest lawyers in North Carolina?"

I said, "You're probably a pussy cat."

When we had that exchange, I knew I had made a friend.

"Oh, all right," he replied, agreeing to meet with me the following week.

Later, when we became dear friends, he said he knew I had his number when I answered him the way I did.

I returned to Charlotte the next week, and Bill Diehl assigned a young attorney, Mark Calloway, who had recently joined the staff of the law firm, to work directly with me in the case. In those first few meetings with Bill Diehl and Mark Calloway, I told them everything I knew about PTL, everything I had done, and everything I was aware of that had transpired at Heritage USA. We covered all of my activities at PTL. Those long, tedious sessions often lasted until one or two in the morning.

When we were informed that a grand jury was being called for the month of August 1987, my concern heightened. Still I hoped that when the truth came out the problems being investigated would be resolved. At the time, I knew absolutely nothing about criminal law, but in the months that followed I received a quick education.

Mark Calloway and Bill Diehl tried to find out what the government wanted to know. Once my lawyers were informed that I was one of the targets of the grand jury investigation, they advised me not participate in the grand jury activities.

The Honorable Robert Potter, chief judge of the United States District Court of Western North Carolina, admonished the grand jury not to divulge any information spoken in the grand jury room. He must have done a splendid job of convincing them. In the sixteen months they were in session, at no time did I or my attorneys hear any disclosure, by anyone, of what took place in the grand jury room.

Witnesses who testified before the grand jury, however, were permitted to tell what they had discussed before the grand jury. That was our only source of information.

From the beginning, I told my wife and children that, if indicted, I would not agree to go to trial. Emotionally drained by the events of the last year, I could not bring myself to think about the distress and publicity a trial would bring.

I told my family and my dearest friends, "I am as much afraid of developing a malicious attitude as I am of being found guilty." I knew that a sour, mean spirit, once it is given life, grows until it consumes the person and everyone around him. I wanted no part of that.

"Going to trial would be an ugly, divisive procedure," I told them. "If I am charged with something, I will admit my guilt to whatever I have done wrong and seek to resolve it. If there is a penalty, I will have to pay it."

As the grand jury proceeded, word came to us from witnesses about the kinds of questions they were being asked. This information indicated the likely possibility that I would be indicted.

That was confirmed, when in October of 1988, my lawyers and I were served with letters from the United States Attorney's office stating that if we wanted to volunteer to come before the grand jury, we would be welcome.

"What does that mean?" I asked my attorneys, Mark and Bill.

"That's usually the last thing that's done prior to a federal indictment," they told me frankly. "But we don't think you should appear before the grand jury."

I followed their advice, hoping and praying for the best but expecting the worst.

On December 6, 1988, Bill Diehl called me in Clearwater about two o'clock in the afternoon and said, "It's happened, you've been indicted."

Dismay and unbelief swept over me. I didn't know what to think. At that point, the significance of the event hadn't dawned on me.

Then I received by fax a copy of the indictment. It seemed I was reading about someone else. I had never been in legal trouble before.

Jim Bakker, David and James Taggart, and myself had been indicted. How could I a pastor — a long-time denominational official, an ordained minister of the gospel — be indicted? It seemed unreal.

In laymen's language, the principal charges stated that we had offered lifetime partnerships on television, had used the mail and the telephone to do so, and were charged with wire and mail fraud. It further declared that we had committed these acts in conjunction with another person, thus a conspiracy. In the recitation of the articles of indictment, other allegations were made, but the core of the indictments were the charges concerning lifetime partnerships.

This can't be happening, I told myself. *I'm not a criminal. After all, I have preached in penitentiaries and gone to jails to get people out of trouble,* I argued with myself. *I've even had judges put people on probation under my authority and worked on cases helping prosecutors and defense lawyers.*

Now none of that seemed to matter.

All I could do was cry. The strength of my wife Mildred made it possible for me to go on from day to day. Somehow I had to face the reality of the situation.

From the beginning of this whole ordeal, my commitment to God remained the same and, to this day, has not changed. Through it all, I never questioned God. I knew He had not forsaken me and that ultimately I would see His hand of deliverance in this entire episode. That thought gave me hope.

I took great satisfaction in the fact that God also knew my heart. His understanding and forgiveness drew me closer to Him, deepening my love and commitment to my Saviour. I knew that when I went to PTL I had never intended or planned to defraud anyone.

Intent, is taken into account by our heavenly Father. In the legal process here on earth, I quickly realized that intent is a perception, it only comes into play on "Perry Mason" and "Matlock." In my memory, not once in the process of determining my involvement at PTL did the subject of intent surface. It was what you did, not why you did it. Perhaps we were all paid too much, but every penny I received from PTL was approved by the Board of Directors.

At the time the indictments were handed down, I secured the services of another attorney, Mr. George Tragos, a former chief assistant United States attorney in Tampa, Florida. Mr. Tragos' experience in federal cases and understanding of the federal process made him a valuable asset.

After conferring with federal officials to determine where we stood, my attorneys decided to start the normal legal process and see what developed. A trial date had been set and was quickly approaching. I realized that if God was going to deliver me, it would have to be soon.

The greatest part of what Mildred and I had worked for and saved during the thirty-eight years of our ministry was being spent toward legal fees. We had sold much of what we had. It seemed pointless to prolong the spending or the agony any longer.

At that point I held firm to my decision and was finally able to convince my attorneys and my family what I had been telling them all along. "I will not go to trial."

"If we get a change of venue and a severance from your co-defendant, Jim Bakker," my lawyers argued, "we might have a chance. Who knows? We might even win if we go to trial."

"I'm willing to go that route," I agreed, "if the Lord works out something."

The wheels of justice turn slowly. By the time I found out that the judge had denied both the change of venue and the severance, I was already in the process of making my guilty plea. That convinced me, more than anything, that I was walking in the plan God was permitting.

"I want to talk to the federal prosecutors," I finally insisted.

"Okay," my attorneys agreed reluctantly, "but they are the ones to make that decision, not us."

The United States officials were willing to talk, and a meeting was arranged.

"We're afraid for you, Pastor Dortch," my lawyers objected. "We don't want you to do anything that could be harmful in the future." At that point, my lawyers gave me a letter stating they would not be responsible for what happened.

I appreciated their concern but felt confident God was leading me. "I feel this is the right thing to do," I told them.

Although I didn't know fully what pleading guilty meant, I reasoned in my mind and told my attorneys: "I do not have several sets of testimony, and I don't know different twists to the events. I only have one story to tell about what happened to me at PTL, and my knowledge of the incidents

UNITED STATES DISTRICT COURT FOR THE
WESTERN DISTRICT OF NORTH CAROLINA
CHARLOTTE DIVISION

UNITED STATES OF AMERICA   )   DOCKET NO. C-CR-88-205
)
vs.   )
)
JAMES O. BAKKER AND   )
RICHARD W. DORTCH, Defendants)

DEFENDANT DORTCH'S MOTION FOR CHANGE OF VENUE

Defendant Richard W. Dortch, by and through counsel and pursuant to Federal Rule of Criminal Procedure 21(a), moves the Court for an order transferring the trial of this matter from the Western District of North Carolina. In support of the Motion, Defendant shows the following:

1. Rule 21(a) of the Federal Rules of Criminal Procedure provides for a transfer of the criminal proceeding on motion of the defendant upon a showing of prejudice:

> The court upon motion of the defendant shall transfer the proceeding as to that defendant to another district whether or not such district is specified in the defendant's motion if the court is satisfied that there exists in the district where the prosecution is pending so great a prejudice against the defendant that the defendant cannot obtain a fair and impartial trial at any place fixed by law for holding court in that district.

2. Rule 21(a) "is intended for cases in which prejudice in the community will make it difficult or impossible to select a fair and impartial jury." Wright, Federal Practice and Procedure: Criminal 2d §342, p. 247 (1982). The widespread, adverse and sensational media coverage of the various controversies surrounding PTL, the grand jury investigation and subsequent indictment of the Defendants in this case, has created so great a prejudice against this Defendant that he cannot obtain a fair and impartial trial in this district.

3. Defendant is compiling evidence that will show that not only has there been years of widespread and often times unfavorable publicity in this district concerning the operation of PTL, a central issue in this case, but that in recent times the grand jury investigation, and the resulting indictment of Defendants Dortch

and Bakker, have received widespread publicity (both on television and in the newspaper) in this district which is highly damaging in this Defendant's ability to get a fair trial.

4. By way of example, since 1986, the Charlotte Observer has published thousands of news articles on PTL, co-Defendant Bakker, or Dortch. With respect to local newspaper coverage of the grand jury investigation alone, the <u>Charlotte Observer</u> has published numerous news items. Particularly damaging were the ill-advised comments of Bankruptcy Judge Rufus Reynolds concerning Defendant Bakker and his management of PTL, which were published in the <u>Charlotte Observer</u> on Sunday, January 1, 1989.

WHEREFORE, Defendant Dortch moves the court (1) to hold a hearing on this matter at which Defendant will offer evidence and legal argument in support of his Motion, and (2) thereafter enter an order transferring this case to another district.

Defendant requests additional time to file legal memorandum and documents in support of this Motion within such reasonable time as the Court sets.

This the *13th* day of April, 1989.

JAMES, McELROY & DIEHL, P.A.

By _____
William K. Diehl, Jr.

_____
Mark T. Calloway
600 South College
Charlotte, N.C. 28202
(704) 372-9870

George Tragos
1755 U.S. Highway 19 South
Suite 333
Clearwater, Florida 34624

UNITED STATES DISTRICT COURT FOR THE
WESTERN DISTRICT OF NORTH CAROLINA
CHARLOTTE DIVISION

UNITED STATES OF AMERICA	)	DOCKET NO. C-CR-88-205
	)	
vs.	)	
	)	
JAMES O. BAKKER AND	)	
RICHARD W. DORTCH, Defendants	)	

DEFENDANT DORTCH'S RULE 14 MOTION FOR SEVERANCE

Defendant Richard W. Dortch, by and through counsel and
pursuant to Federal Rules of Criminal Procedure, Rule 14, moves the
Court to order that the trial of this Defendant be severed from
that of Defendant Bakker.   In support of the Motion, Defendant
shows the following:

1.   Federal Rules of Criminal Procedure, Rule 14 provides for
separate trials if a defendant would be prejudiced by a joint
trial:

>   If it appears that a defendant...is prejudiced by
>   a joinder of defendants in an indictment...or by such
>   joinder for trial together, the court may...grant a
>   severance of defendants or provide whatever relief
>   justice requires. In ruling on a motion by a defendant
>   for severance, the court may order the attorney for the
>   government to deliver to the court for inspection in
>   camera any statements or confessions made by the
>   defendants which the government intends to introduce in
>   evidence at the trial.

F.R.Crim.Pro. Rule 14

2.   There is a reasonable likelihood that Defendants Bakker
and Dortch will assert different and antagonistic defenses, such

that unless a severance is granted, Defendant Dortch will be prejudiced in his ability to receive a fair trial.

3. It appears that at trial Defendant Dortch will want to use the testimony of co-Defendant Bakker. Defendant Dortch cannot require Defendant Bakker to testify at a trial in which both are charged. Therefore, a severance is necessary.

4. There has been relentless adverse publicity surrounding Defendant Bakker, and he appears to have an endless desire for publicity in general, such that this adverse publicity will spill over to Defendant Dortch and prejudice his ability to receive a fair trial unless a severance is granted.

WHEREFORE, Defendant Dortch moves the Court to (1) hold a hearing on this matter at which Defendant will offer evidence and legal argument in support of his Motion, and (2) thereafter enter an order severing the trial of Defendant Dortch from the trial of Defendant Bakker.

Defendant requests additional time to file legal memorandum in support of this Motion within such reasonable time as the Court sets.

This the 14th day of April, 1989.

JAMES, McELROY & DIEHL, P.A.

By: _____
William K. Diehl, Jr.

_____
Mark T. Calloway
600 South College Street
Charlotte, N.C. 28202
(704) 372-9870

George Tragos
1755 U.S. Highway 19 South
Suite 333
Clearwater, Florida 34624

Attorneys for Defendant Dortch

involved is accurate.

"Besides, if Jim Bakker and I have to stand trial," I further reasoned. "I'll be subpoenaed to testify at his trial. When I testify I'm going to tell the truth, so why delay the issue and go to trial? Why not just tell the truth now?"

My argument prevailed, and a date was set for a private meeting to discuss the issues with the government prosecutors.

Mr. Tragos, our attorney from the Clearwater area, my wife Mildred, and I went to Charlotte where we met Bill Diehl and Mark Calloway.

"How do you think the prosecutors feel about me?" I asked, quizzing my lawyers at great lengths about their impressions.

"All we can tell you," they answered, "is that the government attorneys have heard the testimony about you and seen hundreds of television tapes. But they don't really know you."

My lawyers were convinced, as I was, that as I talked to the prosecutors I would have a better opportunity to let them really know the man, Richard Dortch. I was willing to accept responsibility for any actions that I had taken.

I walked into the room with my three lawyers. Sitting around a large table were an assistant attorney general of the United States, several criminal investigators for the Internal Revenue Service, several United States postal inspectors, and two United States attorneys, one from Washington, D.C., and the other from the Western District of North Carolina, and others.

My lawyers and I sat down and began to discuss the issues at hand with the officials of the government. When it came time for me to speak, I said something like this:

> I am here today against the advice of my attorneys. Their counsel is that I proceed on with these issues. I'm here because my lawyers tell me that you are the ones who hold my fate. You are the prosecutors. Whether or not there is some way we

can bring this to an end without going to trial, I suppose will be determined by this meeting. My lawyers tell me that you are not interested in discussing an end to this case without first interviewing me.

I have been wanting to talk to the government since the investigation began, but have been advised not to do so, because I was a target. Since this investigation began I have been destroyed financially, physically, mentally, and emotionally. I have been humiliated. My family and friends know that it has crippled me physically.

I want you to know that I have not intended to defraud anyone, anytime, any place. I was at Heritage USA, PTL, for three years and three months. I went there with an agreement to work there for five years, and I have worked hard to accomplish what I could while I was there. I did not, before I came, while I was there, and since, control the leadership of Jim Bakker. The suggestion that I intended to bring harm to anyone is erroneous. We made mistakes, we may have been fiscally irresponsible. We may not have listened to advice when we should have. If I had it to do over again I might try to exert more control than I did. But at no time was there an intent, or even a feeling, that we were going to offer something that we could not produce.

I will tell you the truth during this meeting today about what I know. If you have a document about a subject, show it to me and I will do my best to explain it. I would like to leave this meeting feeling that whatever your opinions were of me before we met, you have a little better understanding of who I am. It is my hope and prayer that we will bring to an end, very soon, this tragedy. I do not want to experience a six to eight week trial. I want to do what is right.

As I spoke, my fears left me. I knew I was telling the truth so I was not afraid of anything I had to say. My lawyers were concerned. But they, too, knew by my disclosures that I had told the truth from the beginning.

As the day progressed, I was questioned for many hours by the officials of the United States government.

After a lengthy period of time, they commented, "We want to thank you for appearing today, Mr. Dortch. We believe you have made an effort to be candid with us. We will assess the information you have provided." The session ended with the understanding that they would be meeting again with my attorneys to discuss my future.

Assessing the information and working with my lawyers, however, took much longer than expected. We were quickly approaching the deadline for making any kind of a plea agreement before trial. Soon we'd reach the point of no return.

Finally, our attorneys, together with the officials of the United States, began negotiations on the possibility of a plea agreement.

During this process, I walked around like a zombie, being led from place to place. Knowing I was going to plead guilty before a judge left me drained and stirred up an unusual bag of emotions. One moment I would feel relief at the prospect of getting the matter settled; the next I'd be overcome with terror at the thought of possibly going to prison.

Working on the plea agreement was not an easy process. There were at least nine different revisions. Because of the intense negotiations, my lawyer felt it best for Mildred and I to come back to Charlotte for the four or five days it would take.

Every version of the plea agreement had to be agreed upon by the United States attorneys in Charlotte and be approved by the Justice Department in Washington. Working toward the deadline set by the Western District of North Carolina for finalization of a plea agreement, we ultimately presented our final offer to them. It was accepted.

As the agreement shows, I consented to give truthful answers whenever called upon by the United States. At no time, was Jim Bakker, or any other defendant, mentioned.

The Charlotte Observer and the media in general, however, posed the lie that I agreed to testify against Jim Bakker. I never said that — ever. I agreed to tell the truth when called upon. For that reason, I included in this book, the complete true and accurate copy of my plea agreement with the United States.

After the plea agreement was accepted by the federal prosecutors, it had to be approved by the judge. My lawyers thought it best that Mildred, our son Rich, and I, go with them and the United States attorneys, Deborah Smith and Jerry Miller, to the chambers of the judge, the Honorable Robert Potter.

After my lawyers introduced us to Judge Potter, they explained to him — for the first time — who I was, the kind of work I was involved in, and what I had done with my life. The prosecutors presented their case, and Judge Potter was presented both sides of the reasons for the plea agreement. This took a good deal of time.

At the conclusion Judge Potter looked at me and asked, "Do you know what you are doing? Are you doing this of your own volition?"

"Yes, Your Honor," I replied.

"Has anyone promised you anything?" he questioned.

"No, sir, they have not — other than the terms that are written in the agreement," I answered, knowing it was going to be a public document.

"I will accept the plea agreement and the limitations of it," he stated.

I had agreed to plead guilty to offering lifetime partnerships on "The Jim and Tammy Show," and that I did so by phone, by wire, and by mail. That made the charges wire fraud and mail fraud. That I did it with someone else made it a conspiracy.

There were four counts of those three offenses. For purposes of sentencing, each of the two were grouped to-

UNITED STATES DISTRICT COURT FOR THE
WESTERN DISTRICT OF NORTH CAROLINA
CHARLOTTE DIVISION

UNITED STATES OF AMERICA	)	DOCKET NO. C-CR-88-205
	)	
v.	)	PLEA AGREEMENT
	)	
RICHARD W. DORTCH	)	

NOW COMES the United States of America, by and through Thomas J. Ashcraft, United States Attorney for the Western District of North Carolina, and the defendant, Richard W. Dortch, in his own person, and by and through his attorneys, William K. Diehl, Jr. and Mark T. Calloway, who state the following unto the Court:

1. INTRODUCTION

This document contains the complete plea agreement between the United States Attorney's Office for the Western District of North Carolina and Richard W. Dortch, the defendant. No other agreement, understanding, promise, or condition between the United States Attorney's Office and Richard W. Dortch exists, nor will such agreement, understanding, promise or condition exist unless it is committed to writing in an amendment attached to this document and signed by Richard W. Dortch, an attorney for Mr. Dortch and an attorney for the United States Attorney's Office.

2. THE DEFENDANT'S OBLIGATION

A. Richard W. Dortch shall appear in open court in the Western District of North Carolina and plead guilty to Counts 7, 10 and 14 as set forth in the Bill of Indictment against Richard W. Dortch that was filed December 5, 1988 and Count 24, as stated in the Indictment and amended by consent in Paragraph 4(K) of this agreement. Mr. Dortch admits and avers that he is, in fact, guilty of counts 7, 10 and 14 of the Indictment and Count 24 as stated in the Indictment and amended by consent in paragraph 4(K) of this agreement.

B. Mr. Dortch shall cooperate with the United States Attorney's Office and the Department of Justice by providing truthful, complete, and forthright information whenever, wherever, to whomever, and in whatever form an attorney from the United States Attorney's Office or the Department of Justice requests. The term "whatever form" includes, but is not limited to, oral responses to questions; sworn, written statements; interrogatories; sworn testimony before a grand jury; sworn testimony in court; and documentary materials. The term "whomever" includes, but is not limited to, all Federal criminal law enforcement agencies.

3. <u>THE UNITED STATES ATTORNEY'S OFFICE OBLIGATIONS</u>

If Richard W. Dortch completely fulfills all of his obligations under this plea agreement, an attorney for the United States Attorney's Office or the Department of Justice shall:

A. At sentencing and any subsequent Rule 35 hearing, fully inform appropriate probation officials and the sentencing judge of the extent and value of the defendant's cooperation under the terms of paragraph 2(3) of this plea agreement;

- 2 -

B.   Ask the sentencing judge at the time of sentencing to
dismiss any remaining charges contained in the indictment against
Richard W. Dortch that was filed December 5, 1988.

C.   Bring no additional criminal charges in the Western
District of North Carolina, or the District of South Carolina or
elsewhere, against Richard W. Dortch relating to or arising from
his activities and employment at Heritage Village Church and
Missionary Fellowship, Inc., also known as PTL.   Nothing herein
shall prevent the Government from using appropriate process to
collect a fine or restitution if any is ordered.

D.   Bring no additional criminal tax charges based on matters
investigated by the Grand Jury of the Western District of North
Carolina, convened August 1987 through December 5, 1988.   Nothing
herein will preclude the Government from initiating and/or
continuing civil tax proceedings against the defendant.

E.   Contact the Attorney General's Office for the State of
North Carolina and the State of South Carolina to recommend that
no further prosecutions of Richard W. Dortch, arising from his
activities and employment at PTL, commence in those states.

4.   SENTENCING

A.   The defendant Dortch agrees and understands that Counts 7
and 10 shall be consolidated for the purpose of sentencing and
Counts 14 and 24 shall be consolidated for the purpose of
sentencing; and as a result, the defendant's maximum exposure at
sentencing shall be equal to two counts of the Indictment.
Nothing in this paragraph, however, shall limit the Court's

discretion to further consolidate all four counts together for
sentencing. The defendant may argue for further consolidation of
the counts at sentencing; likewise, the Government may argue
against further consolidation.

B. The defendant Dortch understands and agrees that he shall·
be required to pay a penalty assessment of $200 pursuant to
Title 18, United States Code, Section 3013.

C. The defendant Dortch understands that he may, in the
Court's discretion, be ordered to make restitution pursuant to
Title 18, United States Code, Section 3663. The Government will
refrain from recommending any specific amount of restitution;
however, the Government reserves the right to recommend
restitution. The defendant may request that no restitution be
required.

D. The defendant Dortch understands and agrees that he may
be required to serve a period of probation.

E. The defendant Dortch understands and agrees that the
sentencing judge alone will decide what sentence to impose subject
to the limitations imposed in paragraph 4(A).

F. The defendant Dortch understands and agrees that even if
he should later not be satisfied with his sentence, he shall have
no right to withdraw his guilty pleas after acceptance of his pleas
by the Court.

G(1) The defendant Dortch understands and agrees that the
United States Attorney's Office and the Department of Justice
reserve the right to describe fully, both orally and in writing,
to the Court, the nature and seriousness of Mr. Dortch's

misconduct, including misconduct not described in the charges to which he shall plead guilty. The United States also reserves the right to correct misleading or inaccurate statements or information, if any, presented to the sentencing court by the defendant. Likewise, the defendant reserves the right to correct misleading or inaccurate statements or information, if any, presented to the Court by the Government.

G(2) The defendant Dortch understands and agrees that the Government shall refrain from recommending that the sentencing judge sentence Mr. Dortch to a specific term of imprisonment, but reserves the right to recommend that the defendant receive a sentence of imprisonment. The defendant may ask for a probationary or any other type of sentence.

G(3) The defendant Dortch understands and agrees that the Government will not oppose defendant's requests that:

a. if a period of incarceration is imposed, he be designated to a specific institution. The Government's position is that the designation of the institution is entirely within the discretion of the Bureau of Prisons, giving due consideration to any recommendation made by the Court.

b. if a period of incarceration is imposed, the sentence be imposed pursuant to Title 18, United States Code, Section 4205(b)(2). The Government does not join in such request; rather, the Government recognizes that it is entirely within the Court's discretion as to which of the available sentencing options shall be applied. Further, it is the position of the Government that considerations as to parole are completely within the

- 5 -

jurisdiction of the United States Parole Commission or its
successor, giving due consideration to the recommendation of the
Court.

    c. if a period of incarceration is imposed, the
defendant's reporting to the designated institution shall be
delayed until his cooperation with the Government, as called for
by this agreement, is complete.

    H. The defendant Dortch understands that the issue of a
fine, if any, will be left to the discretion of the Court. The
Government agrees to refrain from recommending a specific fine;
however, the Government reserves the right to recommend that a
fine be paid. The defendant may request that no fine be imposed.

    I. Defendant Dortch understands and agrees that if he should
file a motion for reduction of his sentence pursuant to Rule 35(b)
of the Federal Rules of Criminal Procedure, the United States
Attorney's Office shall inform the judge handling the motion of
the extent and value of Mr. Dortch's cooperation under the terms
of paragraph 2(3) of this plea agreement.

    J. The parties consent to amend Count 24 of the Indictment
to allege that defendant Dortch's involvement and culpability in
Count 24, conspiracy, concluded on or about April 28, 1987.

    K. All parties agree that this case is governed by the
sentencing law applicable to offenses committed prior to
November 1, 1987.

5.   USE OF INFORMATION PROVIDED BY THE DEFENDANT PURSUANT TO
HIS OBLIGATION TO COOPERATE

    A. Defendant Dortch understands and agrees that any
information he had provided to date or provides pursuant to the

cooperation paragraph of this plea agreement, paragraph 2(B) above, shall not be used directly against him as an admission in a Federal, state, or local criminal prosecution; however, such information may be used as proof of the charges to which he shall plead guilty, by probation officials and the sentencing judge, and in connection with any Federal prosecution for impeachment and rebuttal, or for investigative leads. Any information and statements made by Dortch pursuant to this agreement could also be used in any subsequent perjury, false statement to a federal official or obstruction of justice trial against him pursuant to Rule 11, Federal Rules of Criminal Procedure. In addition, such information may be used without limitation as set forth in paragraph 5(B) immediately below. Mr. Dortch understands that statements made pursuant to the plea agreement may be subject to disclosure pursuant to the Jencks Act and **Brady v. Maryland**.

(B) Mr. Dortch further understands and agrees that if he should fail to fulfill completely each and every one of his obligations under this plea agreement, then the Government will be free from its obligations under the plea agreement; the agreement shall become null and void, and Mr. Dortch shall be fully subject to criminal prosecution on all charges contained in the Indictment herein of which he has not already been found guilty. All guilty verdicts and sentences thereon shall stand.

6. WAIVER OF THE APPLICABLE STATUTE OF LIMITATIONS

Defendant Dortch understands and agrees that if the Court should determine that he has failed to fulfill completely his obligations under this plea agreement, the Government shall be free to prosecute him for any of the offenses named in the indictment filed December 5, 1988 that would be barred from being prosecuted because of the expiration of the applicable statute of limitations. Such prosecution must, however, be commenced by indictment or information within 180 days after Mr. Dortch has received written notice that the plea agreement has been voided. The United States District Court shall be the sole judge of whether or not Richard W. Dortch has complied with the plea agreement.

7. <u>EFFECT OF WAIVER OF A TRIAL</u>

Mr. Dortch understands that by pleading guilty he will waive his rights (1) to be tried by a jury, (2) to be assisted by an attorney at trial and to have an attorney appointed to assist him at trial if necessary, (3) to confront and cross-examine witnesses against him, and (4) not to be compelled to incriminate himself.

8. <u>ACCEPTANCE BY THE COURT</u>

A. The United States and the defendant acknowledge that this plea agreement limits the Court as to sentencing and is thus in part of the type specified in Rule 11(e)(1)(A) and (C) of the Federal Rules of Criminal Procedure. Accordingly, under Rule 11(e)(2), (3), and (4) the Court will have the discretion to accept or reject this plea agreement, before or after considering a presentence report on the defendant. If the Court rejects this plea agreement, the defendant may withdraw the guilty pleas tendered under the agreement and stand trial on the indictment herein. In such event, the United States is ready to proceed to trial against the defendant.

B. In order to minimize potentially prejudicial publicity
and to insure the defendant's right to a fair trial should the
Court reject this agreement, the parties agree that they will
request the Court to place this plea agreement under seal until
such time as the Court may set an expedited in camera hearing to
determine whether or not the Court will accept this agreement.
Such an in camera hearing is specifically allowed under Rule
11(e)(2) and (4) of the Federal Rules of Criminal Procedure.

C. If the Court rejects this Plea Agreement, then the
agreement shall be maintained under seal until a final judgment in
this case is entered or until such other time as the Court may
direct. If the Court accepts this plea agreement, the agreement
shall be unsealed as directed by the Court, and the proceedings
under Rule 11 shall be calendared in open court at such time as
the Court shall determine.

9. SIGNATURES OF ATTORNEY(S) FOR THE DEFENDANT, THE DEFENDANT
AND THE ATTORNEY(S) FOR THE DEPARTMENT OF JUSTICE

I have read this plea agreement and have discussed it fully
with my client, Richard W. Dortch. It accurately and completely
sets forth the entire plea agreement. I concur in Richard W.
Dortch's pleading as set forth in this plea agreement.

8/8/89	William K. Diehl, Jr.
Date	Attorney for the Defendant
8/8/89	Mark T. Calloway
Date	Attorney for the Defendant

- 9 -

I have read this plea agreement and have discussed it with my attorney(s). I fully understand the plea agreement and accept and agree to it without reservation. I do this voluntarily and of my own free will. No threats have been made to me, nor am I under the influence of anything that could impede my ability to understand fully this plea agreement.

I affirm that absolutely no promises, agreements, understanding, or conditions have been made or entered into in connection with my decision to plead guilty except those set forth in this plea agreement.

I am satisfied with the legal services provided by my attorneys in connection with this plea agreement and matters related to it.

August 8, 1989
Date

Richard W. Dortch
Richard W. Dortch
Defendant

We accept and agree to this plea agreement for the Department of Justice.

August 8, 1989
Date

Jerry W. Miller
JERRY W. MILLER
Assistant United States Attorney
Western District of North Carolina

August 8 1989
Date

Deborah M. Smith
DEBORAH M. SMITH
Trial Attorney, Fraud Section
U.S. Department of Justice

gether, so I was only sentenced for one count on each issue — wire fraud, mail fraud, and conspiracy. The maximum I could receive was a five-year sentence on each count for a total of two five-year sentences.

I understood that I could possibly receive a prison term. I was promised absolutely nothing.

At that point, Judge Potter went into his inner chambers, and our group proceeded to the courtroom. For the formal execution of the plea agreement, the judge emerged wearing his robes.

Five or six people who worked at the courthouse also came in to observe the proceedings. Otherwise, no one else was seated in the courtroom except myself, Mildred, Rich, and the attorneys. No reporters were present.

Without ceremony, the judge asked me the standard questions required by law of any defendant pleading guilty to a crime. I pled guilty, and the judge set a sentencing date for the month of August.

It was over in what seemed like five minutes.

The judge returned to his chambers, and the federal prosecutors, along with Bill Diehl, Mark Calloway, my wife, our son Rich, and I started to leave the courtroom.

As we neared the door, it opened and in walked two journalists. Raising both hands in exclamation, they appeared bewildered and asked, "What's happening?"

I responded by raising my hands and said nothing. My lawyers kept moving toward the door, and we walked out. Whatever information those reporters got, they used. But they didn't get it from us.

The headlines on *The Charlotte Observer,* which came out at ten o'clock that evening for the next morning's paper, shouted, "DORTCH PLEADS GUILTY." Newspapers around the country picked up the press release and repeated the report.

As it would be, the biannual national conference of the Assemblies of God was being held at that moment in Indianapolis, Indiana. In my thirty-six years of ministry, I had attended regularly and had addressed the group.

That fact was very much on my mind as I realized what the 15,000 plus people at the convention would be reading the next morning. I could imagine the discussions and conversations in the coffee shops.

Richard Dortch, the man who had been respected, and, hopefully, loved, in the Assemblies of God, had fallen.

Richard Dortch and Dale Evans Rogers.

15

Eight Years!

What am I, of all people, doing in a federal courthouse in Charlotte, North Carolina? A pastor for thirty-six years. How could I have gotten to the point of being sentenced? Why am I even here?

As I sat in the courtroom waiting for Judge Potter to appear, those and other thoughts raced through my mind.

A few days before, I had briefly seen the pre-sentence investigation, and I knew to expect the worst. Now, sitting in the courtroom, I had been given the final copy and the recommendations of the probation officers.

I sat there hoping and praying, wanting to believe that somehow the judge would see fit to give me probation and not a prison sentence.

Scores of people — PTL viewers, long time friends and associates — had written letters to Judge Potter on my behalf, asking for leniency.

"This is the nearest thing to attending your own funeral," I had jokingly told Mildred, "having so many people say such kind things about you."

As I looked around the courtroom, I noticed the familiar faces pastors, businessmen, executives, and friends. Relatives had driven many miles to be with us.

My lawyer handed me the complete report. Turning my attention back to reading the pre-sentence investigation, I came to the report of the chief probation officer for the Western District of North Carolina and saw his recommendation. Suddenly, I felt like the floor had opened up and I was falling through it.

The word "IMPRISONMENT" in capital letters jumped off the page at me. Reality set in. I was in court waiting to be sentenced to jail!

I thought, *What have I done to deserve this? Haven't I already paid a heavy price? How can I ever regain what I have already lost — my reputation, my job, my life's savings? What more do they want from me?*

The answers to those questions didn't matter now. In a few moments I would stand before a federal judge whose history and reputation was to give severe sentences.

I had approached the day's events with a great deal of fear on one hand, but also with a consciousness that no matter what happened, God was going to see me through.

The night before, I had spent some time at the attorney's office, but had left after only a few moments. I couldn't seem to find the right place to go or the right thing to do. Later, in the silence of our room, Mildred and I prayed with our children, "God, give your angels charge over us, and please keep us in all of our ways. God, make us adequate to accept whatever happens."

From the time I had been indicted in December, 1988, I had faced a smorgasbord of possibilities. I could plead innocent, or I could plead guilty. I could go to trial, or I could plead no contest, if permitted.

I chose to plead guilty because I felt, for me, that was the best course — as the outcome has shown it was. I had offered lifetime partnerships by phone, mail, and with someone else. I was guilty as charged.

Suddenly, Judge Potter entered the courtroom, and I stood with my attorneys. The place was packed, not only with friends, associates, and relatives, but with publicity seekers and government witnesses. At one point, there had been a lively exchange between the witnesses and my attorneys.

Even though the plea agreement had previously been settled, the sentence hearing took on the atmosphere of a trial and lasted for several hours. First, the United States prosecutors presented their case and their witnesses to the judge. Part of the plea agreement was that they would not make any recommendation as to sentencing. They would simply state the issues as they saw them. During this time, my attorneys, the proficient Bill Diehl and the brilliant Mark Callaway, countered the testimony of the prosecutions' witnesses.

Then suddenly they were finished, and my lawyers gave me the nudge to stand. The sentencing time had come.

I had asked Mark, who had been the law clerk for Judge Potter several years ago, what I should look for and expect.

He had told me, "Judge Potter usually looks down when he's reading what he has prepared to say in the sentencing. It might be difficult for you to catch the legal jargon for the counts and the amount of time of the sentence. Most people won't understand exactly what is being said."

Mark was absolutely correct.

The judge hastily read his statement, put the gavel down, and walked out of the courtroom. Still standing, I didn't have any idea what he had said.

When court was dismissed, I turned around and looked at Mark and asked, "What was it?"

Mark, thinking that I wanted to discuss the terms of the sentencing, said, "Let's wait and talk about it outside."

I was perplexed and numb! Moving quickly through the crowd, the reporters, and interested people, my mind reeled with confusion. I knew the judge had sentenced me to prison, but I didn't get the counts and the amount of time to be served. Maybe I had filtered out the things I didn't want to hear.

My pastor, Larry Freeman, and his wife Pat, approached me, along with Pastor Dale Edwards and businessman friend, Jerry Leeth. Everyone was embracing me and holding me. At least, I thought, whatever my sentence, I'm not going to walk through it alone.

Mildred, Rich, Deanna, and my two attorneys got into the car, and we started down the highway.

Finally, I cried out, "Will somebody please tell me what my sentence is?" Shocked, everyone looked at me.

"You don't know?" Mark asked.

"No, I don't!"

Then he soberly explained, "You have received two four years sentences for each of the counts. Not running concurrently as most sentences do. Eight years. In the language of prison they were 'stacked,' four years for each count. You have been sentenced to eight years, with an exposure for ten. You did well!"

Probably in Judge Potter's mind he had been lenient with me and had given me twenty percent less than he could have. I took little comfort in that thought.

Having prepared myself for the worst, the sentence didn't impact me too much. I was numb. Also, I knew that the plea agreement might make it possible to have the sentence reduced. That gave me hope. How much that would be, no one knew. Whatever it was, I believed God would make me adequate.

On the way back to the lawyers' office, someone turned on the radio. The program was interrupted by a special bulletin from the federal courthouse. "Richard Dortch has just been sentenced to five years probation and has been fined $500," the announcer read. Where the press got that information I'll never know.

That afternoon, Mildred and I flew back to Tampa, arriving just in time to catch the evening news broadcasting the story of my eight year sentence.

At one o'clock in the morning, as usual, I was on the air with "You and Me," my late-night Christian call-in program. After the theme ended, the director pointed at me, and the red light went on the camera.

I said simply, "During the life of this program we have

never made an issue of my problems or my needs. We have been concerned about your problems and your needs. Nothing has changed tonight. Where is our first call from?"

Not one person mentioned my sentencing on the program that night. Who would have believed, with calls coming from all over the United States, nobody mentioned my sentencing? I considered that a miracle.

That was the first of many miraculous events that would take place in the next few months.

In the fall of 1989, I returned to my home town, Granite City, Illinois, for a brief visit. During that time, the pastor of my home church, Rev. Dale Edwards, called pastors and others throughout Illinois, inviting them to a special luncheon.

To my delight and surprise over seventy pastors came. At first, I was embarrassed to see them, but they were not judgmental. I had pled guilty, been sentenced to eight years in prison, and yet they reassured me of their sustaining love. I felt, and needed, the strength of their support.

In my sentencing I had asked for a recommendation from the judge to be sentenced to Eglin Prison Camp, located at the giant Eglin Air Force Base near Pensacola, Florida. Even though Eglin was approximately five hundred miles from our home, it was probably the closest prison camp with minimum security that I could obtain.

After talking to my lawyers and several former inmates of the prison, I realized that Eglin was probably the best choice. The judge could simply recommend it. The Bureau of Prisons would decide where I would ultimately go. Mildred and I began to pray.

We waited and prayed, hoping I would not have to live in a prison with hardened and violent criminals for the next eight years. Finally, when I was contacted and informed that I was being assigned to Eglin Prison Camp, Mildred and I rejoiced. We knew God was still in control. His mercy and grace overwhelmed me. He had answered our prayers. Another miracle.

Just three months before having to leave for Eglin, our

daughter remarried. God brought into her life a wonderful man, the son of a Southern Baptist pastor from Alabama. Deanna had known Mark Moody for several years. He had been the pianist in the lobby of the Heritage Grand Hotel at Heritage USA.

As Tammy Faye's personal secretary, Deanna had watched the PTL scandal develop from the beginning and felt betrayed by what had happened. Deanna and our son Rich had both worked at PTL, giving of themselves 150%. The outcome had been devastating. All of a sudden they were without jobs and, for a while, had lost their ministries.

About a year and a half after we settled into the Tampa Bay area, Mark Moody moved to an apartment in Clearwater just a few blocks from our house. After a few months, it became obvious that Mark and Deanna were going to marry.

Deanna had gone through great heartbreak and sorrow, but now she and her son, Michael, were eagerly anticipating a new life with Mark. That meant for me nothing but joy. The daughter and grandson that I loved so dearly were beginning a new life together as a family.

Nothing thrills the heart of a parent more than to see their child contented. I was going to Eglin Prison Camp, but once again God was looking after our family. All was in place.

Not long after my sentencing, I was subpoenaed to testify in the trial of Jim Bakker. I dreaded going to court again, especially to face a man I loved as a brother. My appreciation for him had not changed. Several years ago, I had trusted Jim enough to walk away from my career as a churchman to work beside him in the PTL ministry. As far as I knew, he was the same man I had known from the beginning.

Knowing I had told the truth in my plea agreement and that I was going to tell the truth now, gave me strength. Still I didn't want to hurt him. I also had to be honest with Jim Bakker and with myself.

When the day came, Mildred and I flew to Charlotte. I thought I would be spending a good deal of time with the federal prosecutor in preparation for the Bakker trial. To my surprise, I only talked with him about twenty minutes.

One of the prosecutor's instructions to me was, "During the course of your testimony, if there are things that will help Mr. Bakker, feel free to tell them as long as you are truthful. It is not our responsibility to convict him, it is our responsibility to get out the facts." I did just that.

I testified for two whole days and was cross-examined by Jim Bakker's attorneys. I knew in my heart that I was simply telling the truth. It was painful but necessary.

The truth has an incredible weight to it. You don't have to have an outstanding memory to tell the truth. Just simply presenting the facts can put a different face on things. The greatest concern for me wasn't that the truth had not been told at PTL, the problem was that the facts were not all out in the open.

At the conclusion of the two days, I was weary.

When I left the courtroom at different times, during the recesses, some of the Bakkers' supporters would speak directly to me, making nasty remarks and asking, "How can you do what you're doing?"

I wanted to reply, "Would you expect me *not* to tell the truth?"

When people complained about my testimony, especially Christians, I was puzzled. What would they want me to do, lie? To tell something I knew was not true?

After the testimony in the Bakker trial, my attorneys asked for a continuance, extending the deadline for me to enter prison. The judge honored our request for me to remain home during the holiday season. The United States Marshall recommended that I enter the prison on the second day of February, 1990.

I continued my television program and my ministry of Life Challenge up to the end of the year. I preached in churches, shared the love of people, and visited my parents for the last time before I had to enter prison.

Since the indictment on December 6, 1988, I had been reporting by telephone each Monday morning to the United States Pretrial Services, a federal agency in Tampa, Florida.

It is a part of the United States Probation Service. Living in the Tampa area could have been a problem, having been indicted in Charlotte, North Carolina.

My immediate supervisor, Mr. Haywood Polk, was a probation officer in Charlotte. This distinguished gentleman represented everything a federal law enforcement officer should be, using his authority with compassion. He was very serious about his job, which he knew well, Mr. Polk handled himself and his job in a way that left the person under his authority with their self-respect. Since Mr. Polk was the first law enforcement person I came in contact with, my expectations were high.

I awakened on January 28, 1990, knowing it would be my last Sunday in our church for the length of my sentence. I had learned so much from our pastor, Dr. Larry Freeman, and the wonderful, kind people in the congregation.

After breakfast, I sat on the couch to relax for a few moments when despair and depression suddenly overtook me. I began to cry.

I couldn't bring myself to face the people of our church. I knew that they loved me. They had demonstrated that over and over. I just couldn't go. The thought of leaving all those dear people, the pastor and his wife we loved so dearly, overwhelmed me! I got undressed, went back to bed, and wept. It was also pounding in my mind, *You are going to prison!*

I encouraged my wife to go to church, but she wouldn't leave me alone. Mildred wanted to be by my side to understand, to care, to love.

The consciousness of what the future held had abruptly become abundantly clear. I'm going to prison. I have no choice. I can't evade it — I must go! The certainty of it all hit me hard!

That was the beginning of what had to be the most painful day of the entire experience. I had never known grief like I sensed that day.

Reflecting on the things that the media had said about me and the way many colleagues had frozen me out opened old wounds that had never healed. Considering the separation from my family that I knew was coming tore at my insides.

How foolish I had been to let myself get caught up in something that was not God's best for me. I knew God was permitting it, but why?

I was experiencing true remorse, but there was nothing I could do to reverse the consequences. It was only the second time in my life that I had hit an unmovable object that would not move. It kept coming back: I'm going to prison. Like it or not.

Nothing mattered, nothing. I felt like a sinking ship being sucked down in a whirlpool. That day I died to Richard W. Dortch. I was learning what it meant to submit. I totally yielded myself to my Heavenly Father. The cup was bitter.

Crying out in prayer, I groaned in deep contrition. It was a wailing — eerie and foreboding — an out of earth journey in my spirit. In my wrenching travail, every fiber of my body was expended.

Our daughter Deanna, her husband Mark, and our grandson Michael had come to the house after church. "What is wrong with dad?" Deanna inquired. Mildred knew I could hear their discussion so she came to my room with Deanna.

Falling on their knees beside me, Deanna touched my face. "Don't cry Dad. God will take care of you. He always has, and He always will. The Lord will see us through this."

For almost the entire day, I travailed before God in deep humility. My hour had come. I had experienced pain from Crohn's disease and from recently passing kidney stones, but the pain in my soul was different from anything I had ever known.

I had been caught in a big scandal and could do nothing about it. My heart did not condemn me, but the feeling of helplessness tore at my insides.

For the past few weeks, after we'd go someplace or visit people or do something, I would reflect — sometimes silently, sometimes verbally to Mildred, "This is the last time that I we will be doing this until I get 'out'." I could not bring myself to say the word. I avoided it at all cost. I could not get the word "prison" out of my mouth. It happened constantly. The details of each day's activities were chronicled in my mind. This is the last time that I will be doing . . .

Having to go to prison is an experience that only those who have done it can understand. I cannot transmit the pain and humiliation, fear and hopelessness, depression and agony.

When the realization became so intensely clear, I'M GOING TO PRISON, it filled my mind, blocking out everything else.

I thought, *One week from now, I'll be an inmate in a federal prison.* For me it was so unreal, yet I knew that it was true.

The next day I thought, *Six days, and I'll be in prison.*
The next day I thought, *Five days, and I'll be in prison.*
Then it was four days, three, two.

Every night Mildred and I would lie in bed, holding each other and weeping, weeping, weeping. *Why Lord? You know my heart? What did I do to deserve this? What did I do that was so wrong?*

If you are going to prison you obviously want to know why. What act did I do? What did I steal? What was the criminal activity that I was involved in? None of it made any sense. It all counted for nothing. I was going to prison, and that was it! The government said I was guilty. I was. I did what the judge said I did.

Two days before I was to enter prison, January 31, 1990, I watched the most beautiful sunrise from our house in Safety Harbor, Florida. This was to be my last day and night at home.

When the media attention had been so intense, our family had needed the shelter of a home. This house had become a haven of rest for me. It was a house, yes, but it had truly become home.

I knew I would never return to it. The house was no longer ours. We were losing almost everything. It was just a matter of time. There was nothing I could do about it. It was a melancholy day at our house. Each moment was a treasure. The inevitable had come.

That night Mildred and I once again prayed, cried, and committed ourselves to God. I knew in my own heart who I was and what I had done. I released myself to God's keeping grace.

I began February 1, 1990 by reading Psalm 112 from *The Living Bible*:

> Praise the Lord! For all who fear God and trust in him are blessed beyond expression. Yes, happy is the man who delights in doing his commands. His children shall be honored everywhere, for good men's sons have a special heritage. He himself shall be wealthy, and his good deeds will never be forgotten. When darkness overtakes him, light will come bursting in. He is kind, and merciful . . . and all goes well for the generous man who conducts his business fairly. Such a man will not be overthrown by evil circumstances. God's constant care of him will make a deep impression on all who see it. He does not fear bad news, nor live in dread of what may happen. For he is settled in his mind that Jehovah will take care of him. That is why he is not afraid, but can calmly face his foes. He gives generously to those in need. His deeds will never be forgotten. He shall have influence and honor. Evil minded men will be infuriated when they see all of this: they will gnash their teeth in anger and slink away, their hopes thwarted.

Mildred had pointed out this Psalm to me months before. I knew we would see this come to pass.

I awakened with confidence and a peace that I had not known would come to me. Fear was gone. Our prayers had been answered. Constantly I thought, *Underneath are His wings, and in Him will I trust.*

I prayed that day, "Oh, God, make me adequate for what

I face in the days to come."

The facts concerning where I was going, and the physical characteristics of the prison camp were all known to me. Three months before, I had preached in a nearby city at the church of a friend, Rev. Ronald Meade. That gave me the opportunity to get the "feel" of the place where I could spend the next eight years of my life.

The mammoth Eglin Air Force Base near Pensacola, Florida, the largest military installation in the world, measured sixty miles east and west, and twenty miles north and south. At that time about eighteen thousand military personnel were stationed there. Including dependents and civilian staff, the military complex supported over 25,000 people.

I had promised Al Reuchel, a TV anchorman at the local ABC affiliate, that I would give him an exclusive interview the day that I left for prison. We met him in the parking lot of a supermarket on our way out of town.

Then finally the journey began. I was anxious to make the eight hour trip and get on with the task at hand.

It was an overcast but pleasant day. As I drove, I tried to put everything behind me. The fear, the hurts, anxieties, disappointments, they were all secondary. There was a larger task at hand.

I tried that day to minister to my wife; I probably failed. But she was, for those hours, pre-eminent in my thoughts. We'd have one more night together.

How had all this affected her? I wondered and decided to ask. Her answer surprised me somewhat, but knowing her deep sense of commitment to people and to God's work, I knew she was being honest.

"I saw and lived the other side of PTL," she began, "not just the fantasy world that everyone talked about. I saw the hard work that went on behind the scenes and the load that you carried." I turned toward her to see a weak smile cross her face.

"I was able to see the good that was done and some of the things that were accomplished," Mildred continued, obviously reliving pleasant scenes in her mind. "I felt it was worth putting that much effort into it if that many people were being helped. Only eternity will reveal the countless lives that were changed because of the ministry of PTL."

Somehow, when she said that, a great burden lifted from me. *Maybe it had been worth it all,* I thought. She then changed the subject and talked about our whole lives, saying, "There are moments when I wonder, *Have I been fooling myself all this time? Have we been living in a fantasy world believing that all of this was real?* I try to put a lot of the PTL problems out of my mind, telling myself it can't be." Mildred struggled to control her emotions.

"When it all fell apart, I felt I had been so naive. When I thought about what I'd been taught, what I'd believed, and even what I'd taught others, I was disappointed to find out it's not always that way," she said, her voice shaking. "The hurt went very deep."

"After many years as a Christian, I felt I should have had all the right and spiritual answers. I think, in reality, I was more disappointed in myself than in God." I didn't try to stop her. These were things, I knew, she needed to unload.

"I felt at a loss not being able to do something for you, — and the children. As a mom, I was always the one who carried the first-aid kit. I was supposed to be able to make everything right and heal everyone's hurt." At that point, Mildred broke down and wept.

It was all I could do to keep my eyes on the road and see through my own tears.

"You know," she said, dabbing a tissue at her eyes, "maybe if it had happened more suddenly, if they had come and arrested you and taken you away, it would have been a lot easier than living in a state of shock and disbelief month after month, year after year. But at least I learned to take it a day at a time. And that's what I plan to do now."

Those last words, confirmed what I already knew — her strength, her faithfulness, and her godliness would see us both through the difficult days ahead.

How much she meant to me! Separating from her was

the most difficult thing I had to come to grips with. Mildred had given her all for me and to me. Through this terrible ordeal, we had been together more in the past two and a half years than we ever had before. We had been married for thirty-seven years, and I loved her at that moment more than ever.

We had no doubts about our relationship or our love for one another or about our relationship with our children. We had always been a family filled with loving devotion for each other. Nothing had changed. Although we were devastated by the strange turn of events in our lives, we were more committed to God, His will, and His plan for our lives than ever before.

Our son Rich had said to me at the time of my sentencing, "I know, Dad, if you and Mom were in a missionary service, and a call was given to go to a mission field where there were people who needed help, you would respond. You would probably be the first ones on your feet. Look at this as a mission field, and you'll be all right." What profound words.

A rainy mist was falling when we arrived in Crestview, Florida, one of the towns adjacent to the air force base. It all seemed so unreal. Another trip, another place, we were accustomed to that. But now I was eighteen hours from becoming "07423-058," a federal prisoner.

Pastor and Mrs. Ron Meade; Air Force Colonel Bill Rimes and Mrs. Rimes; Mr. and Mrs. Bill Landreth; and Mr. and Mrs. McLain, owners of a restaurant nearby; our daughter and her husband, Deanna and Mark; and Mildred and I met for our last meal together prior to my entry into prison.

These friends knew I was in one sense confident of the assurance that God had given me, but still somewhat like a robot going about what had to be done. After a wonderful meal and a time of prayer, we went our separate ways, acknowledging that we would meet at ten o'clock the next morning.

I had received a list from the United States Marshall Service of the things that I could bring into the prison:

6 undershirts
6 briefs
1 belt
1 collared shirt
1 pair of dress slacks
1 pair of leather sole shoes or boots
2 pairs of socks
1 sweatsuit
1 tennis racket
1 racketball racket
4 tennis balls
4 racket balls
1 pair of sneakers
1 single edge razor (Electric razors, hair dryers, and such cannot be used in a federal prison because they can be converted to other uses that are unauthorized.)

As Mildred and I were driving back to the motel after eating, it occurred to me that I didn't have a razor blade. I had used an electric razor for over thirty years. It was 9:30 p.m. when we entered K-Mart to buy a razor the night before I entered prison.

Richard Dortch and Franklin Graham (Billy Graham's son).

16

Eglin Prison

That Friday morning, I awakened to an unreal world of peace — a deep, settled peace that only God could bring.

I looked Mildred longingly in the eyes, took her hand, and said, "Mildred, honey, at this moment I feel as confident entering prison today as I did when we returned from the mission field. Honey, God will somehow take care of us. You will see, everything will be all right."

After a quiet breakfast, we returned to our room to wait for Pastor Meade and the others who were going to the prison camp with us.

The press knew I would be entering prison that day and were already staking out the west gate of the air force base. A dear friend had access to the Eglin base for commercial reasons and volunteered to take us in one of the smaller construction entries, where we knew no reporters would be expecting us.

As we drove through the gate, I paled, knowing this possibly could be my place of residence for the next eight years.

Before driving over to the prison camp, we were met by a dear friend, Air Force Col. Bill Rimes who was stationed at the base. He could see by my expression that I needed a diversion before checking into the prison. Col. Rimes was responsible for a unit at the base that he thought I'd be interested in seeing. He took us by the facility. Seven months later, when the Desert Storm operation began, I was excited to see some of those same planes in action.

I sensed all of these delays were expressions of the loving concern of friends who wondered, "Is he ready now?"

The United States Marshall Service had told me to be at the prison by 1:00 p.m. It was now 12:30 p.m., and I knew the hour had come. "Let's go," I said, "I'm ready."

The mist from the day before had continued. This second day of February was cold, unlike most perceptions of Florida.

We drove up to the front of the administration building. It was an army barracks type of building with the entrance in the middle of the long span. Two young ladies descended hastily from the office, and surprisingly they came straight toward our car.

"Are you Richard Dortch?" one asked.

"Yes, I am," I slowly answered.

"Members of the press are on their way to this building. You may want to come inside," she politely cautioned me.

We entered quickly. We each said our little pleasantries and made a few comments about the pictures of previous wardens on display in the lobby. Then a distinguished man appeared, coming out of an office. "Are you Mr. Dortch?"

"Yes, sir."

"I'm Rick Harris. Would you please come with me?"

"Yes, sir."

"This is it, Honey. I love you." For a moment I felt my legs were going to give way.

I must be strong and brave for my family, I thought.

"I love you Deanna. I love you Mark. Pastor Meade, thanks for your prayers and concern." We all embraced.

Once again I embraced Mildred and held her close to me. I knew God was there, but for this moment I needed the closeness and tenderness of my beloved wife. I whispered to her, "I love you. I love you."

To my surprise and dismay my "Rock of Gibraltar" whispered back, "This is the darkest day, the top of the mountain of pain. But it is all downhill from here. I love you, Honey."

Slowly I let her hand drop, and I followed Mr. Harris down the hall, daring not to look back. Knowing Mildred would be able to visit the next morning helped me deal with the agony of separation.

My wife told me later that an inmate who was cleaning and doing maintenance work there in the building, stepped through one of the doors as she was watching me walk away. He looked over and whispered, "Don't worry, he'll be all right. We'll take care of him." Mildred was touched and found great consolation in his words.

Mr. Harris took me into what they called, in prison language, R & D, Receiving and Discharging. There I was stripped and searched, even into my body cavities, for drugs. I was photographed, fingerprinted, and a urine specimen was taken.

The clothes they gave me seemed specifically designed not to fit. Everyone in R & D wears shirts that are either too big or too little, and pants that are too short or too long. These are temporary garments that you wear until you are issued clothing more suited to your size.

I had taken my medication for Crohn's disease early in the morning. By the time the processing was finished, it was about 4:00 p.m. At that point, I was taken to an office where I was asked if anyone in the prison population knew me, and if I had any co-defendants there. They gave me a CIM rating, which means Central Inmate Monitoring. High profile inmates who have received a lot of publicity are given this designation because of the danger they face from others within the prison population.

After that briefing I was taken back to the R & D area where I sat and watched the office employees go home. A lot of people walked in and out until approximately 5:30 p.m. But nobody said anything to me. I felt the aloneness of being a nonentity — an inmate of no consequence to the outside world.

After a while I became nervous and afraid and wondered, *Have they forgotten about me? What is the delay? Why am I being kept here? God, please assist me. Send someone to help me! I'm frightened! Please, Lord!*

Dear Jesus, what is going to befall me? What is life going to be like on the other side of that door? I was feeling sick and wanted to get where I was going and bed down for the night. I had heard so much about what life was going to be like and simply wanted to get on with it.

By that time the mounting anxiety and the fear had caused my Crohn's disease to act up. I was in deep pain. I had learned through the years that if I double over and press my hand under my left rib area, the pinching relieved some pain. I was in that doubled up, bent over position, when a gentleman that I later learned to be Mr. Kramer, walked through the R & D area, and politely asked, "What are you doing here?"

I explained, "I just arrived today, and I really don't know what I am doing here."

He asked, "Are you in pain?"

I told him, "Yes."

He said, "I'll call somebody from the hospital."

In a few minutes one of the physicians assistants came and took me to the prison hospital, a small medical clinic. He called the prison physician, Dr. Rossi, and received permission to give me some pain medication. He then advised me to lie down in their ward and try to get the pain eased. After a few minutes, someone asked if I had had anything to eat since I had been admitted to prison.

"No, I haven't eaten since early this morning." I was brought a cold meal. With no microwave to warm up the mashed potatoes and gravy, I ate what I could. After resting for about an hour and a half, the pain subsided, and I was taken back to R & D.

An officer, Mr. Spencer, a big man, young, and very caring, helped me put my things together on a dolly. He took me over to Dorm 2, to a large room, better known at Eglin

Prison Camp as the "Fishbowl." To my disbelief it was a room about 12'x16', the size of Mildred's and my motel room the night before. It housed twelve inmates in six bunk beds. This was to be my new home until a modular cube became available.

The prison was greatly overcrowded, with over 900 inmates (it had been built for 460). I stood there and looked around at a room jammed with men. Because of my physical problems, I was assigned a lower bunk where my sheets and a pillow case were placed. My things were unloaded, and suddenly I was facing eleven unknown prisoners.

Thank God I was not alone. Immediately, Jimmy Levine, who I later learned was from Tampa, Bill Eckard, Alan Burkett, and some other inmates began to help me make my bed and get things put in a locker. They knew what it was like to enter prison life.

"We have been expecting you for about six months, ever since you were sentenced and the judge recommended that you be placed in Eglin," Jimmy Levine said.

All of them expressed their concern and gave me a quick education in prison life. I learned some "facts" in those first couple of hours. What life was going to be like, things I shouldn't do, where the boundaries were for the camp, and the consciousness of time.

"At certain times," Bill told me, "you shouldn't be in an unauthorized area. A total prison count is made at 12:30 a.m., 2:30 a.m., and 4:30 a.m. while you are sleeping, and at 7:00 a.m. and 1:00 p.m. on your job."

"At 4:00 p.m. the entire federal prison system has a stand up count," Bill Eckard added, "and every inmate is to be standing beside his bed. There must be total silence when the officers come through to get each count. This is when the population is counted to see if everyone is there."

I thanked them and laid down on my bunk, hoping to rest. But instead of sleep, the tears came.

My education in prison life began.

We were housed in dormitories, not cells. Open dormitory living is very difficult. Some inmates prefer cells because there is more privacy. There is a code of life all of its own in prison. There is a clearly defined set of items that you are allowed to keep in your small locker. Officers "shake down" your lockers periodically, looking for contraband. One of the first things you learn from your new found friends is "don't let the 'hacks' get to you." After I was there a few days, a fight began on the ball field. An inmate standing nearby turned me around and said, "You don't see nothing here!"

There is a language all of its own. "How long have you been down?" means "How long have you been in prison?" "Getting short" means "I'll be going home soon."

The Eglin Prison Camp was a work camp. The prison compound was comprised for five dormitories; a small hospital (clinic); a large cafeteria; a laundry and clothing room; chapel; classrooms; administration building; recreational area; ball diamond; work-out rooms; tennis, basketball, and handball courts; soccer field; library (both legal and lending); and large visiting areas (both inside and outdoors).

In the line of my work at the prison, I would see the area where the "hole" was located. It was a special housing unit, much like a cell, for the few men who had broken the rules and were being disciplined or sent to a higher level of prison.

You are not permitted to have a wallet in prison, no paper money, and no jewelry except a wrist watch valued at less than $50. You are only permitted to have $20 in coins. If you have money in your account, you are limited to withdrawing $15.00 a week from the account. If your funds are sufficient you can spend $60 per month at the prison commissary for personal items and food products which are sold there.

The thing I feared the most when I arrived was going to the cafeteria. I noticed that when I walked into a building or area, the conversation usually ceased. I knew that the 925 men knew very little about the rest of the inmates who were outside of their circle, but they had read many articles about me. I wanted to make sure that I would make it on my own. I asked for no special treatment and I received none.

One of my first remembrances is when an officer told me

to abide by my medical restrictions. Once she noticed I had been on my feet for more than thirty minutes, so she told me to lie down on my bunk. After I was there for a few moments, the captain, who is the chief of security, came through the area, saw me, and asked why I was lying down. I told him I was there because of the officer's instruction and my medical condition. "What did you do on the street?" he asked. I didn't know what he meant. The only thing I could connect with "street," was drugs. So I explained that I didn't know what he meant. "What did you do before you got here?"

I said, "I'm a preacher."

He looked at me in total puzzlement, half-scared, and walked away.

The principal objective in prison is to survive, make the time there serve you, obey the rules, and stay out of trouble.

One day towards the end of a meal, when the cafeteria was not very full, an inmate stopped beside me. With a fierce look he said, "I hope you burn in hell!" This was a new experience.

I lived from visit to visit with my wife. The days of the week were unimportant. The only thing that mattered was, "When does Mildred come?" I was unlike many inmates. I wanted to see my wife as often and as long as I could. We needed each other.

You are permitted to submit a list of twelve people who can visit you if they meet the requirements of the Bureau of Prisons. Those were the special times when family and friends came.

Rumor mills are a way of life in prison. Sometimes an inmate would tell a story, knowing it wasn't true. They just wanted to see how long it took for the story to get back to them, and to see how much it had changed since they started it.

It was at night, when it was quiet and I was on a bunk in the midst of twelve men, when I felt desperately alone. The feeling grabs you . . . strong . . . hard . . . *I'm alone; I'm missing days out of my life!*

The next morning as I anxiously went through the new

routine, all I could think about was seeing my dear wife and family. I knew they'd be there early at eight o'clock, one of the first in line. It broke my heart to think of my lovely wife and precious daughter standing outside the prison door.

Seeing them brought mixed emotions. I needed to look on familiar faces, but I hated to put them through this ordeal.

"Honey, this morning an interesting thing happened that really disappointed me," Mildred told me. "We were standing in line, waiting to be allowed into the prison. We had been told we could bring a picnic lunch, so last night I bought a small thermos to bring you some gumbo. We had a tablecloth and napkins, and were going to have our own cute little picnic, making it as pleasant as we could. While standing in line I noticed no one else was carrying a picnic basket. To our dismay we were told that the rules had been changed. We could not bring anything in, not gum, candy — nothing. So we toted our picnic back to the car. I am really sorry."

Mildred told me later that as soon as she saw me, she thought, *This is not the man we left the day before.* She described me as someone who appeared lifeless and drained. "How my heart ached for you," she told me later, "and I could do nothing to relieve your anguish. That was the worst part for me."

My face and eyes were swollen from crying all night long. Even then, I could hardly speak without weeping.

It was a very emotional day for all of us and especially difficult for our daughter Deanna. She came back in a few weeks and then didn't return until about September. Deanna couldn't handle seeing her father in prison.

I returned to my cube, more broken and distraught than ever.

Life turned around for me the next day. I met a man who helped me so much. Jim Humphrey became my friend. I met him at work the next morning. Out of a group of approximately eighty men, why I don't know, but I focused on him. He became a true brother. I'm not glad that I went to prison, but I am delighted that Jim Humphrey is my friend.

Going to prison is like no other trip. It affects the family as much as the person going. Many believe that the greatest pain is borne by the family. The one who goes to prison enters another world in which where you go, what you do, and why you do it is totally controlled by others. You have few choices. Some measure of bonding occurs between inmates because you are insulated from the normal activities of life.

It is just simply, "Do it," and "You do it." Very few questions are asked. It is a very unreal world. No one asks your opinion. It is not wanted. Among our prison population there are a lot of former decision makers, but for this period of time there are no decisions to make.

The Bureau of Prisons at the federal and state level is a tremendous growth industry. I knew most of these things. They were bearing down on me. I was like a robot. Someone punched the buttons and I moved.

These things are minor compared to the big issues of life. When a father, husband, or sweetheart goes to prison a new set of priorities begins. Here's what we are told in prison. When you are there for a sentence of three years or more, there is an eighty percent chance that you will leave divorced.

In most cases the bread winner is gone, and the adjustment to life without husband, father, or sweetheart begins. You can't understand unless you have walked the road yourself. The public humiliation and the scorn is something that a family faces from the public each day. The prisoner is isolated from that.

Many families have no choice but to go on welfare. The incarceration of people in prison for non-violent crimes is a loss because it often destroys the fabric of society — the families.

Punishment is needed and necessary. Surely there is a better and more efficient way to penalize non-violent law-breakers. Making a person non-productive, losing the taxes on his income, having to pay for his care, and making it necessary for the family to be supported by the public is not the logical or sensible choice.

There are many alternatives to the government spending between $10,000 and $30,000 a year for the care of each prisoner, and also having to support their family. The level of security determines the cost. A prison camp is operated for approximately $10,000 per inmate, per year. High level security costs much more, up to $30,000 per year for each inmate. Add to that the loss of income tax and the cost of welfare, and it is nearly $50,000 per year.

Within the next few days, I entered a four-week program called A & O, which is Arrivals and Orientation. Grouped with other new inmates, I was given orientation classes covering all aspects of prison life: health, education, psychological care, spiritual care, and medical care. The warden explained his expectations of the inmates, what they can do and not do, and the dangers involved. Then the officer of custody told how to avoid conflicts.

A & O training was interspersed with manual work every day. Basically, the system is designed to immediately grab the new arrival's attention, get him thinking in a prison way, and to totally humble him.

When a person, like myself, who has received wide publicity, the stories surface that they are now scrubbing toilets in prison for eleven cents an hour. The facts are, when you're in A & O, you don't get eleven cents an hour. You simply work, do your job, and get used to prison life.

I did a broad range of work including picking up cigarette butts, cleaning toilets, mopping floors, taking out the trash, washing windows, polishing brass, and cleaning up the visitors room. There was constant change of my activities, which integrated me into all aspects of prison life, and helped me to get to know the facility and the people.

On the fourth day I was assigned to go to the clothing area to get my shoes and clothing. I went to the clothing area, got my clothes, and was sent to the shoe room. I handed the blue card I had been given to the inmate working there.

When he took the card he looked at me and snarled, "So you're the rat."

At that point, I didn't know anything about prison life or prison language, and I didn't understand what he meant.

He raised his voice and hollered again, "So, you're the rat. How much time do you have to do?"

I said, "Well sir, you must know or you wouldn't be asking the question."

"How much time has Jim Bakker got to do?"

"Well, you must know that or you wouldn't be asking the question," I repeated, hoping I wasn't pressing my luck.

"We've been waiting for you to get here because there's not a man here that's got any use for you. You're nothing but a rat."

Somehow, I have always had the ability to think at my best when I'm under pressure — when I'm really, so to speak, up against the wall. At that moment, I had a little grace flowing in my veins.

I looked at the inmate and said, "Sir, perhaps I knew you, or you knew me real well prior to my coming here. You sound like you know all about me, and about the PTL problem. Evidently I hurt you or I disappointed you. If that is the case, I must ask you to forgive me. Would you please forgive me?"

That enraged the man all the more. Fellow inmates who knew him told me that had I cursed him, he would have been pleased. But the fact that I humbly looked at him and said, "Please forgive me, I'm so sorry I offended you and hurt you," upset him. He simply didn't know what to do, so he snarled and walked away.

I walked over to another clerk in the clothing room, who became a very trusted and dear friend. Mr. Paget said, "Don't worry about it, Dortch. We'll take care of you."

Eglin Prison Camp is a federal minimum prison in a Class 1 category for the Bureau of Prisons. As the level goes up, level 2 through 6, the prison becomes more controlled in movement. The most secure federal prison in the United States is located in Marion, Illinois, where prisoners are locked down twenty-four hours a day.

FPC Eglin

Eglin Air Force Base, Florida 32542
904-882-8522   FTS: 534-9100
Federal Prison Camp, *Southeast Region.*

Location: In north-west Florida's panhandle, 45 miles east of Pensacola on Eglin Air Force Base. The area is served by Pensacola Airport and Greyhound, and Eglin AFB has an onsite airstrip.

Security Level: Minimum/Male.

Judicial District: Northern District of Florida.

Capacity: Rated–480. Population, March 31, 1990–874.

Staff Complement: 134.

Overview: Opened in 1962, FPC Eglin houses male offenders primarily from the southeastern U.S. who do not have records of escape, violence, sexual offenses, or major medical/psychiatric problems. Inmates serve as an auxiliary work force for Eglin AFB.

Housing: 5 double-bunked cubicle dormitories.

Education: ABE, GED, ESL. College courses through Okaloosa-Walton Community College. Classes are conducted in English and Spanish.

Vocational Training: Diesel engine mechanics, marine engine mechanics, woodworking, and drafting.

UNICOR: None.

Medical Services: 1 physician, 1 dentist, 7 physician assistants, and 3 other health services staff.

Religious Services: 2 staff chaplains and community volunteers provide services for all faiths.

Psychological Services: 2 full-time clinical psychologists.

Accreditation Status: Yes.

The Eglin Prison Camp was what the name indicates — a twenty-eight acre facility within Eglin Air Force Base. In the years of the bootleggers and later when white collar crimes increased, the Bureau of Prisons realized that it would be much more cost-effective to put non-violent first offenders in camps.

The principal purpose of the Eglin prison camp is to provide workers for the air force base. Daily, about 500 men leave the camp to take care of the grass, landscaping, and roads on the base. Inmates also work in the air force base hospital and offices. It is obviously cheap labor, at an average salary of twelve cents an hour.

There are no fences, barriers, or walls around the prison camp, and none of the officers carry guns. They wear gray trousers and navy blue blazers. It's a much more relaxed environment, although occasionally officers who are transferred from higher level prisons forget that Eglin is a camp and not a walled institution.

After four weeks of A & O, guess where they assigned me to work? Because of my health, they gave me a job in the clothing room, only a few feet away from the shoe room and my snarling friend.

My medical restrictions said I couldn't pick up any object over fifteen pounds, nor was I permitted to stand for over thirty minutes. Although I was required to work, my physical condition was taken into account.

I began my job in the clothing room and settled into prison life. Some of us who worked together became close friends.

During that time, I always smiled and said, "Hello," to the shoe man. In all those months, he never grunted or spoke a word to me, not once.

After a few months, I was put in what is called the "cage." That's where the clothing is handed out to the inmates. I was told that working there was a position of trust.

There are two major things that control prison life: what you wear and what you eat. Many times in prison those items are bartered.

An officer told me that he believed I would not use the dispensing of clothing for personal gain.

How ironic, I thought. *I have such a trusted position.*

17

How Long,
Oh Lord?

Each day at Eglin we were awakened at five o'clock in the morning. Breakfast was at five-thirty, and everyone who was leaving the prison camp reported at the gate for processing to go to work at 6:40 a.m.

Those who remained and worked at the camp took care of the needs of the facility. There were approximately 250 people who did the cooking, cleaning, maintenance, construction, and worked in the offices and hospital for the 500 inmates who worked outside on the base.

Each inmate had a bed and a built-in modular unit. Twenty-eight inches across from the bed we each used a locker about eighteen inches high and fourteen inches wide. Everything we possessed had to be either on hangers in the locker or stored under the bed. Coming from a three-bedroom home to a 14" x 18" facility, in itself was a shock!

Each inmate owned three changes of clothing, prison issued shoes, four pair of socks, four pair of underwear, and a prison jacket. At Eglin the uniforms are a dark navy blue, somewhat like the Air Force personnel wear on the flight line at the base. There were no markings on the pants or shirts.

A few high profile people, like myself, were not permitted to work on the Air Force base, partly to avoid degrading us in front of the public. That policy was fine, but in the things that really mattered to me as a prisoner, my high profile worked against me.

After being in prison for approximately ten and one-half months, in a category such as mine, most inmates received a pass every three months. They began with a fifteen hour pass, then an overnight pass, then two days and one night. After that they could qualify for a five day furlough to return home. Then it became a seven day furlough to help the prisoner adjust to reentering normal life.

Because of the publicity in my case, I was not permitted to leave the camp for any reason, unless for medical care. But God had other plans. On two separate occasions, I had the opportunity to spend time with my family outside of the prison.

The first time, a federal judge released me to testify in the case of *United States* vs. *Samuel Johnson*. Unaccompanied, I got in a taxi, went to the airport in Pensacola, Florida and flew to Charlotte, North Carolina where my lawyer met me. For eight days, I was under house arrest in our son's home in Charlotte. Mildred came to be with me, and the family spent a wonderful time together. Although I could not leave the house unless accompanied by my lawyer, I thanked God for another miracle.

Immediately after the Johnson case concluded, I had a hearing before Judge Potter on the reduction of sentence petition my attorneys had filed 120 days after my sentencing.

On another occasion, in November 1990, I was ordered released for five days by a federal judge to return to Charlotte to testify in a civil case. Both plaintiff and defendant attorneys had petitioned the judge for me to testify.

In over sixteen months of being in prison, I was permitted to spend thirteen glorious days with my family in our

IN THE DISTRICT COURT OF THE UNITED STATES
FOR THE WESTERN DISTRICT OF NORTH CAROLINA
CHARLOTTE DIVISION
C-CR-88-205-02

FILED
CHARLOTTE, N. C.
APR 2 5 1990
U. S. DISTRICT COURT
W. DIST. OF N. C.

UNITED STATES OF AMERICA	)	
vs.	)	O R D E R
RICHARD W. DORTCH	)	

THIS MATTER is before the Court on Defendant Dortch's Motion for Reduction of Sentence pursuant to Rule 35(b) of the Federal Rules of Criminal Procedure, timely filed December 5, 1989. A hearing was held at Charlotte, North Carolina on April 12, 1990. Jerry W. Miller, Assistant United States Attorney, represented the Government. William K. Diehl, Jr. and Mark T. Calloway, Attorneys at Law, represented Defendant Dortch, who attended the hearing.

Mr. William Fawcett, Attorney at Law, also attended the hearing and made a statement to the Court. Mr. Fawcett represents the lifetime partners in an unrelated civil class action seeking reimbursement for purchases of lifetime partnerships. Mr. Fawcett informed the Court that Defendant Dortch is the only executive from PTL to step forward to assist the class of lifetime partners and that Defendant Dortch has cooperated completely in the lifetime partners' civil class action.

I. FACTUAL BACKGROUND

Along with co-Defendant James O. Bakker, Defendant Dortch was indicted on twenty-four counts basically for conspiracy, wire fraud, and mail fraud. Each count exposed Defendant Dortch to a maximum term of imprisonment of five years, totalling a possible maximum exposure of 120 years.

Shortly before trial, Defendant Dortch entered into a plea

agreement with the Government in which he agreed to plead guilty to four counts in the Indictment: Count 7 (mail fraud), Counts 10 and 14 (wire fraud), and Count 24 (conspiracy). The Plea Agreement provided that Counts 7 and 10 would be consolidated for the purpose of sentencing and that Counts 14 and 24 would be consolidated for purposes of sentencing, which effectively limited Defendant Dortch's maximum exposure to two counts of the Indictment, or ten years.

Paragraph 2(B) of the Plea Agreement provided as follows:

> Mr. Dortch shall cooperate with the United States Attorney's Office and the Department of Justice by providing truthful, complete, and forthright information whenever, wherever, to whomever, and in whatever form an attorney from the United States Attorney's Office or the Department of Justice requests. The term "whatever form" includes, but is not limited to, oral responses to questions; sworn, written statements; interrogatories; sworn testimony before a grand jury; sworn testimony in court; and documentary materials. The term "whomever" includes, but is not limited to, all Federal criminal law enforcement agencies.

Paragraph 4(I) of the Plea Agreement provided as follows:

> Defendant Dortch understands and agrees that if he should file a motion for reduction of his sentence pursuant to Rule 35(b) of the Federal Rules of Criminal Procedure, the United States Attorney's Office shall inform the judge handling the motion of the extent and value of Mr. Dortch's cooperation under the terms of paragraph 2(B) of this plea agreement.

On August 8, 1989, the Court accepted the Plea Agreement executed between Defendant Dortch, his attorneys, and the Government. At sentencing on August 24, 1989, in accordance with the Plea Agreement, the Court consolidated Counts 7 and 10 and consolidated Counts 14 and 24 for purposes of sentencing. The

Court sentenced Defendant Dortch to an active term of imprisonment as follows: On consolidated Counts 7 and 10, four years imprisonment, plus a $100,000.00 fine, and on consolidated Counts 14 and 24, four years imprisonment, plus a $100,000.00 fine. The Court also imposed a $50.00 special assessment on each count, totalling $200.00.

II. DISCUSSION

The Court has deliberated extensively over this matter and has considered, among other things, Defendant Dortch's maximum exposure if he had been convicted on all counts at trial, Defendant Dortch's maximum exposure under the Plea Agreement, and Defendant Dortch's eight-year sentence actually imposed by this Court.

It appears that Defendant Dortch has followed the terms of his Plea Agreement, specifically Paragraph 2(B) quoted previously. Defendant Dortch has cooperated with the Government in three criminal prosecutions, all of which were tried before this Court: United States v. James and David Taggart, United States v. James O. Bakker, and United States v. Samuel Johnson.

In reference to the prosecution of the Taggarts, Defendant Dortch has produced a letter addressed to one of his attorneys from David A. Brown, Assistant Chief, Department of Justice, one of the attorneys who prosecuted the Taggarts. In the letter, Mr. Brown essentially stated that even though Defendant Dortch did not testify at the Taggarts' trial, his failure to testify was not attributable to any reluctance by Defendant Dortch to testify, but was rather a purely legal decision by his attorneys. Mr. Brown pointed out that Defendant Dortch was present at the Taggarts' sentencing hearing and was available to testify. Mr. Brown concluded his letter with these words:

> In summary, Mr. Calloway, your client exhibited uncharacteristic candor and his unrestricted cooperation exceeded my expectations. Coupled with his plea of guilty which we recognized as large step on the road to rehabilitation, Mr. Dortch is, in my opinion, deserving of due consideration of his motion to reduce his sentence.

In reference to the prosecution of his co-Defendant, James O. Bakker, Defendant Dortch did in fact testify at trial before the undersigned. In accordance with Paragraph 2(I) of the Plea Agreement, Mr. Miller, one of the attorneys who prosecuted Mr. Bakker, informed the Court at the hearing on April 12, 1990, that Defendant Dortch cooperated in every way with the Government both in assisting the Government to prepare for Mr. Bakker's trial and by testifying at trial. Having presided at Mr. Bakker's trial and listened to Defendant Dortch's testimony, the Court is of the opinion that Defendant Dortch was forthright and truthful.

In reference to the prosecution of Samuel Johnson, which also was tried before this Court, Defendant Dortch testified at trial. Mr. Miller also informed the Court at the April 12, 1990 hearing of Defendant Dortch's cooperation in the grand jury investigation and in the Government's presentation of its case. Having presided at the trial of Mr. Johnson and listened to Defendant Dortch's testimony, the Court believes that Defendant Dortch was forthright and truthful.

This Court has said in the courtroom time after time that acceptance of responsibility and assistance to the Government are two of the most important ways a defendant may help himself and impact the sentence ultimately imposed by this Court

III. ORDER OF THE COURT

NOW, THEREFORE, IT IS ORDERED that:

1. Defendant Dortch's Motion for Reduction of Sentence be, and hereby is, **GRANTED**; and

2. The Clerk **AMEND** Defendant Dortch's Judgment and Commitment Order, entered August 24, 1989, by:

    a. Striking the language "Counts 7 and 10 consolidated for sentencing: FOUR (4) YEARS IMPRISONMENT plus a $100,000 fine plus a $100 assessment; Counts 14 and 24 consolidated for sentencing: FOUR (4) YEARS IMPRISONMENT to run consecutively with counts 7 and 10 plus a $100,000 fine plus a $100 assessment."; and

    b. Substituting in place of the above-stricken language "Counts 7, 10, 14, and 24 consolidated for purposes of sentencing: THIRTY (30) MONTHS imprisonment, plus $200,000 fine, plus a $200 special assessment."

The Clerk is directed to certify copies of this Order to Defendant, defense counsel, the United States Probation Office, the United States Bureau of Prisons, and the United States Attorney.

This the ~~25th~~ day of April, 1990.

ROBERT D. POTTER, CHIEF
UNITED STATES DISTRICT JUDGE

son's home. It was so wonderful to embrace my wife in the seclusion of a house; to eat homecooked meals; to have privacy in the bathroom; to spend time alone. Maybe that's what I hated most about prison —you're never alone, and the noise level continually grates on your nerves. The loud speaker in the dormitory is a must, but it is mind altering.

On any given night the Eglin camp rallied with activity. I liked to sit in the center of camp on a bench, turn full circle, and watch men working in the wood shop, playing soccer or softball, practicing musical instruments, working out in a weight-lifting room, exercising with stationary bicycles, playing handball and tennis, or walking the 1.1 mile road that circled the camp. Others were taking college courses, finishing their high school education, participating in Bible studies, practicing for musicals in the chapel, or reading in the library. Inside the recreation room others were playing cards and dominoes, enjoying a snack of popcorn and Coca Cola, or watching television.

Most of my personal time was spent walking or reading or talking. I did attend a Bible study with several of the men, and we grew together in our faith and love for one another.

At the prison we were permitted visitors every Friday night and every other weekend. Visitation was from 8:00 a.m. until 3:30 p.m. on Saturday and Sunday. Mildred usually arrived on Friday and left to return home on Sunday, making it possible for us to spend most of the weekend together.

During the sixteen months and ten days that I was at Eglin, my dear wife Mildred, made that thousand mile round trip fifty-two times. She drove the equal of around the earth two times to be with me.

When I asked her once if she minded, she replied, "I never dread the trip. It's a pleasant time to be alone and think and pray and sing. I listen to cassettes and communicate with the Lord."

On Sunday mornings I was able to sleep a little later — until about seven-thirty. Then a little after eight, I would be informed that my wife had arrived. It was sort of like dating again. We'd sit in the visiting room, drinking hot chocolate and eating coffee cake until time for the church service.

I remember, in particular, Chaplain Johnson's message on "Wax or Clay." "By the light of the Son, He can either melt or harden us, depending on His plan for our life at that time," he had preached. "When clay hardens it becomes strong. When wax is melted, it can be formed into a new image."

What will my outcome be? I wondered. What does God want me to be? It was then I realized that *being* is more important than *doing*.

The chapel program at the prison camp was excellent. The senior chaplain, Rev. Stephen Johnson, and Rev. Arthur Bectin ministered to our spiritual needs. Inmates were told they could find help in the chapel program, and many did.

The chapel sponsored work programs. The prison, in conjunction with Prison Ministries Fellowship, repaired the homes of poor people. The prison choir conducted services in local churches, sponsored musical events, and arranged for Bible studies with teachers from the community. On holidays the chaplains invited local church choirs to perform at the prison chapel. The programs were splendid.

At night I often listened to the Christian radio station. Hearing the song, "To Be Used of God, To Sing To Preach and Pray," made me ask, "What will God make of me?" I wept thinking of how I had failed Him.

I still found it hard to believe that I was incarcerated in a federal prison. Depression would set in, often for days at a time.

Then I would turn to my Friend, who sticketh closer than a brother, my Saviour, Redeemer, and constant Companion. *I do have a friend,* I thought, *who understands everything that has happened.* I didn't understand, so I yielded to Him, asking for His grace to be able to bear "all things."

I was convinced that being in prison was somehow in His plan and in His will. He will bring me through as an overcomer, I reminded myself. To know the fellowship of Jesus was the cry of my heart.

Only God's presence, the love of my wife and family, and the encouragement of some true friends sustained me during that time. Without them, only God knows what would have happened to me.

Jim McDonald, a long-time friend from our Illinois days, visited me regularly. On the day that I entered Eglin Prison, Jim took over as the general manager of the local Cadillac/Buick car dealership in Fort Walton Beach, Florida, located only five minutes from the prison camp. Other than two weekends when he was out of town, Jim McDonald visited me every week during my entire sixteen months and ten days of incarceration. I couldn't have had a more dear and wonderful person to spend time with.

As everyone has, Jim and Rita McDonald had gone through their own tough times years before. Mildred and I had the opportunity to walk through that experience with them. Anytime you go through conflict with someone, a certain bonding takes hold. Jim McDonald and I had that kind of a friendship.

The dearest friends we had during this experience were Dr. and Mrs. Arthur Parsons. They came to see me many times.

Other friends, like Sandra and Larry Sims, also came to visit. Since April of 1987, they had stood by our side from the day of the indictment up to the sentencing time. Now they continued to show their support to Mildred and me while I was in prison.

One day in April, 1990, while in the cafeteria, Mrs. Anderson, my case manager, called and said my lawyer, Mark Calloway, was on the phone. I went to the phone with much anxiety, wondering if this could be the answer I'd been waiting for.

"Is this about the judge's order on my reduction of sentence hearing?" I asked excitely.

Mark answered cautiously, "It's probably not what you wanted, but it's good. Judge Potter has reduced your sentence from eight years to thirty months."

I had hoped he might give me house arrest or probation.

At the Rule 35 (Reduction of Sentence) hearing, the judge had asked some questions that made me think he would end my prison sentence. Although deeply disappointed, I respected his decision.

On May 2, I began the next quarter of my now thirty-month sentence. I had been in Eglin for three months. Facing the stark reality that I wouldn't be up for parole for at least another year filled me with dread. I knew the judge's decision on my Rule 35 hearing was final. That was the last chance of getting my time shortened. I felt like I couldn't go on. Would I endure to the end? I wondered.

That day faith was put to the test in more ways than one.

I made the mistake of walking into the bathroom at the wrong time. An inmate, whom I knew from the clothing room, had just mopped the floor and it wasn't quite dry. I did not know that.

The man went into a rage, cursing me voraciously.

I pled with him for forgiveness and volunteered to mop the floor myself. But there was no appeasing him; he was livid.

I wept at his anger in front of him.

Many of these men had so much hostility bottled up inside them that they lashed out for no reason at the slightest infraction. The jealousy I saw among inmates also amazed me. But then, I thought, it's probably not any more than the average church deals with on a regular basis.

More and more Mildred's visits became my life line. I felt God had blessed me with a jewel of jewels. Her faithfulness to God, the way she stood by my side, and the godly example she set for our family overwhelmed me with love. When all else fails, I thought, her bedrock foundation in God remains secure.

In the fall of 1990, I had a hernia that needed to be repaired. Knowing that I would probably be paroled sometime in the summer of 1991, I thought it would be a good idea to get it taken care of because it had been bothering me for some time.

The medical staff approved the very apparent need for

the surgery, and I entered the hospital on January 4, 1991. At the Air Force hospital, the Gulf War occupied everyone's thinking. One hundred and ten medical personnel were preparing to leave for Saudi Arabia the next day to join the Desert Storm initiative.

The night before surgery, Col. Razor, the Chief of Internal Medicine at the Eglin Air Force Hospital, came into my room with the Chief of Surgery.

As he was walking out of the room, he noticed that my legs were swollen. He asked, "Do you know why your ankles are swollen?"

"No, I don't, but I have been concerned about it," I replied.

Col. Razor suggested to the Chief of Surgery that they do a CAT scan several days after the hernia surgery to see if I had any obstruction in my leg causing this swelling.

He added, with a twinkle in his eyes, "Besides that, we can see then the beautiful surgical job you've done, Colonel."

The hernia operation went well, and I made excellent progress. Several days afterwards, I was taken to the radiology department and had a CAT scan.

It was a very sober and solemn Chief of Surgery who came into my room that night. He said, "Pastor Dortch, you have a large cyst on your right kidney that I feel we should keep watching. However, what deeply concerns me is that your left kidney has a mass that needs to be analyzed. I am going to send you by ambulance down to the MRI facility in downtown Fort Walton Beach to take a closer look at this mass."

The next day Air Force personnel took me by ambulance to the MRI facility, where I was put in a capsule for forty-five minutes and analyzed.

About an hour after I was back at the hospital, I received a telephone call from the doctor. "You have a cancer, unquestionably, and we have to remove your kidney as soon as we can arrange it."

Hearing the word "cancer" brought new waves of shock, fear, and uncertainty. Being in prison had already put a tremendous emotional strain on Mildred and me, and now this additional burden seemed more than we could bear.

I have always been confident in God's wisdom to take care of me, but having gone through the PTL experience, the prison sentence, and now being diagnosed with cancer, I wondered, *When will it end?* I must admit that I felt like saying, "Lord, tell Job to move over. I want to sit down beside him."

In less than a week, I underwent major surgery for the second time. Having a kidney removed left me feeling very vulnerable, especially knowing my other kidney already had a cyst.

After the operation, I awakened from the anesthesia in tremendous pain. Using a special device, I could push a button and give myself morphine. Not in the habit of taking pain medication, I was reluctant to do so. But the nurses convinced me to "push the button" and get some relief from the constant agony. For the next ten days, I struggled through a living hell. Then gradually I began to feel myself growing stronger.

I have talked to a number of people who have had a heart bypass or major organs removed. A few weeks after the surgery almost every patient goes into a state of depression. I was no exception, but I remained confident in the fact that I was going to get well.

The Bureau of Prisons Camp Medical Director, Dr. Rossi, and the medical staff at the Air Force Base Regional Hospital were very kind to Mildred and me. Counting the time for the surgical hernia and the kidney removal, my stay in the hospital came to four weeks.

During that time, the chaplains from the Air Force Base, who were people of prayer, came by the room frequently and prayed with me. The hospital turned out to be an oasis of spiritual help, and the entire experience bolstered my faith in our merciful Heavenly Father.

My major concern was, when was this all going to be over? In some strange way, I thought, maybe my bout with cancer will be a way of getting out of prison. Although I was incarcerated for another four and a half months after my surgery, I was released twenty-eight days earlier than was planned.

When it became apparent after my cancer surgery that I would be released soon, I noticed that Chaplain Johnson, the senior prison chaplain, became much more friendly. He had always been kind to me, offering to do what he could to help me, but suddenly his interest in me took a different approach.

While the chaplain talked about helping to get me out of prison, he mixed his conversation with accounts of his own personal financial needs. At that point, a red light came on in my mind. Could what I had heard be true, that there are occasions when someone might try to trap inmates into a situation that is either embarrassing or illegal? Was this a scam, or an undercover job, to entice me to do something that I shouldn't do?

I was concerned. What was really going on? I wondered. I didn't know, but something appeared out of kilter. Whether it was an attempted plan to "get me" for something, I never knew. All I know is what took place.

Chaplain Johnson told me that his son was going to college, and they needed financial help for his tuition. One day in the visiting room, I introduced Chaplain Johnson to a very prominent man who was the head of a large corporation in the Tampa Bay-Clearwater area. I told the chaplain that he was a businessman.

"Perhaps you could ask him for help with the tuition for my son?" Rev. Johnson asked me. "I also need help getting to Europe for a chaplain's conference. I'm an officer in the prison chaplain association, and I really need to attend that meeting." It didn't make sense. Why wouldn't the Bureau of Prisons supply the funds for the trip?

In the course of conversations, I had mentioned that our son worked for a computer firm.

One day he called me into his office and said, "I need a computer."

I asked him, "Is it for the chapel?"

I didn't quite understand his response, but he did state that the computer would be put in his home.

"Come into my office," he urged and pointed to the telephone. "Why don't you call your son?"

I hesitated but did as I was told. After all, Rev. Johnson was a prison official, and I was only a lowly inmate.

I called Rich and asked if it would be possible for his company to give a gift of a computer to Chaplain Johnson

Rich responded with a question. "Could this be a tax-deductible gift?"

I quite naturally turned to the chaplain and asked, "Is this a tax-deductible gift?"

His response was, "Yes."

I related that to Rich, who responded quickly, "In whose name would it be given?"

With a wink, Chaplain Stephen Johnson responded, "It can be given to the Saint Stephen's Ministry."

I left the matter in Rich's hands, exited the chaplain's office, and went on about my tasks. I felt very uncomfortable. Later I conveyed to Rich the wink that accompanied the chaplain's reply. I knew he would know what to do about the situation — forget it!

After I was released from prison and had returned home, on two occasions the chaplain called me. According to regulations, officers of the camp are not permitted to call or contact inmates for two years following their release. So, once again, I wondered, *What's going on here?* I would not respond to the chaplain, even after his second call.

If this book dealt with some other subject, it wouldn't be necessary to have told this story. But in my search for integrity, this incident proved to be a personal test for me. I would not allow myself to be sidetracked by anyone or anything that could keep me from finding my way back to the integrity I had known before.

Knowing I would soon be going home encouraged me to take an internal audit. What had I learned in prison? How did this experience mesh with the integrity I sought?

I had obeyed the rules — not just the letter of the law —

I had tried to keep the spirit of them also. If I failed, it was in the head, not in the heart.

"I think you've been paroled," Mark Calloway said when he called me at the prison around the first of May.

"NBC television contacted me," he continued. "They want my comments on the decision of the United States Parole Commission to release you. I told them I hadn't heard anything."

"The Parole Commission won't make a public statement until the prison and the party involved have been notified," I told Mark. "I'll check it out and let you know."

One of the case managers at Eglin Prison Camp kindly called the Parole Commission to see if the report was true. He was told they could not release the information to him.

The next morning my wife called the Atlanta Regional Office of the commission, and knowing she was, in fact, Mrs. Dortch, they confirmed my imminent release. We were ecstatic.

All I had to do now was wait and pray.

Near the end of my prison term, nights and days became a blur. At times I found it difficult to express what I was really thinking and feeling deep inside myself.

Maybe it would help to keep a daily diary, I thought. The following are a few entries from those last agonizing weeks:

Thursday, May 3, 1991. I am asking the Lord what He is trying to teach me. I'm so very conscious of His presence guiding me. Just as Jesus made himself of no reputation, so must we. I will live for God. Not just for the earthly church, but for Him.

I'm thinking for the first time about my exit from Eglin. When that time comes and I'm released from my obligations to the government, how can I help people best?

God will take care of me. I know He will. Mildred and I will be starting anew. What will it be like? I wonder what God has in store for us. "Commit thy way unto the Lord and He will direct thy paths."

Monday, May 7. The ultimate question is, what is God

saying to me about all I've been through?

1. Share your experiences with others in ministry.
2. Be still and know that I am God.
3. Spend more time reading the Bible
4. "Do not conform to this world but be transformed by the renewing of your mind, that you may prove that which is good and the acceptable will of God."

Tuesday, May 8. Got up at 5:15, got a blood test. Need to check cholesterol and triglycerides. Had breakfast, then back to the cube reading God's Word.

What will God teach me today? I need to pray more and read the Word more.

He will not forsake me now. The timing of my release is in God's hands. I called my darling wife. We must pray more to get our house in order that we may be used of God.

Monday, May 13, 1991. Mildred is here. When I got up this morning. I felt that I should begin to pack. All the papers are put away, and I cleaned out almost everything.

If it happens today, if I'm able to leave, I'm ready. I sense it will be soon. The Lord has taught me, and is teaching me, patience. God is leading by His Spirit.

Let me go home, Lord. I rejoice at the deliverance You have given me.

Tuesday, May 14. Mildred is here. She will be talking to someone at the Parole Commission today, trying to get some information. Oh God, grant that I may return home today. Is it possible, Lord?

Wednesday, May 15. Mildred called the Parole Commission. There's no news. No hurry or rush in the case. It will be circulated among the other commissioners. Some questions arose because of original jurisdiction in the case. Will probably be several weeks. God knows.

What a disappointment! How long, Oh Lord, how long? God, please hear my cry. I beseech thee, Oh Lord. Please deliver me out of my affliction.

Thursday, May 16. I'm spending all the time I can with my Christian brothers. Reading, waiting on the Lord, praying for the Parole Commission. Mildred is here tonight.

How long, Oh Lord, how long? Why, Oh Lord, why?

Monday, May 20. Went to the Full Gospel Businessmen's meeting tonight. Mr. Purcell spoke. It was good. Mildred is home safely. I worry about her so much. Thank God for her gift of love.

How grateful I am that Marvin Tragash is going home. He is very ill, we must all continue to pray for him.

Wednesday, May 29. What will this day bring forth? Chapel service was a blessing. Thank the Lord, time is passing quickly. Parole Commission is meeting this week. It has been a day of toil. Oh God, deliver me. I'm tired, I'm weak, I'm worn. This is the Lord's day. "He leadeth me beside still waters; He restoreth my soul."

Friday, May 31. My sweetheart comes tomorrow. She's on her way. My love for Mildred is so deep. Has this episode made a difference in our love for each other? No. Never. Absolutely not. Has it enriched our love? Yes. The Lord has made of us tender vessels, and I appreciate her so much.

What a wonderful day. What a wonderful time of fellowship in God's Word.

Sunday, June 3. Up at 6:55. What a beautiful day. I want to walk with God today, enjoy His fellowship and know His direction in my life. Today I will serve Him, love Him, commit myself to Him.

Mildred and I spent most of the morning talking about parole matters and personal decisions that affect us. My sweetheart left today at 2:10 to begin the trip home to Clearwater with Uriah and Ivory. What precious grandchildren! I am so blessed.

Tuesday, June 4. PAROLE GRANTED. It was in *USA Today.* Mark Calloway called. TV stations have contacted the prison. A custody person told me that something is about to happen for me.

How can I get treatment for my illness? I trust the Lord will allow me to go home. He leadeth me, He leadeth me by His own hand, He leadeth me.

Wednesday, June 5. A day of great physical pain. My guts hurt so bad. I went to the hospital trying to get help.

Thank you, Lord. How long, Oh Lord, how long? I hurt so bad. God, please heal me.

I talked to Mildred again. "Lord, You are our only source. We need Your help. It appears that we're still on target. I hope and pray I will hear soon. God, You are our source, our only source."

Thursday, June 7. Pastor Ron Meade will be here today. When will I get the date. "Lord, You know today is Your day."

It finally happened! It really did. Mr. Rick Harris told me. I'm going home about the first of the week. Thank you, loving Lord. I can't believe it! It's drawing so close. God is so good. I still can't believe it.

I called Rich, not there. I talked to Rhonda, Deanna, Ed and Dot, Bill and Pam, and Pastor Meade. I tried to reach Jim McDonald and Mark Burgund.

A man died today. Oh, what a scene at the ball diamond when the inmate passed away. I am concerned about some of my brothers here who are in spiritual need. Their lives appear so hopeless. Aside from completing their sentence, they have no goals, no purpose in life.

Friday, June 8. "A friend loveth at all times and a brother is born for adversity" (Ps. 17:17).

"Lord, let this day be a day crowned with thy blessing of love, and thy blessing also on those who minister to us here at Eglin. We pray for Chaplain Johnson and Chaplain Bectin. We pray for the warden and all the team that serves with him, each official, staff member, Mr. Harris, the captain, the staff officers."

Tonight at ten o'clock I listened to the fine Christian station in this area. The songs filled me with worship. "Worthy is the Lamb That was Slain," "Behold, the Lamb of God that Taketh Away the Sins of the World," "Precious Lamb of Glory," "Tell the Wondrous Story," "Rock of Ages," "Pipe Organ Anthem." It was great.

Wednesday, June 12. I leave today at 8:45 a.m. Going to St. Petersburg. I'm on my way home!

President and Mrs. George Bush with Richard Dortch.

18

Integrity

Several days after I entered Eglin Federal Prison Camp, I was asked to go for a walk with a man who said he had some important things to tell me. He asked me if I knew who he was. I responded, "I'm not quite sure, but your name is Joe LaMotta, isn't it?"

"Yes, it is. When you came into the camp, I didn't think I was going to like you, but something has happened to me during the last few days. You have been polite to me and there's something you need to know. You be strong, God sent you here!"

I wasn't looking for a message from anyone about how God felt about my being in prison, but when the son of the legend, Jake LaMotta "the raging bull," a former boxing champion, said that to me — I paid attention. Hardly anyone ever disagreed with Joe LaMotta, nor did I. I believed him. I did have a certain sense that even through this experience my paths were being set by One much bigger than me. That's why I approached the writing of this book with such solemnity. I do not take it lightly that God has permitted me to go through this experience, through the justice system, prison, the loss of a malignant kidney, and all that I have been through.

I am very mindful that questions can well be asked in reading such a book as this, "What right do you have in writing such a book about integrity?" That's a fair question. But through the pages of this book, I have not dealt with people's rights. I have tried to approach the subject of our relationship to one another and our relationship to God. Lest we all forget it, a loss of integrity can happen to just about anyone. Oftentimes when we come out of a good work environment, a good home, and an environment that is wholesome, we can well think we are immune to any kind of a flaw that concerns integrity. The loss of integrity is an ugly thing. It is immensely painful and there is a supreme price to pay when it happens. Most of your acquaintances won't be there with you.

I have learned that a friend is one who walks in when the rest of the world walks out! Only your true friends will be there. When I was an asset I was wanted by some people, but when I became a liability my presence was not desired or sought. So many people are living close to the line of integrity, on the fence, or are falling across the line, just "living on the edge." We must come to the tough truth. This is not a question of you or me. It is *us!* The kind of persons I was with in prison were not what I really expected. For the most part they were people who would be the most unlikely to fall victim to their crimes.

In almost every facet of life there have been revelations about a lack of integrity. The academic community was shocked to learn about the public disclosure of hyped and falsified scientific research. A study accused forty-seven scientists at the Harvard and Emery University Medical Schools of producing misleading papers. Some of the most prestigious universities have had to admit that they illegally took money from the government. It didn't develop into much of scandal, but tens of millions of dollars were taken by Stanford and other universities.

A House subcommittee estimated recently that one out of every three working Americans is hired with educational or career credentials which have been altered in some way. Sooner or later somebody asks the questions, "What's going on?" "Are the American people dishonest?" A great American, John Gardner, founder of the Common Cause, recently said, "Duplicity and deception, in public and private life, are very substantially greater than they have been in the past."

I was in a meeting recently when someone said that a survey has shown that ninety-one percent of the American people lie regularly. Interestingly, people are firm in their conviction that "others," up to and including public officials, should be held to high standards of honesty. Seven out of ten Americans say the president of the United States should never tell a lie. That being stated by the ninety-one percent of people who admit that they regularly lie.

Integrity involves everything about the wholeness of our inner person, our heart, mind, and will. Integrity simply means singleness: singleness of our purpose, singleness of our will, singleness of our hearts. There is no dividing of the truth that splits the wholeness of what we are about.

It is said that adversity tests our ability to survive, and prosperity tests our integrity. That's when the problem usually occurs, in the times when we are high, and above it all.

Arrogance of Integrity

We have all been told at one time or another that our good name is our most valuable asset. A commendation from our boss or the adoration of a congregation reinforced the notion that we were building a good reputation.

While we might tolerate certain accusations against our activity, we will not stand for attacks on our character or our good name. To a point, this is admirable, but there is a subtle temptation that lies just beneath the surface of this sort of motivation.

Once our reputation grows among the circles in which we live, travel, work, or worship, that reputation begins to take on a life of its own. A certain synergy takes place that allows us to think more of ourselves than is safe to do.

The Scriptures warned of this centuries ago, that this sort of pride in oneself will produce the perfect setting for failure.

David returned victorious from battle, and with great presumption about his own weaknesses looked upon another woman. Peter shared a meal with his Lord and boldly proclaimed that he would follow Him until death. Before the morning sun, Peter broke that vow.

The Book of Proverbs warns, "The Lord detests all the proud of heart. Be sure of this; They will not go unpunished" (Prov. 16:5).

James writes, "God opposes the proud, but gives grace to the humble" (James 4:6). In the Lord's work we can easily forget that these words are not written for someone else, but for us.

I went to PTL in this kind of circumstance. My reputation preceded me. I heard people say, "We can quit worrying about PTL now, Richard Dortch is there and he wouldn't put up with anything that would be dishonest, illegal, or anything of the kind. He will have a straight arrow, squeeky-clean operation."

When I went to PTL, I was Mr. Clean. I believed, as did others, that nothing could go wrong. I knew it and everyone else knew it. I was proud of the fact that in thirty-five years of public life, there had never been a rumor or scandal attached to me.

I had never made a "deal" with anyone.

I didn't have a "Jessica Hahn" in my past.

I had not stolen money or anything else.

I was proud of it.

The problem was that I was in an arrogant state and I lost my sensitivity. I lost sight of the big picture of what was going on. People had told me over and over, "There will be nothing going wrong at PTL with you there." I believed that. I was above it all.

I believed that, and in my entire career had tried to practice that. Slowly, however, I began to believe that what others said about me and my reputation was not only true, but something I could depend on to make certain that nothing illegal or crooked took place.

As PTL began to grow rapidly, my confidence in my own integrity began to blur the need for humility before the Lord. The confidence in my own integrity had gradually became an arrogance that I did not recognize as such.

Paul Cedar, a respected pastor on the west coast, wrote about the danger leaders can face in this dilemma:

> Pride tells us to go it alone; God tells us to go with Him. Pride tells us to follow our instincts; God tells us to follow Him. Pride tells us to utilize human knowledge and rational approaches; God tells us to acknowledge Him. Pride tells us to "fake it;" God tells us to allow the truth to set us free. Pride tells us never to appear weak or uncertain; God tells us that His strength is made perfect in our weakness. Pride tells us to have people focus upon us; God tells us to invite people to follow us with their eyes upon Jesus![1]

The arrogance of integrity is blind. I couldn't see what was going on around me. I took satisfaction in what others had said, that I could be trusted. That still, small voice that can warn of danger could no longer be clearly heard over the roar of what was being done for the Lord.

I became so intoxicated with the growth of Heritage USA, so enamored with what was developing around me, that I refused to see what was happening. The sins of adultery, fornication, embezzlement, etc., was so far removed from me that I was confident of a moral and godly life.

Being on television, speaking to adoring crowds, having favorable articles written about me, was enjoyable. I thought that because of my character, nothing could happen. What accusation could possibly be made?

This kind of arrogance of integrity is not the exclusive sin of church leaders. It is natural to man regardless of his profession. The temptation to believe that your strength comes from yourself is alluring.

Mark Ritchie was a successful commodities trader who, by his own confession, fell victim to his own arrogance:

> It wasn't just the realization that I genuinely thought myself better than others, but it was the fact that my goal in life was to improve myself to the point that it would, in fact, be true; so I could, with honesty, face myself in the mirror and say that I was good, better, maybe even best — all relative terms that can only be defined in relation to other people. Even then, some objective measurement must be employed; quantity of money, power, influence, sexual attractiveness. Incongruous as it seemed, my life goal was to become stuck on myself, the very thing everyone agreed to be the worst of qualities.[2]

I was too proud to see what was really happening. That had always been my strength, sizing up situations and problems and knowing what was really going on. Not the secret agenda that is apparent to everyone else, but to perceive what isn't being said, what has not been spoken. That's where the problem would usually lie.

Each week seems to bring another revelation that a leader previously thought invincible has committed a fatal error.

A respected savings and loan executive is found guilty of violating the trust of his shareholders and depositors. Members of the United States Senate are implicated in the matter.

Did he set out in the beginning to defraud? Probably not. When arrogance about our own reputation and integrity is dominant in our life, then we get out of kilter and make the wrong decisions.

Robert Linder, professor of history at Kansas State University, has analyzed United States presidents and found that an arrogance of one's own integrity can result in duplicity:

> Ulysses Simpson Grant (1869-77), for example, attended services with considerable regularity with his devout wife at the Metropolitan Methodist Church in Washington. When as president he was requested by the Sunday School Times to compose a message for its readers, he advised, "Hold fast to the Bible as the sheet anchor of your liberties; write its precepts in your hearts and practice them in your lives."
>
> Although relatively honest, Grant allowed corruption to run rampant during his eight years as president.[3]

Church leaders, business executives, politicians, professionals, and people from all walks of life, must guard against this subtle temptation. Few people, if any, start out with the intent to fail or disappoint others. In an effort to achieve their goals and make their organizations successful they choose a demanding responsibility.

It is for that very reason that their original intentions were good and honorable, that arrogance becomes such a personal enemy.

Steven Covey, in his *Seven Habits of Highly Effective People*, underscores the importance of an uncompromised integrity within ourselves:

> . . . Integrity is, fundamentally, the value we place on ourselves. It's our ability to make and keep commitments to ourselves, to "walk our talk." In other words, if you are an effective manager of yourself, your discipline comes from within; it is a function of your independent will. You are a disciple, a follower of your own deep values and their source. And you have the will, the integrity, to subordinate your feelings, your impulses, your

moods, to those values.[4]

David said, "Do not lift up your horn on high, do not speak with insolent pride." God simply states, don't toot your own horn, and don't let anyone else toot it. Whether you are in the valley, or on the mountain, the tilt of the neck should always be the same. You have to look up to see God. God takes and God gives away. God raises up or brings down. We are not nearly as important as we sometimes think we are.

In reflecting back, in studying what I was about, and in listening to my own heart, I believe that I felt that the reputation I had was clear and spotless. That it would hold me. I only focused on issues that were obvious and forgot about the little things that were going on all around me. I set aside the fact that I knew that life, as a whole, was made up of the little things.

Certainly, all of us have been shocked by the things that have happened in the last five years in the world of religion. The Catholic Church has been severely wounded by the accusations of impropriety in the relationship of priests to their followers. The evangelical community has been rocked by the PTL scandals, Jimmy Swaggart's failures, the revelations of ABC television about well-known evangelists and their fund raising and spending practices. Government employees, the savings and loan fiasco, office holders, and a big slice of the business community, it's all there. It involves all of us. The sad thing is that most of us have not seen those who are involved step forward and say, **"I was wrong. I have sinned! What I didn't do, or what I did do was wrong, and I am sorry. Please forgive me."** Dr. Arthur Parsons, the man who helped me the most of all the Christian leaders, said to me on one occasion, "To be honest, you have to be honest." Profound? Yes, if you are seeking to be honest!

Reverend Theodore Hesburgh, former president of the University of Notre Dame, recently stated, "To the extent family life is disintegrating, kids are not being taught values about lying, cheating, and stealing."

I recently read that twentieth century Americans have

grown cautious about making value judgments. There is a growing degree of cynicism and sophistication in our society, a sense that all things are relative, and nothing is absolutely right or wrong.

When a New York City student turned in a purse she had found, complete with the $1,000 cash, not a single school official would congratulate her on her virtue. Her teacher explained, "If I come from a position of what is right and wrong, then I am not their counselor." The apparent translation: We no longer believe in black and white, only shades of grey.

Most Americans believe there is dishonesty in the business community today. The philosophy seems to be, "Do whatever is necessary to succeed and beat the competition."

"People come to feel like suckers if they're honest," a recent article in a *Business News* magazine reported.

Paul Harvey, the noted ABC news commentator, recently observed that Sears, one of America's great retail institutions, had lost $48 million in the last quarter to shrinkage. Most retailers agree that the greatest loss in shrinkage is to theft. It's a known fact that four times more is stolen by employees than by the public in the retail industry. There is an impersonality, an anonymity that makes it difficult to affix responsibility. Some of my fellow inmates were in prison because of bank failures and savings and loan scandals. I also shared the dormitory I was in with quite a number of government officials. Among my friends in prison were quite a number of lawyers; they were probably the largest number of professionals with me in prison. There were medical doctors there because they had wrongly taken Medicare and Medicaid funds. There were also former prosecutors, a former member of the Secret Service, and a former judge. It is a given fact, that many have failed the public. Some have admitted it, and some have not. People have a right to expect more from us in leadership positions than others. It seems that many of us find it so hard to come straight forward and admit that we are wrong.

This subject involves much more than just a few people

in and out of the church. It's more than Jimmy Swaggart having an illicit affair, Ivan Boesky taking money wrongly from Wall Street, and the *Washington Post* writer who made up the story for which she received a Pulitzer prize. It involves people in church work and in the secular community. Nothing could please the enemy of our soul more than to point fingers at Jimmy Swaggart and forget the tens of thousands of ministers whose private lives have not yet been made known. It's more than Jim Bakker and Richard Dortch who got caught up in something. It involves all of us.

I have never accused anyone of having committed my sin and I bear no responsibility to accept the blame for others. But one thing we must universally understand is that we are in the problem of integrity together. Without question, it is the issue of the '90s. For many of us, it's quite obvious that we really don't know what is going on in our own personal lives. We don't sense how deep we have sunk: telling lies, implying untruths, cheating on our income tax, taking money, or anything that is not ours, infidelity to our companions, doing things to hurt someone, not doing what we should have done, coveting something of someone else's, and having a multitude of gods.

Integrity in its most simple form means wholeness, completeness, entireness. It's from a root word that means intact. It means that our heart is not divided. There is no hidden agenda, nothing! As an administrator, I had one criteria for what we would do. I taught, believed, and practiced a very simple philosophy about integrity. "If we can do what we are proposing and explain it to our supporters, and feel totally comfortable in doing it, it's probably the right thing to do. If we have to remain silent on it, or compartmentalize it, it's probably wrong, and we'll suffer if we do it."

Integrity has to be with completeness. I must know in my heart that I have done everything that I can do to admit my errors, acknowledge my sins, ask for forgiveness, and know that "there is now no condemnation to them that are in Christ Jesus . . . who walk not after the flesh, but after the spirit." It is wonderful to be free! No fears! To know that there is nothing that is about to be revealed, nothing not yet told. Arrogance, pride, and a haughty spirit always come before the fall. A law enforcement officer told me, "I was surprised that you were as forthcoming as you have been." I knew I had told the truth.

Summary

The arrogance of integrity is the result of pride that begins to take root in the life of someone who has earned a reputation for integrity. It is borne out of a failure to realize daily that what the Bible says about people is true of us all — our flesh is constantly seeking to fulfill itself in pride.

How do we guard against this dilemma? First, we must remember that we are never more right with God than when we admit we are wrong. The grace of our Lord is His response to our need, not our good work.

Secondly, everyone needs a select group of people to whom they can be totally accountable. This group does not have to be large or influential, rather they must simply care enough about you to tell you what you need to hear.

Selective Integrity

"You can't ask me to leave my position as the leader now, we're having the most successful time we've ever had here." That is what the top man in the organization said to me when I confronted him with his apparent problem that seemingly everyone knew except him. In the many years that I have served as a leader and person in a place of responsibility, I have made some observations. Almost every person that I can think of who has fallen, layman or minister, did so because they believed they could commit the terrible thing they had done, but they were going to be the exception. They thought they could pick and choose. They could sin . . . even if only occasionally . . . even for a good cause, and it would make no difference. They could have a public persona, but no one would ever see the other side of their life. I saw it in Christian television and I saw it a lot of other places where

I served. A top executive in Christian television recently told me, "The biggest motivator in Christian television is the check book. It has less to do with the purpose and will of God than revenue — who pays the most gets in the mainstream of the 'will of God.' The time slot opens up for those who have the check book. Our soul is for sale. When will we learn that God's economy is not ours? Once your persona overshadows your ministry, it is as if you are waving your alms before men. Therefore, you have your reward." It is an honorable, safe man who speaks like that.

Yes, money was a factor in the way we were all thinking at PTL. There were occasions when, I am convinced as I reflect back, the greater good took second place to the money that was involved. There is an obvious reason that the Master of our souls said, "The love of money is the root of all evil." When greed gets into our spirit we are usually the last one to know. Others can see it but, seemingly, we can't. When you're living close to God He has a way of rubbing off on you. When your affections are on money, it, too, has a way of rubbing off on you. It's really not worth it. Self-denial is the best and wisest course.

There seems to be two people in many of us, the one who can do something for someone in a kindly act, and the one who is unfaithful to their companion. There often is the person who can correct others, even in a helpful way, and yet cannot see the iniquity in their own person. They thunder to their children, "Don't you cheat!" Yet they bring things home from work that do not belong to them. Every person faces the sin, the calamity of selective integrity. **If others do it, it's wrong; if we do it, God understands.** So often we expect and demand more of others than we deliver ourselves.

Americans have developed a passion for the scoop on public figures. It doesn't matter whether they are politicians or pastors. If someone has a picture, a tape, or an eyewitness — people want to know.

This seeming demand for high morality would be a welcomed trend if it reflected a concern that all of us should be more conscious of our actions.

Sadly, most polls indicate that we demand one standard of others and quite another of ourselves. Some actions have been labeled taboo, while others are acceptable — if we can get away with it.

The pastor who would abhor infidelity might think nothing of cheating on his tax records. The extra income that came in December can be rationalized away from being taxable — or even reportable on the form 1040.

The politician who speaks openly in opposition to certain behavior may have no qualms about violating his own marriage vows.

In fact, most of us have become so good at selective integrity that our attitude reflects it. A recent study found that most Americans agree that the American family spends less time together and is in trouble — all except their's, that is.

This selective integrity leads to a life of extreme self-centeredness. David Halberstam, writer and journalist, described this attitude in his book, *The Next Century:*

> Not surprisingly, most Americans, faced with a new equation, wanted it both ways. They wanted a sort of no-fault patriotism — to keep enjoying the far greater personal freedoms and entitlements of the seventies and eighties with the vastly improved lifestyle and greater professional possibilities, while their neighbors were to revert to the more disciplined lives of the fifties. We were, in effect, a great free people, anxious for everyone to start making sacrifices, except, of course, ourselves.[5]

The late Joseph Fletcher caused quite a stir when he wrote his controversial work on situation ethics. To many he seemed to be promoting the notion that lying was acceptable, perhaps even honorable, if it served some higher good.

The idea of selective integrity was certainly not original with Fletcher, but his book proved to be a watershed on legitimatizing the subject.

One man who found himself in the middle of an integrity crisis that impacted the world was Chuck Colson. When it was first announced that Colson was born again, many people, including church people, were skeptical.

After a decade and a half, however, his testimony has borne fruit. In a recent publication, entitled *Kingdoms in Conflict,* Colson reflects on how the Nixon White House would use the White House church services for political rather than spiritual purposes:

> People in power use power to keep themselves in power. Even if they are genuinely interested in a special interest group's agenda — or naturally disposed to their position — they will work that relationship for everything they can get out of it.[6]
>
> The weekly church services Nixon scheduled most Sundays for the East Room provided great opportunities as well. To select the preacher, we determined who would give us the greatest impact — politically, that is, not spiritually. At the time I was a nominal Christian at best, and had no way to judge the spiritual. And there were always two hundred or more seats to be filled, tickets that were like keys to the political kingdoms.[7]

The practice of selective integrity has long been suspected in business. Countless dramas of the tension between profits and people have been played out with the theme of integrity.

Business schools enjoyed record enrollments in the eighties when the barometer of success was financial. Much of the stigma of being totally profit driven was replaced with a generation of graduates ready to move up.

At the same time, the American marketplace was threatened by overseas competition, a shrinking consumer base, and a growing emphasis on quality.

These changes became a challenge for corporate leaders in choosing between what was perceived to be best for business, stockholders, employees, or themselves.

While pursuing integrity on many fronts they often selectively chose areas where they might not get caught.

Tom Peters, celebrated management consultant, illustrates one example of selective integrity:

> To use the psychologist's terms, integrity is not only absolute (stealing is bad, period), but it involves "perceived equity." That is, fairness is in the eye of the beholder. Paying bonuses to management and withholding worker bonuses in a problematic year is perceived to be unfair, regardless of the extenuating circumstances.[8]

Peters goes on to conclude that integrity may be far more important in the smaller areas of an executive's life:

> Integrity may be about little things as much as or more than big ones. It's about executives taking friends, rather than customers, to sit in the company's box seats at the ballpark. It's about pushing salespeople at the end quarter to place orders, knowing that many will be canceled within the week — but that the cancellations will count in the next period for accounting purposes.[9]

Such action has not, however, gone unnoticed. Litigation against business executives for breach of integrity has been on the rise in recent years. The rash of legal activity on Wall Street concerning insider trading and fraud has become legend.

Were these business leaders untrustworthy? Did they lie or cheat in every area of their life? No, they selectively chose areas where the potential return was the greatest when compared to the risk of being caught.

The private sector has not been alone in pursuing selective integrity. And, while such action is reprehensible anywhere, it can be no more frightening than when it occurs in government.

Government leaders serve in a sacred trust with the electorate. In America that trust is considered essential to a democracy. Local, state, and national leaders swear to uphold their respective constitutions. When government's integrity is called into question, the future of our culture is at stake.

Sadly, in the past two decades one leader after another, from both parties, has been accused of swearing to an oath one day and breaching integrity the next. Alvin Toffler put the deceptive practice of cooking the books into a contemporary perspective:

> Governments, of course, have been "cooking their books" at least since the invention of double-entry ledgers by the Venetians in the 14th century. They have been "cooking" all sorts of data, information, and knowledge, not just budgetary or financial, since Day One. What's new is the ability to fry, broil, or microwave the stuff with help of computers.[10]

Each time we experience selective integrity, whether as the one who is doing it or being harmed by it, something happens inside us. I believe we lose respect for each other and, ultimately, ourselves.

Peters suggests that we cannot view these as mere lapses:

> These minor lapses set a tone of disrespect for people, products, systems, customers, distributors, and relationships that can readily become pervasive. That is, there is no such thing as a minor lapse in integrity.[11]

In the maelstrom that affected all of us at PTL, I've heard others define precisely what happened to me there. The stories were totally untrue, yet they told them as facts.

When you ask any one of these people if they are a person of integrity, they respond quickly, "Of course, that's what I believe in!" Do they tell the truth? No, the story was simply too good to not comment on, whether or not it was true.

Truth cannot be selective. That is how integrity is lost, becoming so involved in something that we lose a sense of our honesty. We say it when we flatter people and we don't mean it and are totally insincere — often even when we despise them.

Selective integrity is the hypocrisy of knowing that there is duplicity in our lives. It is saying to someone, "We sure do love you," when we know in our heart of hearts we seldom, if ever, think of them, and have never extended a helping hand to do anything for them. It is making up our minds about something or someone, and then going out and looking for facts to prove what we have already decided. It's sending mixed signals to people. In one moment we are pledging our covenant of commitment, and the next turning upon them. There have been moments of hurts in my life in recent days when someone has said to me, "I certainly do love you." I have restrained my spirit and thought to myself, "I do hope that you don't treat everyone you love the way you have demonstrated your love to me."

Integrity is telling the truth and not picking and choosing our facts. Selective integrity, however, is our doing evil and expecting good to come from it.

When we are trying to develop a philosophy about right and wrong, picking and choosing, we need to pull back and listen to our hearts. That's also what integrity means, fullness of heart, wholeness. Using selective integrity you can tell the truth with the intent of leaving the impression of something other than the truth that you have spoken. David did some very foolish and sinful things, but interestingly, the Scriptures say, he had "a heart after God." God said, "This is a man after my own heart!" Why? David said, "Let integrity and uprightness preserve me, I wait on thee!" Spoken by the man who went to bed with Bathsheba and fathered two illegitimate children. The man who killed

Uriah, talked about integrity. God never said that David was always righteous. God never said that David was always spiritually correct. God did say that he was a man after His own heart.

There is hope after failure! There is light after dying to yourself. We must be willing to admit to our mistakes, clean up our duplicity, and live again.

Is it any wonder that our nation is so soundly confused on the issue of selectivity in our integrity. President Reagan vows that he never traded American arms for hostages in Iran. We all have come to recognize that it turned out that he apparently did just that. The humorous Mark Shal said, "George Washington said, 'I cannot tell a lie.' Richard Nixon could not tell the truth. Ronald Reagan couldn't tell the difference." Slowly a web of misinformation and half-truths have told us that high officials in our government were deceiving each other and the public, and perhaps themselves. It is a fact of life that there is a crisis of confidence in most areas of life today because selective integrity is being practiced.

Integrity says that we must not lie, but selective integrity says that the only real test of a lie is whether or not people are enraged by a particular deception or a distortion that they have learned.

It's obvious that the American public has had it. *U.S. News and World Report* has said that seventy percent of the American people are dissatisfied with the current standards of honesty. It's obvious that for many of us the yellow light has been blinking in our minds for a long time, the red light comes on, and in our mad rush to tell our story, picking and choosing, we have gone straight ahead. We knew it was wrong, but we thought we would not be caught.

Summary

Selective integrity is common to us all. While we may hold truth with passion in one area, there are other times when we wink, or worse yet, close both eyes.

The problem of selective integrity has become epidemic in public life. Sadly, if something is pervasive enough for long enough, it can be accepted as the norm.

What can we do to guard against this problem? Like the issue of arrogancy, an accountability group is vital. But the first line of defense against selective integrity is with those closest to us — our spouse, our children, our work associates.

We must create an environment at home and at work where others will sense that it is alright to point out an area that they feel we are not facing up to. I know this is risky, but the one who ultimately loses the most in selective integrity is the one practicing it.

The benefit of a more open environment at home and at work pays a valuable dividend. When I must be accountable for all of my actions, then, as Paul wrote to the Corinthians, "The power of Christ can rest upon me" (2 Cor. 12:9; NAS).

Judgmental Integrity

When the disaster hit PTL and voices began to cry out, and the screaming began, one thing became very obvious. The finger pointing had begun. Any time someone starts the finger pointing process . . . especially publicly, it always has spelled danger for me. I certainly was not in a place to be judging others myself. It was interesting to sit back and note the people in this process who were the meanest and the least redemptive. They were often harsh and inaccurate in their statements. Now some are out of the Lord's work. Their lives were later revealed, unknown to me, but known to the Almighty.

The Greatest Man who ever lived asked the question, "How can you say to your brother, let me pull out the mote in your eye, when you can't see the beam in your own eye?" Most people know that a mote is just a tiny piece of dust or a speck of material that can get in your eye. A beam, obviously, is a support, either wood or metal, that holds up the roof of a building. Jesus said, "Can't you see that?" We must desperately seek an integrity that is whole, not divided by a judgmental spirit. The person who finger points actually thinks that darkness is light, and they don't know the difference. That's why deterioration sets in. When we go about fantasizing on the issue that we are something that we are not, the question of our own integrity becomes an immense problem. "If we say that we have no sin, we deceive ourselves and the truth is not in us." Somehow we must learn to step back and listen to our hearts and deal very severely with ourselves. Otherwise, a judgmental attitude will let us lie to ourselves, believe it, and begin to point fingers at others. In our quest to straighten the world out and to correct those we target, we lose the sense of what we have become ourselves. We see nothing wrong in what we are doing. We hardly recognize the darkness in which we are walking. When such a spirit has grasped us, we are determined to conquer and enslave someone.

We must come to recognize that denouncing, charging others, and accusing often reveals more about ourselves than it does them. Each of us has a Referee who adjudicates right and wrong and makes the choices. That person is not us.

The sad thing is that judgmental integrity has no healing, it explodes into matters where we injure rather than ultimately bring healing. It starts a fire in the soul, a blow to the innocent. We must seek to arbitrate our spirits, not go off in haste and bring hurt to the community of our fellows. Being judgmental is like a bomb waiting to detonate. It is a flaming spirit. It has a condemning effect and it gives a person a feeling of condemnation. "Always leave something to build on" is the admonition I heard as a young executive from a very wise man. Are we attempting to slay our foe, or bring help, hope, and healing? That's a choice each of us must face.

A judgmental concept of integrity puts a spirit into our hearts that begins to loathe, detest, and despise people. We get carried away in our own importance. Very often jealousy and envy comes into us. The Apostles' perception of integrity was to take care of ourselves first. How often have we wounded someone? Our negative comments (that we were not certain were true) have slain our enemies! This kind of attitude reflects much more about ourselves than those we are trying to judge.

It's not enough to make ourself a little god! We are taught to forgive and make friends of our enemies.

Every generation needs someone who will stand in the place of the prophet and declare, "Thus saith the Lord." Someone who will unashamedly point out where we as a people have fallen short of God's standard.

The oft quoted, "a prophet is without honor in his own country," reveals how tough this job can be. Just read a few stories in the Old Testament and you will gain a fresh appreciation for the man or woman with the courage to call a nation and her people to righteousness.

A prophet, however, faces temptation and challenges as all mortals do. If he yields to those forces then he must repent quickly lest his guilt be manifested in even harsher judgment of others.

As the guilt gnaws at him this exhorter will pound the table even harder while demanding integrity and purity from others. He will often exercise judgment by penalizing others for the very thing he is doing privately.

Pastors and preachers, especially, have been accused of judgmental integrity. They will decry sin in the community while carrying on a secret affair. Television has magnified this experience.

I can recall an evangelist who preached against pornography passionately. His private judgment for others was no less harsh. After many years of fruitful ministry, his hypocrisy was revealed when he was caught with a prostitute.

While the television evangelist has a wider audience for his indiscretion, the scene can be repeated each week in communities across America. A minister who rallied against gay rights in Florida was arrested for soliciting an undercover policeman, is just one more example.

Judgmental integrity is practiced just as fearlessly in non-sexual settings as well. Tom Peters describes the boss who brags about service on one hand, while acting hypocritically:

The boss who preaches quality, but puts wholly unrealistic schedule demands on the plant of operational center, is seen as a hypocrite. Trust, integrity, fairness in dealing with others (all under the gun to do unrealistic things and sign up for unrealistic promises), and quality/service all go kaput.[12]

Over the past century America has witnessed a tug of war between labor and management that is borne out of a basic mistrust of each other. Both sides demand that the other practice impeccable integrity, but neither side will trust the other to carry through without a contract.

During this past year one of America's largest and longest flying airlines went first into bankruptcy and then into demise, as the union accused management (specifically, the ownership) of siphoning off profits for other ventures while demanding 100% of time and effort from labor.

The union leadership has argued, unsuccessfully, that management knew their actions would bankrupt the company and rob long time employees of future benefits.

As the world grows smaller and information becomes more pervasive, the double standard practiced by governments around the world is becoming painfully obvious.

Nowhere has this been more explosive than in Eastern Europe. For almost a half century leaders in places like Romania demanded loyalty from the people, and fidelity to the law of government.

The overt immorality of Western type dress, music, and movies was officially prohibited. A breach of integrity in these areas was dealt with swift punishment.

As the economy faltered and hundreds of thousands of people began to starve, the people grew restless. A shortage of food and staples began to make the people wary of the promises of the government.

When the dictatorship of Romania was toppled and their leader executed, the horrible truth began to come out. First to the people of Romania, and then through Western news agencies to the rest of the world. While children starved to death in orphanages, the government leaders ate as royalty from hidden supplies.

The anger and resentment for being judged so harshly by a government that practiced their own secret sins was the fuel for revolution.

In country after country throughout Europe people have begun to demand the truth. And those who lived by the sword have begun to die by the sword.

Here in America the situation has not reached this crisis point — yet. There is, however, a growing resentment against those in authority who have been holding the American people accountable while playing loose with integrity themselves.

This past summer the media heralded the scoop that members of Congress were writing bad checks at a bank controlled by the House of Representatives. That was followed closely by the revelation that some members had failed to pay their tab at the Congressional Restaurant.

At first, Americans seemed to respond with more ridicule than anything else. The story made great fodder for the late night comedians.

As the fall of '91 settled in, however, pollsters began to report that Americans were getting fed up with incumbents and their perceived hypocrisy.

In Tampa a rally entitled "Throw the rascals (incumbents) out" drew a record crowd. The president's popularity began to plummet despite a previous record of confidence from the American people.

When our concern for integrity is rooted in covering up our own misdeeds rather than for the benefit of truth to everyone, we have become judgmental.

When a leader, no matter his position, whether private or public, business or profession, clergy or layman, begins to harshly judge the actions of others he may be simply trying to drown his own guilt.

Summary
Everyone in leadership is called upon to pass judgment

on issues of integrity. That is a fact that no leader can escape. The danger lies, however, in the leader's temptation to ignore his own guilt by treating others more harshly.

Unresolved guilt lowers our self esteem, and out of that poor self image a leader will use his influence or authority as a bloody pulpit.

How can we guard against this? Dr. Stephen Olford, a Baptist leader, advises people to keep a short account with God. Confess our sins frequently.

The human mind has no mechanism for handling guilt. Our hospitals are filled with people, many of whom have attempted to resolve guilt through abuse of drugs and alcohol.

Leaders, unfortunately, can often attempt to soothe their own conscience by judging others harshly. They abuse not only themselves but others in the process.

How do we guard against this danger? First we must remember as the apostle Paul said, "So were some of you." There is no sin we could not commit save for the grace of God. Therefore, as leaders, we must evaluate others with a contrite heart that depends wholly on the Lord himself.

Secondly, we must confess our sins daily for the Lord's healing. This is not a confession for salvation, but rather for unhindered fellowship with the Father. Apart from His grace, sin and the judgment of others will be our constant companion.

Consensual Integrity

There is a supposed integrity that I call consensual integrity. My dear friend, Dan Johnson, told me a story of a missionary who was preaching. An older, wiser minister sat with a friend listening to the story being told. The question arose in the mind of one who heard. Reflecting, he asked the senior clergyman, "Do you believe what he is preaching?"

The response was quick, "He does."

It is a deadly sin. Perhaps my greatest sin at PTL was consenting to some of the things that happened. It wasn't a deliberate decision. I just did nothing. No man should be accountable for what others do. I must bear my own responsibilities. I never verbalized my objections, never spoke for it, and was often not against it. I just did nothing. I wanted to be a good person, but I should have lovingly but firmly spoken up and asked, "What is going on?" Men and women can live lies, teenagers can live a lie, families can live the big lie, institutions can live a lie, a church, college, or ministry can be living the big lie, and we do nothing. We seemingly consent to it by the actions that we do not take. We assent morally with our accord and unconsciously bring agreement to what is taking place. In our desire to be in harmony we lose sight of what's really taking place. Somebody says something in our clique. We know it is not true, but we do nothing. It is very uncomfortable to not consent. We know to do better, but we don't do it, and we let in the enemy of our souls. We all must be brought to the truth. I admit it. I want to be liked, so do you. That's a part of our humanity, and it's also a part of our problem. There are things on which we need to focus. Like simply, lovingly, and firmly moving into people's lives who are not living the truth. All of us must take the mantle and do it.

The question needs to be asked when we see some fallen person gasping for breath, "What do we do to respond to that person's need?" Do we just watch his expiration? Who do you know that you lovingly believe has lost their integrity? Have you kindly and in a gentle but firm manner moved into their lives, asking what is happening to them? What have each of us done about this question about consenting to people's failures? Leaders fall by the wayside and some of us never notice. Why do we wait until it is too late to realize that someone has lost it all? The Good Samaritan wasn't sent by a church, a club, or a committee. He was one who stopped and cared. When your heart tells you to do something, to reach out to someone who is failing, do it, and as quickly as possible. Don't consent to what is going on in their lives.

Yes, our motives must be right, and if it is we will not consent to things that are displeasing to our Heavenly

Father. Every group and person's decision should be reviewed by all of us who have an interest in that decision. For the sake of those deciding we must not consent to what we know is not right. None of us are ever too big or mighty to be wrong. We have passed the time when institutions will make an effort to speak to this problem of consensual integrity. It is the responsibility of each of us. We become too busy and insensitive to what our heart is saying to move into someone's life and speak in a loving, firm way to the problems they face.

There is a common phrase among frequent churchgoers that is used when describing the exaggeration of a preacher. The phrase is "evangelistically speaking." That is a euphemism for being less than honest.

How is it that someone can mislead people for so long without anyone knowing it? Do they simply fool everybody? Are they like the people who are caught for impersonating a doctor, who go for years without getting caught because they are so competent?

While there might be some in this category of professional con, there is a far more subtle explanation. Others who know the truth simply go along; they acquiesce to what the group thinks.

Politicians applaud vigorously as their candidate promises the voters prosperity and peace, all the while knowing that he cannot deliver either.

Church leaders will listen to a mission report that they know couldn't be accurate. They sit in silence, however, so as not to hurt the "faith" of others.

Advertisers make bold claims that the businessman knows cannot be wholly substantiated, but tolerate it as part of the marketing effort. After all, who will really be harmed?

A president denies any knowledge of wrongdoing while his staff and closest aides know better. But in the interest of national security his remark goes unchallenged.

The problem, of course, is that people are harmed by such consensual integrity. The truth does make a difference regardless of who chooses to turn their head away.

The recent U.S. census is vital to everything from the

appropriation of tax money to voting districts. There is perhaps no research carried out by the U.S. government that impacts more Americans at once than the census.

Yet, the census, too, has become political. Congressmen know that integrity is breached. Nevertheless, it is accepted as simply "part of the process." Alvin Toffler summarizes the census problem:

> The ten year census questionnaire used in the United States must be approved by Congress. Says a senior census official: "Congress puts various pressures on us. We do a sample survey on farm finance. We've been directed by Congress not to collect that data because it might have been used to cut federal support for farmers." Companies in every industry also pressure the Census Bureau to ask, or to avoid asking, certain questions.[13]

The census has become not an instrument for raw data, but rather politically correct data, regardless of veracity.

When those whom we trust to provide oversight and protection to the people choose to ignore the truth, the results can be devastating. The recent savings and loan scandal, which will cost the American taxpayer billions, has left people asking, "Who knew about these lapses in integrity, and why didn't they do something?"

As the cost of consensual integrity in the marketplace grows, so does the concern of people everywhere. In the closing weeks of 1991 a painful example has come to light from the financial empire of the late Robert Maxwell.

Business Week of December 23, 1991 reported on what appears to have happened:

> Robert Maxwell, 68, may have defrauded his two publicly traded companies of at least 1.4 billion, mainly by filching money from the companies' employee retirement funds, before his mysterious death at sea on November 5.[14]

How could this happen? Wasn't someone somewhere responsible for regulating the activity of a publicly traded company? Was Maxwell a master of fraud, or were others simply turning their head in their own best interest?

Unfortunately, the latter appears to be the case. Even with little or no government regulation, *Business Week* went on to conclude,

> Maxwell would have been able to do little without the willing aid of his bankers . . . more likely, they were enticed by Maxwell's profligate borrowing, which generated handsome fees.[15]

As the blame is passed around, the people lose when consensual integrity is practiced. While losing one's life savings is disastrous, the practice of consensual integrity can be even more costly.

The fatal train derailment in Maryland where the operator was under the influence of drugs is a sad example. The airline pilots who fly too soon after drinking alcohol, with the rest of the crew knowing, risks countless lives.

Recently the media has focused on television evangelists who seem to be using less than honest practices. Was the media the first to know, or did fellow ministers know all along that this was going on?

Many people might cowardly back off from being a whistle blower by quoting the Lord's admonition that, "He who is without sin cast the first stone." But remember that crowd had gathered for a one-sided lynching, not total truth.

To the contrary, the Scripture admonishes us that to choose not to do what is right is a sin of omission, and is serious.

Consensual integrity is tolerated for one reason — selfishness. And that reason has two points. First, I don't want to get involved because it might cost me something. Secondly, I don't want to say anything because I might lose money or prestige from the very person I am confronting.

Either way we fall short, for the Scriptures call for us to be men and women of integrity. The roar of the crowd must never entice us to go along with a lie, or to hide from one. The price for ourselves and others is too great.

Summary

Consensual integrity is borne out of a person's own bent for self preservation. The cost of going against the popular consensus for the moment seems frightening.

No one understands this better than Jesus. His message of redemption ran counter to both the religious and secular culture of His day.

How can we guard against this strong temptation? First, we must cultivate a passion for the Lord's will to be done rather than our own. It begins with a simple question: Given this same set of circumstances, what would Jesus do?

That question, made popular in a book by Charles Sheldon, is very powerful. By asking it before you act, and by searching the Scripture for the answer, you will more often than not make the right decision.

The apostle Paul warned us that our battle would not be of the flesh but of the spirit. Ultimately we resist the lure of consensual integrity not by our own strength but by the power of the Holy Spirit.

Remember Peter's failure on the night Jesus was arrested when he went along with the rest of the crowd and denied knowing the Lord? Yet in Acts 4 he stood before the council and, under threat of his life, proclaimed Jesus as Lord.

What happened? What made the difference? The answer is found back in Acts when the passage reveals, "Then Peter filled with the Holy Ghost spoke" (Acts 4:8; NAS).

Ultimately our dependency, day by day, and moment by moment, upon the Holy Spirit is our only sure defense against consensual integrity. As we take the sinner's place, He empowers us to serve Him — faithfully!

19

Free At Last

My friend, Emilio Sanchez, helped me take the cartons of books, legal papers, and letters to the taxi. I had received many hundreds of letters, and had kept every one of them. I hugged him and noticed the tears in his eyes. He had become my son "in the faith." Now it was time — June 12, 1991 — to say goodbye.

Prisoners doing their work in front of the administration building began to wave and call out, "Rich, we're pulling for you, buddy."

As the taxi backed up, I glanced behind me at the door I had just exited, the same one I had entered February 2, 1990. My mind flashed back to the way I had felt that day — scared and hurting, physically, emotionally, and spiritually. The eight year sentence had loomed darkly before me.

Now I was leaving, having served only 18% of my original sentence. I had learned an important lesson: God is not faithful to us because He gets us out of a jam or out of a prison, whether physically or emotionally. He is faithful because He is God, the loving, caring Saviour.

The taxi eased its way through the giant Eglin Air Force Base. *What would life be like for me now?* I asked myself, brushing tears away from my eyes. Finally I looked at the driver.

"Going home?" he asked.

"Yes, sir! I'm on my way home."

The trip to Pensacola Airport was a montage of cars whirling by. Everything appeared so full of color and beauty. It was hard for me to take in all the different people and places passing by.

The taxi driver never quit talking from the time we left Eglin until we got near the airport, over an hour away. I was relishing what I was seeing, and he was having a good time talking. We were, during those moments, in two separate worlds.

"What's that?" I asked, noticing what looked like a new kind of restaurant.

"That's one of many new hamburger joints you can drive through. This one is called Crystal's. There are many others. You can't eat there. All you can do is drive through."

I responded quickly, "Please, let's drive through. Do you like hamburgers?" I asked.

"Love 'em," was his response.

We approached the window and I said, "Make mine with lettuce, pickle, onion, ketchup, and bacon."

"You can't get that much stuff on the little things," the taxi driver said.

I responded, "Well, let's take two each then."

Our last few moments together, the driver and I reveled in total communication, talking about the simple joy of a forty-five cent, very small hamburger. It was a big deal to me. My first meal out of prison. I was on my way to freedom.

At the airport, I checked my luggage and headed for the nearest telephone to call our son, Rich. When I heard his voice on the phone, with no beeps, my first words were, "Free at last! Free at last! Thank God Almighty! Free at last!"

Although for the next five more months I would be living in supervised confinement at a halfway house, I was still basically on my own. Now out of prison, I had the certainty that the God, who has been, and is, would be the Lord of my life in this new experience — re-entering life, or as the inmates call it, "on the street." My heart had a deep assurance that God was working and walking far ahead of me.

When I had received information from the "team" — my case manager, counselor, and unit manager — that I was going to be sent home on June 12, I decided not to opt for the home detention program. For medical purposes, I decided my re-entry into normal life would best be accomplished by going to a halfway house rather than being paroled and confined only to our home. Because of the long-range effect on my health, I felt the halfway house would help me to adjust emotionally.

My rejection of parole was widely publicized in the media. The reason I did not take parole was very simple. I was not ready to face the real world again.

Leaving Eglin had been a deeply emotional experience. I had anticipated the moment from the time I had arrived. After sixteen months and ten days of confinement, I was excited, expectant, happy, and also afraid.

The fears were very real. How will my friends and associates respond to me? How will the church people act toward me? Will my acceptance be the same as before I went to prison?

After I pled guilty and had been sentenced, I really felt no change nor observed any difference in the way people reacted to me. But that was before I was identified as an inmate of a federal institution. Now I was an ex-convict. How would people react to me?

When U.S. Air, Flight 584, lifted off the ground bound for Tampa, Florida, I knew this short flight was, for this day, going to be the beginning of something beautiful. When the door opened in Tampa, I wanted to be one of the first ones off the plane. I was.

I really wasn't expecting anyone to be there to greet me. Suddenly, eight of my dear loved ones ran toward me. What a surprise! What a delight! What a joy! My wife, daughter, son-in-law, grandson, my wife's sister and her husband from Illinois, and their two grandchildren were all there. It was a very special blessing that I will never forget.

I held Mildred in my arms and said, "Honey, I love you. It's almost over. We've made it."

When an inmate transfers from a federal institution to a halfway house, he must use a public conveyance. I was required to take a taxi to the Goodwill Rehabilitation Center. That morning I had my light breakfast at five o'clock, and it was now 1:00 p.m. I called the halfway house and asked for permission to eat a meal at the airport.

After a quick lunch, I jumped in the taxi and arrived twenty-five minutes later at the Goodwill halfway house.

The United States Bureau of Prisons contracts with various organizations like the Salvation Army and Goodwill Industries to run halfway houses. They provide lodging, food service, and key personnel to help inmates in their re-entry into a normal life.

When a certain accountability level is reached, the inmates are given passes to spend time with their families. Getting a job is a requirement. When the criteria is met, going home and other social visits are permitted. Strict time frames are followed so that the halfway house always knows where their "client" is at any given time.

I was assigned to the halfway house in St. Petersburg, Florida. This unique facility housed a Goodwill Industries showroom, a rehabilitation center for the physically handicapped and the disadvantaged, and the corrections facility.

Paul Norris, the supervisor of the Goodwill house, and his dedicated staff were committed to serving the people lodged at the halfway house. I tried to remind myself and the other inmates that the staff members were simply doing their jobs and had nothing to do with how or why we were there.

On June 16, 1991, my case manager, Mrs. Eke, kindly helped me arrange a schedule for my first day to go home in sixteen and one-half months. That is a day I will always remember. I was permitted to shop for two and one-half hours. Big deal! Yes, it was to someone who hadn't been able to get out among people and into a store for almost a year and a half.

Mildred arrived a few minutes early. As I walked out the door of the halfway house and started toward the car, I began to cry. It was my first day out in public in such a long time.

After shopping, I had to go home and report in by telephone at one o'clock and five. I had to return to the halfway house at eight in the evening. What a great day it was. To be with my wife, to be free to be myself.

My schedule at the halfway house provided the structure I needed along with a time at home each evening:

7:30 a.m. — personal Bible study and prayer.
8:30 a.m. — staff prayer.
9:30 to 12:00 noon — writing and assignments.
12:00 noon — lunch.
1:30 p.m. — things that needed to be done. (At the church)
2:30 p.m. — back to the halfway house for checkout to go home.
9:00 p.m. — check back in to the halfway house.

Part of my probation included working at the Pinellas Park Wesleyan Church where, my friend, Pastor Freeman gave me the opportunity to do the things closest to my heart: caring for people, writing, and preparing myself spiritually and emotionally for the days to come. Today, as never before, I know for certain that I will only be fulfilled by serving people, speaking in churches, and doing the work of a minister.

The ministry I had at Pinellas Park provided an additional time of healing for me. Pastor Larry Freeman, his wife Pat, and the staff were not only gracious and helpful, but vital in my entry back into normal life. The people of the church, without exception, have been living examples of New Testament Christianity. I have a better understanding of 1 Corinthians 13 because of them.

I felt at last I was well on my journey back to restoring my integrity. My confinement in prison had provided countless hours for me to study the Word of God and meditate on where and how I had failed.

I was scheduled to be released from the halfway house to home confinement on October 12, 1991. My complete release from the Bureau of Prisons had been set for November 10.

On the 22nd of September, I received a phone call from Victor Mims, my case manager at the halfway house, requesting me to be in his office at eight o'clock the morning of the 23rd. I could sense in my heart that the meeting was going to be favorable, and it was.

"We are releasing you from the halfway house to home confinement," he said. "That means you do not have to return to the halfway house daily. Two times a week you must return for check-in and review. That won't take too long. There are some restrictions. You must continue working. You are to be at home and call in before nine o'clock each evening. You must remain there until six in the morning."

I can't remember if I floated out of his office or if I walked, but I know for certain I was rejoicing.

Prior to my release from the halfway house, Rev. Gordon Matheny, superintendent of the Assemblies of God in Florida had talked to me about the possibility of being reinstated into the denomination. Mildred and I gave it serious thought. That's what I really desired. My heart has always been there. After much discussion with various people, "I was made to know" that I should fill out the application for reinstatement to the Assemblies of God.

I sent the application to Dr. Cookman and prayerfully waited for the reply. In the letter that I sent with my application for reinstatement, I wrote the following:

"For over forty years I have been in some kind of full-time ministry. I'm so sorry for the hurts I caused you dear people. Please forgive me, and do not keep me in this bondage for the rest of my life."

Dr. Alfred Fireman, the psychiatrist who had helped me so much, had written the national headquarters of the Assemblies of God several years before. In that letter, he stated I would not be completely well until my relationship to the Assemblies of God was healed.

With my cancer experience, the continued Crohn's disease, the removal of a kidney, and the emotional, financial, and physical loss of these past four years, I needed the acceptance of my denomination to put me on the road to recovery. Dr. Fireman believed, as a professional, that would only happen if I were reinstated to my church and to the ministry that I loved so very much. I had to agree. That was exactly how I felt.

Pastor Karl Strader of the Carpenter's Home Church in Lakeland, Florida had asked me long ago to speak to his congregation, one of the largest Assemblies of God churches in America, seating about 8,000 people. On Sunday, November 10, 1991, Mildred and I drove to the church with great anticipation, a little anxiety, and much joy.

All the way there I couldn't help but think this was a key part of my recovery. That morning I would confess publicly that I had lost my integrity and was on my journey back.

When Mildred and I entered the church, we were greeted with kindness, hellos, hugs, and blessings.

As I waited to speak, tears welled up in my eyes. I was so humbled to be in the presence of this mighty congregation. Seated among them were my spiritual overseers, Dr. and Mrs. Arthur Parsons, and Dr. and Mrs. Charles Cookman, superintendent of the Assemblies of God in North Carolina.

I thought, Lord, You are so faithful. Thank You for loving and caring for me.

As Pastor Karl Strader introduced me to the people, his kind words brought more tears of gratitude. Over the past three years, he and his wife, Joyce, had done so much to help us. True friends, they had loved us and reached out to us.

I took my place behind the pulpit. It seemed as though I was about to preach my very first sermon. My heart pounded with expectancy. The service was to be televised to many markets. The press was also there reporting the event.

I looked at Mildred, and the impact of her love and faithfulness hit me. She had stood by me those many months of anguish, separation, and loneliness. She sat waiting, like the others, to hear the Word of God from Richard Dortch. I began by saying something like this.

"Pastor Strader and friends of this congregation, I'm here this morning by the grace of God. This is, for me, a very solemn occasion. I'm here because God cares and a lot of people loved us. Thank you for standing with Mildred and me and our family during this most incredible, hurting time of our lives. I want to thank the American people. I want to thank the church community, and I want to thank each one of you who stood by our side.

"Today I want to talk to you about integrity, how I lost it and my journey back. Thank God this morning I'm on the right road. I trust that this day is the beginning of the end of a long sojourn. I know that my tomorrows will be happiest where I am today — serving God and humanity."

Epilogue

On November 20, 1991 Richard W. Dortch was reinstated as a minister of the Assemblies of God.

ENDNOTES

1 Paul A. Cedar, *Strength in Servant Leadership* (Waco, TX: Word Books, 1987), p.150.

2 Mark A. Ritchie, *God in the Pits* (Nashville: Thomas Nelson Publishers, 1989), p. 134.

3 Robert D. Linder, "Pious Presidents," *Christianity Today*, February 17, 1989, P. 37.

4 Stephen R. Covey, *The 7 Habits of Highly Effective People* (New York: Simon & Schuster, Inc., 1989), p. 148.

5 David Halberstom, *The Next Century* (New York: William Morrow and Company, Inc., 1991), p. 102.

6 Charles Colson, *Kingdom in Conflict* (New York: William Morrow/Zondervan Publishing House, 1987), p. 309.

7 IBID., pp. 307-308.

8 Tom Peters, *Thriving on Chaos* (New York: Harper & Row, 1988), pp. 628-629.

9 IBID., pp. 629-630.

10 Alvin Toffler, *Power Shift* (New York: Bantam Books, 1990), p. 281.

11 Peters, op. cit., p. 630.

12 Peters, op. cit., p. 631.

13 Toffler, op. cit., p. 287.

14 Mark Maremount, Mark Landler, "An Empire Up for Grabs," *Business Week,* December 23, 1991, p. 70.

15 IBID., pp. 71-72.

Index

A

Angley, Ernest 70
Ankerberg, John 139–141, 151, 158, 171, 183
Armstrong, Ben 126, 165, 181, 189, 229
Assemblies of God 15, 25, 26, 27, 32, 34, 41, 51, 66, 84, 126, 131, 141, 142, 144, 146, 169, 170, 218, 258, 345
Assembly of God 91, 228
Atkins, Mike 67
Azvedo, Vi 83

B

Bacon, Brad 175
Bailey, Herman 8, 226, 227
Bailey, Pearl 56
Bailey, Peter 69, 71
Bailey, Sharon 8, 226, 227
Bakker, Jamie Charles 38, 39
Bakker, Tammy 13, 14, 16, 17, 33–34, 36, 38–39, 40
Bakker, Tammy Sue 38, 39, 119
Banther, Dr. Barry 7
Bectin, Arthur 297, 307
Berkey, Dr. Dale 228
Boesky, Ivan 318
Boone, Brian 207
Boone, Esther 207
Boone, Pat 66
Borden, Arthur 229
Brock Corporation 75
Buckingham, Jamie 7
Burgund, Mark 8, 45, 152, 174, 207, 307
Burgund, Wanda 8, 207
Burkett, Alan 279
Bush, George 126, 308
Bush, Mrs. George 308

C

Calloway, Mark 8, 234–236, 243, 257, 261–262, 298, 304, 306
Carr, Owen 27
Central Bible College 34
Chapin, Dick 229
Cho, Dr. Paul Yonggi 130, 222
Clark, Dr. E.M. 26, 162
Cobble, Dr. James 45
Collins, Michael 208, 264, 267

Connoway, Phoebe 94
Cookman, Dr. Charles 35, 144–148, 169, 183, 344, 345
Cookman, Mrs. Charles 345
Cortese, Aimee 35
Cress, Albert 45, 172–176

D

D'Andrea, Molly 8, 226
D'Andrea, Robert 8, 223, 226
Davis, Dr. Durward 8
Davis, Mrs. Durward 8
DeMoss, Mark 139–142, 151, 151–153
Diehl, William 8, 234–236, 243, 257, 261, 261–262
Dobbins, Dr. Richard 138
Documents
  Compromise & settlement 107
  Daily Activity Report 74
  Letter from paralegal 87–92
  Plea Agreement 247
  Proposed Hahn lawsuit 96
Dortch, Harry 19, 19–21
Dortch, Ivory 208, 306
Dortch, Mary 20
Dortch, Rhonda 208, 307
Dortch, Rich 23, 86, 116, 152, 174, 186, 190, 191, 192, 208, 246, 262, 272, 303, 307, 340
Dortch, Uriah 208, 306
Dudley, Cliff 8
Dudley, Tim 8
Dugan, Robert 229

E

Eckard, Bill 279
Edwards, Dale 261, 263
Ellsberg, Daniel 133
Eskelin, Neil 7, 150-151
Evangel College 34
Evans, Dale 66

F

Falwell, Jerry 106, 126, 139–142, 152–153, 155, 158–167, 177, 181–184, 188–190, 200, 205–207, 210, 213, 218–219, 232
Ferrin, Paul 60
Fireman, Dr. Alfred 225–226, 344
Fletcher, John Wesley 14, 83

Ford, Dr. Leighton 131
Foth, Dick 138
Freeman, Larry 228, 261, 266, 343
Freeman, Pat 228, 261, 343
Fulbright, Shirley 57, 61

G
Gaither, Bill and Gloria 163
Gibson, Robert 27
Gorman, Marvin 145–147
Graham, Billy 34, 56, 131, 134, 180
Graham, Franklin 274
Gray, Dr. Bob 214–218
Greenaway, Charles 24
Greisen, V.G. 24
Grell, Mary Ellen 45
Groff, Allen 138
Gross, Dr. Fred 83, 104, 111, 168
Grutman, Roy 106, 151–155, 159, 163–164, 185, 188, 210, 213

H
Hahn, Jessica 13–17, 79–83, 104–111, 127, 132, 134–135, 137, 141, 150, 158–160, 164, 168, 171, 173–176, 178, 183, 184, 186, 200, 210, 213, 218, 219–220, 234
Hargrave, Harry 232, 232–233
Harris, Glenn 228
Harris, Rick 276, 307
Harrison, Henry 28, 54
Hosey, Russell 207
Hosey, Sandy 207
Humbard, Rex 156, 165, 181
Humphrey, Jim 282

J
Janway, Cecil 144–145, 145
Johnson, Bob 78
Johnson, Dan 21, 28, 332
Johnson, J. Foy 228
Johnson, Jeanne 78
Johnson, M.C. 26
Johnson, Samuel 233
Johnson, Stephen 297, 302–303, 307
Jones, Leslie 8, 139, 207

K
Kelley, Jack 211–212
Kevin 62–63

Knox, Eddie 64–65

L
LaMotta, Jake 309
LaMotta, Joe 309
Landreth, Bill 8, 272
Landreth, Mary 8, 272
Lawing, A.T. 35
Lawrence, Carol 56
Leeth, Jerry 262
Levine, Jimmy 279
Leyland, Elizabeth 211
Life Challenge 11, 221–222, 232, 265
Lunsford, Beverly 228
Lunsford, Donald 228

M
MacLeod, Gavin 56
Mainse, David 167
Marcus, Warren 139
Martin, Walter 171
Matheny, Gordon 228, 344
McAdams, Rudolph 22, 23
McDonald, Jim 8, 298, 307
McDonald, Rita 8, 298
Meade, Mrs. Ron 8, 272
Meade, Ron 8, 270, 272, 275, 276, 307
Meese, Edwin 232
Messner, Roe 105–106, 120, 150, 153–155, 184, 186
Miles, Leon 91
Miller, Jerry 246
Moody, Deanna Dortch 21, 24, 86, 116, 174, 192, 208, 262, 264, 267, 272, 276, 282
Moody, Mark 264, 267, 272, 276
Moore, Sam 163, 165, 187, 189
Moran, Bob 8

N
Nichols, Dr. Lester 118
Nims, Jerry 139–142, 151–153, 163, 181, 185, 232–233
North Central Bible College 21, 26, 29, 34

O
O'Guin, C.M. 26
Oldham, Doug 165, 185
Olson, Fern 29–32
Olson, Russell 29

P

Parsons, Dr. Arthur   8, 298, 345
Parsons, Mrs. Arthur   8, 298, 345
Peterson, Richard   45
Polk, Haywood   266
Potter, Robert   235, 246, 246–
    257, 259, 259–261, 290
Profeta, Eugene   93, 94, 111

R

Ragsdale, Bob   207
Ragsdale, Trish   207
Razor, Col.   300
Reagan, Ronald   161, 326
Rentz, Jim   145
Reuchel, Al   270
Rhoades, Dr. Ross   131–133
Richards, W.T.H.   25
Richardson, Walter   70, 144
Rimes, Col. Bill   8, 272, 275
Rimes, Pam   8, 272
Roberts, Oral   21, 56, 70, 131,
    132–133, 155
Robinson, James   204
Rogers, Dale Evans   258
Rogers, Roy   66
Rooney, Mickey   56
Roper, Paul   95, 95–104, 106,
    171, 175
Rossi, Dr.   278, 301

S

Sanchez, Emilio   339
Schmidgall, Robert   26, 131
Schuller, Robert   56, 61, 70
Shal, Mark   326
Shelton, Gene   8, 138–139, 211,
    212, 219
Shoemaker, Lloyd   25
Sims, Larry   8, 298
Sims, Sandra   8, 298
Smith, Bailey   163, 181, 181–182
Smith, Deborah   246
Snider, Bill   45
Spencer, Dr. Evelyn Carter   67
Stanley, Dr. Charles   126, 163,
    165, 179
Stevens, Bill   133
Strader, Joyce   8, 228, 345
Strader, Karl   8, 228, 345, 346
Swaggart, Donnie   145
Swaggart, Frances   143–145, 181,
    181–184

Swaggart, Jimmy   56, 70, 139–
    148, 151, 155, 158, 169–173,
    176, 181–186, 183–184, 206,
    316, 318

T

Taggart, David   57, 233, 236
Taggart, James   233, 236
Tragos, George   8, 237, 243
Treeby, Bill   171
Trinity Broadcasting Network   33

U

Urquhart, Frank   8

W

Wacker, Grant   21
Waldron, Tommy   228
Ward, Dr. C.M.   128–130, 136
Watt, Becky   8, 207, 220
Watt, Eric   8, 174, 186, 186–187,
    190, 207, 220–222
Watt, James   136, 156, 160–161,
    165, 181, 186, 186–187, 189,
    191, 207
Wilkerson, David   112–114
Winan, BB and CC   67

Y

Yaktsis, Ande   7

Z

Zimbalist, Jr., Efrem   35, 230
Zimmerman, Dr. Thomas   34,
    131, 145

Dear Pastor Dortch,

 I want to know more about Life Challenge.

I need help with my integrity. I will be calling you.

I would like someone to contact me for spiritual counseling.

Name _____

Street _____

City, State, Zip _____

Phone (   ) _____

Life Challenge
Office hours 9 a.m. - 4 p.m. EST

Phone (813) 799-5433
(LIFE)

(Fold here - staple and mail)

Life Challenge
P.O. Box 15009
Clearwater, FL 34629